Restorative
Justice Today

This book is dedicated to Audrey Sutherland, Ellen Langer, and the late Insoo Kim Berg, whose collective wisdom and courage to do what seemed impossible inspires us to believe justice can be restorative. Audrey swam around the North Shore of Moloka'i alone in 1962 at the age of 40; Ellen challenges us to "invent" our lives and world not merely "discover" things; and Insoo taught us to change our language to change our lives, and to help others who want to change theirs.

Restorative Justice Today

Practical Applications

Katherine S. van Wormer

University of Northern Iowa

Lorenn Walker

University of Hawaii Honolulu Community College

Editors

Los Angeles | London | New Delhi
Singapore | Washington DC

Los Angeles | London | New Delhi
Singapore | Washington DC

FOR INFORMATION:

SAGE Publications, Inc.
2455 Teller Road
Thousand Oaks, California 91320
E-mail: order@sagepub.com

SAGE Publications Ltd.
1 Oliver's Yard
55 City Road
London EC1Y 1SP
United Kingdom

SAGE Publications India Pvt. Ltd.
B 1/I 1 Mohan Cooperative Industrial Area
Mathura Road, New Delhi 110 044
India

SAGE Publications Asia-Pacific Pte. Ltd.
3 Church Street
#10-04 Samsung Hub
Singapore 049483

Printed in the United States of America

Library of Congress Cataloging-in-Publication Data

Restorative justice today : practical applications / editors, Katherine S. van Wormer, Lorenn Walker.

p. cm.
Includes bibliographical references and index.

ISBN 978-1-4522-1991-2 (pbk.)

1. Restorative justice. 2. Justice, Administration of. I. Van Wormer, Katherine S. II. Walker, Lorenn.

HV8688.R496 2013
364.6'8—dc23   2012017347

This book is printed on acid-free paper.

Acquisitions Editor: Jerry Westby
Production Editor: Brittany Bauhaus
Copy Editor: Dan Gordon
Typesetter: C&M Digitals (P) Ltd.
Proofreader: Carole Quandt
Cover Designer: Anupama Krishnan
Marketing Manager: Terra Schultz
Permissions Editor: Karen Ehrmann

12 13 14 15 16 10 9 8 7 6 5 4 3 2 1

Brief Contents

Detailed Contents

Foreword

Criminology's love affair with restorative justice is now in its third decade, and it has been interesting to watch that love develop. Plato and the ancient Greeks famously distinguished between different types of love, differentiating *eros* (or the swooning sense of being "in love") with *agape*, the deeper sense of "true love" one feels for a life companion after many years. Certainly, our feelings for restorative justice have developed in this sense over the years.

We have passed through the puppy love and infatuation stage, endlessly scribbling its name inside heart shapes: "Crim Loves RJ," "Crim loves RJ" at conferences and meetings. Such crushes quickly wane and can become a source of embarrassment and denial in retrospect. It is hard for any object of worship to live up to the expectations and imagination of the most smitten, so former devotees can turn quickly into denigrators. Indeed, there have even been hard times in the past few decades between criminology and restorative justice. We have fought and struggled and even discussed parting ways. We saw the relationship through those hard times, however, and we even formalized the relationship (made it "legit"). In the past few decades, restorative justice has gone from being a pie-in-the-sky revolution to being the subject of increasingly tedious academic conferences, textbooks, and journals to ultimately becoming part of the bureaucratic machinery of numerous criminal justice systems around the world. The first books on restorative justice had titles like *Changing Lenses*; newer books have titles like *Institutionalizing Restorative Justice*. Yes, our relationship has gotten very serious indeed.

It is hard, of course, not to miss those early days with all of their radical hopes and dreams. We shared a vision for remaking justice as we knew it; it was hard not to get caught up in the excitement of it all. The restorative justice movement today feels less dangerous, less daunting, less dramatic, and less fun. We have moved from beautiful ideas to reality and seen the restorative justice alternative for what it is, warts and all. The movement has suffered missteps, attracted charlatans and con artists, and proven itself to be all too human, like any other social movement fueled and driven by, well, we humans. I understand and sympathize with those of my colleagues who have abandoned the movement and decided to look for another beautiful idea to come around, sweep them off their feet, and rekindle the giddiness of eros and excitement.

Yet, the love that those of us still in "the movement" feel now is still very much real; it is just a more mature, more nuanced, and tempered affection. We see the limitations and shortcomings of the restorative framework, we know it is not perfect, but we continue to be deeply impressed by its wisdom and grace. It may no longer be trendy and cutting edge, but it has survived by proving instead to be timeless, based on ancient principles that accord with hard-wired human intuitions about fairness and morality.

This collection of new empirical and theoretical essays, put together by two of the most interesting thinkers (and doers) in the restorative movement, reflects that wisdom and demonstrates why restorative justice is still an idea to be reckoned with—maybe *the* idea to be reckoned with—in justice debates. The ideas herein may no longer make us swoon with eros, but will strengthen and reaffirm the feelings of agape that so many of us have come to feel about restorative justice over these many years. You'll love it.

—*Shadd Maruna*

Director, Institute of Criminology
and Criminal Justice
School of Law
Queen's University Belfast

Preface

We need to make the kind of society where it is easier for people to be good.

Dorothy Day, *The Long Loneliness*

Today, nationally, we are at a crossroads: some of us seeking after just deserts and harsh punishment, and others of us looking in a new direction. One path, the one we have been following blindly, stubbornly, up until now, leads further down into the mire of fear and darkness. But there is another path, one that is taken less often, that leads upward toward the light.

There is a growing recognition that as a society we are failing victims and failing offenders and the families of all concerned, that if people are to change, meeting evil with evil may not be the best way. There is a steady realization today of the traumatic impact of all forms of violence, including sudden, unexpected assaults and invasions of one's person and continuous bullying and name calling on the school yard and in the workplace. There is a steady realization, too, that the wrongdoers themselves are often the victims of their own lives and of the criminal justice system. In light of the fact that harmful behavior should not be ignored, a paradigm shift is in the wind, a new vision of restoring justice.

The paradigm shift—restorative justice—is about seeking the good in people, about bringing people together face to face, about hearing the pain of woundedness, and about healing. The stories of restorative justice, and you will read of many in this book, are dramatic, beautiful, and life-changing; some have an almost spiritual flavor. You have probably heard of some of the more powerful examples as highlighted in the media and on talk shows. Others, equally moving, are known only in small circles of people who somehow have gotten involved or of professionals who have been to the trainings or workshops and heard the stories, read the narratives, and shared in a sense of awe and wonderment.

Restorative justice is about righting a wrong not only for victims but also for offenders and communities. It is about making amends rather than punishment, restitution rather than retribution. In criminal justice, RJ is about healing individuals, communities, and even nations after harm caused from wrongdoing. While retributive justice asks, "What was the crime that was committed; how can we establish proof; and how harsh should the punishment be?" restorative justice asks, "What harm was done? Who was hurt and how can the harm be repaired? And how can we prevent this wrongdoing from occurring in the future?" The concern of restorative justice is threefold: It is for the victims and offenders, as well as for the community.

Although the basic principles known as restorative justice go back thousands of years in many indigenous communities, it has only been since the 1970s that this way of responding to wrongdoing has been given a modern application. And since the 1970s, there has been a proliferation of restorative justice practices and research worldwide. Because of the recognition of RJ's potential to help right a wrong at the interpersonal level and at the macro peacemaking level, restorative justice is a movement endorsed by the United Nations and one of international ramifications.

Restorative justice (RJ) takes shape in many forms. In the school setting, restorative justice is a meeting between a child who has engaged in tormenting another child and who must listen to the victim of the mistreatment express his or her pain. In child welfare, restorative justice exists in the form of a family group conference in which extended family members seek a solution to the abuse or neglect of a child. Behind prison walls a restorative process involves a facilitator-led session between a prison inmate and members of the family whose loved one was killed by this person. In a community, justice is restored as the perpetrators of the violence and collective abuse are held accountable and assume responsibility for their actions. Restorative justice on a global scale may take place following years of war and hate crimes inflicted upon opposing groups through public hearings involving extensive testimony and confession by the guilty parties. Whether on a small or large scale, when people from opposite sides of a crime or other wrongdoing come together in a carefully structured and prepared meeting and with community support, new understandings can emerge.

Organizing Framework and Rationale

An underlying assumption of this book is that the present system of criminal justice, with its heavy emphasis on standardized harsh forms of punishment and scant attention to the personal dimension, is flawed. For example, how the victim-survivor can be helped to heal and what can be done for the wrongdoer-offender to be reconciled with the community are basically ignored by the system. Relevant to both victims and offenders, an alternative approach is needed, one that can operate within the juvenile or criminal justice system or alongside it or entirely independent of it.

We write this book in a spirit of guarded optimism. Our optimism stems largely from reported shifts in public opinion toward a belief in rehabilitation matched by a parallel belief that victim-survivors should be actively involved in the process. Progressive developments are evident, including a burgeoning interest by social scientists, lawyers, judges, teachers, and social workers in restoring justice where wrongdoing has occurred in a wide range of settings. Recent initiatives promote healing of victim-survivors and their families through victim-offender conferencing. At the same time, in the United States and in other democratic nations, an interest in setting up specialized courts is strong—for example, drug courts, mental health courts, and veterans courts.

This book is geared for students of criminal justice, criminology, and social work, as well as all those who work or plan to work in some capacity with people whose lives have been touched by wrongdoing or crime. Professionals who are already working in the field will find much of interest here. They include probation and parole officers who increasingly are expected to engage in case management of their probationers and parolees, counselors and therapists who work in the fields of victim-assistance programing, mental health, and substance abuse treatment, and of course correctional workers of all sorts. Pastoral counselors, nuns, priests, rabbis, and imams, similarly, will find ideas here to help people cope with the wrongs that have been done to them, including those perpetrated by the religious institutions themselves.

The purpose of this book is twofold. The first and primary purpose is to introduce readers to restorative justice as a form of conflict resolution with practical applications for work with individuals as victims or offenders. Advocacy for social policy change in the criminal justice system is a part of this mission. The goal is to ensure that the interests of people who have been harmed or injured are met and that the wrongdoers, where appropriate, have the option of making restitution.

A second major purpose in assembling this collection is to familiarize the reader with restorative strategies from across the globe. To this end we have invited theorists and policy makers actively involved in direct action in their countries to discuss innovations with which they have been involved. It is our belief that the values on which restorative principles are built are universal and that they can be applied cross-culturally with care to be culturally sensitive to unique cultural norms. You will see, for example, in the case histories presented in several chapters on the topic of school bullying that the anti-bullying programs that started in Norway have spread to North America, and are now established in Hong Kong. Clearly, the transfer of knowledge can benefit us all.

A note concerning terminology: *Mediation* is a term we have taken pains to avoid in this book in the place of restorative justice dialogue or conferencing. The term is fine in its correct meaning as defined by the Oxford University Dictionary: "the process or action of mediating between parties in dispute to produce agreement or reconciliation; the state of being an intermediary." Restorative justice is not about negotiation between parties. Restorative justice is for people who have been affected by wrongdoing. There is no "dispute between parties" that needs to be negotiated. Unfortunately, the first books in the field used the word *mediation*, so it is widely used, especially in Europe, for example, as *victim-offender mediation*. We use the terms *conferencing* and *dialogue* instead. For the person who directs the process, we use the term *facilitator* rather than *mediator*.

Another term commonly used in the restorative justice literature that we avoid is the notion of *reintegrative shaming*. We recognize that shame is an emotion, which is different from the concept of "reintegrative shaming" that denotes a "regulatory practice" (Braithwaite & Braithwaite, 2001, p. 4). Reintegrative shaming is a concept widely used in Australia and Asian countries to describe a passage from community disapproval to reintegration. While reintegrative shaming is not the stigmatizing form of shaming as traditionally practiced in the criminal justice system, we come from a strengths-based and solution-focused perspective and wish to avoid any negativism that the term *shaming* connotes. Braithwaite and Braithwaite (2001), writing in their chapter, "Shame and Shame Management," state that "it is imperative to distinguish between good and bad shaming and harmful and helpful shame. This does not mean that social movement advocates should actually use the word shame as part of their reform rhetoric; with restorative justice.... Responsibility and healing are likely to supply a more politically resonant and a more prudent neoliberal discourse than shame and reintegration" (p. 5). We support this strategy and prefer to use the positive concepts of responsibility and healing rather than shame to describe preferred restorative outcomes.

Organization of the Book

Following the introductory chapters, which provide a historical and theoretical overview, the chapters in this text basically are organized in order from the more individually based, small-group restorative rituals and interventions (for example, victim-offender conferencing), to family and community-level strategies and practices that can be provided by educational, correctional, and religious institutions (for example, Family Group Conferencing), to macro-level peacemaking commissions (for example, truth and reconciliation commissions in the aftermath of war).

Restorative Justice Today: Practical Applications, as the title suggests, provides descriptions of specific programming. The book is divided into five sections: Overview; Prevention Programs and Community Practice; Pretrial: Before or After Arrest—Diversion Programs; In Correctional and Reentry Programs; and Community Restoration and Reparation. Within each section, each contribution is preceded with an introduction by the editors and each chapter contains two critical thinking questions at the end. Seven of the chapters contain boxed readings placed by the editors to provide a more personal or contextual dimension to the text.

The authors come from many parts of the world, including Australia, Canada, New Zealand, El Salvador, Greece, Norway, Hong Kong, New Zealand, Puerto Rico, and the United States. The topics are diverse as well and include the use of restorative strategies in situations of domestic violence, sexual assault, clergy abuse, juvenile justice, adult corrections, reentry to the community following incarceration, anti-bullying programming, practices related to drug courts and mental health courts, environmental justice, and reparations to tribal and racial populations who have been wronged by the society.

About the Editors

We editors bring to this project a dedication borne out of personal life experience and teaching. Both of us have done extensive research on the criminal justice system and have taught restorative justice in our classrooms.

From Katherine S. van Wormer, MSSW, PhD,
Professor of Social Work, University of Northern Iowa

I grew up in New Orleans, was actively involved in two civil rights movements, one in North Carolina and the other in Northern Ireland. After I returned, I became a sociologist with a research interest in women in prison. I taught criminal justice at Kent State for five years and then returned to graduate school to become a social worker.

Attending an international social work conference at the University of Calgary, I first learned of restorative justice. For me, this was a great eureka (I have found it!) moment. Spreading the word about this more humanistic form of justice has been a personal mission of mine ever since. My passion is writing, and in every book, I include sections on different aspects of restorative justice. My most recent books are *Death by Domestic Violence: Preventing the Murders and the Murder-Suicides* (Praeger, 2009); *Women and the Criminal Justice System* (coauthored with C. Bartollas, Prentice Hall, 2010); *Working with Female Offenders: A Gender-Sensitive Approach* (Wiley, 2010); *Human Behavior and the Social Environment* (Oxford, 2011); and *The Maid Narratives* (co-authored with D. Jackson and C. Sudduth, LSU Press, 2012).

From Lorenn Walker, JD, MPH, University of Hawaii Honolulu Community College and Restorative Justice Practitioner, Hawai'i Friends of Justice and Civic Education

I grew up in Japan and Santa Cruz, California, and have lived in Hawai'i most of my adult life. In Santa Cruz, I lived on my own at age 14, did not finish high school, and spent some time in jail. I became a Montessori preschool and kindergarten teacher when I was 19 and taught until I was 23. I was almost murdered by an unknown assailant, which helped motivate me to go to law school. Through my 30s I was a Hawai'i deputy attorney general representing state agencies and employees, including correctional officers, prisons, social workers, schools, teachers and the child welfare system. I also prosecuted people and later was a criminal defense attorney for indigent youth and adults. After becoming disillusioned with lawyering as a means to improve things, I studied public health. Since 1996 I have developed, provided, and evaluated nine restorative justice projects with a range of groups including juveniles; crime victims where no offenders are identified or participate; and people in prison. The projects were all developed and provided in collaboration with a variety of entities including courts, police, prisons, and nonprofits. As a college instructor, I have taught restorative justice for undergraduate and graduate students in criminal justice courses and for the last 10 years included it in personal and public speaking courses. I have visited prisons on all continents except Africa, and taught restorative justice workshops to thousands of people in the United States and internationally. I have facilitated restorative meetings for people involved in all ranges of harm including murders and other serious felony offenses.

Reference

Braithwaite, J., & Braithwaite, V. (2001). Shame and shame management. In E. Ahmed, N. Harris, J. Braithwaite, & V. Braithwaite (Eds.), *Shame management through reintegration* (pp. 3–59). Cambridge, UK: Cambridge University Press.

Acknowledgments

Katherine van Wormer would like to acknowledge her husband, Robert, for his helpful suggestions and careful proofreading of the text. She would also like to thank the University of Northern Iowa for their continuing support and encouragement.

Lorenn Walker thanks her husband, Jim, for editing her articles; all of her co-authors, including Katherine van Wormer for inviting her to assist in editing; the Hawai'i Friends of Justice & Civic Education board and volunteers for supporting RJ programs; Hawai'i judges Leslie Hayashi, Steve Alm, Mike Wilson, Mark Browning, Matt Viola and Chief Justice Mark Recktenwald and retired Chief Justice Ronald Moon for promoting pono kaulike, which retired judge Michael Town introduced and for his continued service on the Parole Board, which she also thanks along with its dedicated parole officers; also David Hipp and Merton Chinen of the Hawai'i Office of Youth Services for helping our incarcerated youth learn through RJ; the Hawai'i prison director Ted Sakai, warden Mark Patterson and Larson Medina for helping bring RJ into our prisons and healing for our community; and big mahalo to Native Hawaiians and the other indigenous people who have never stopped practicing RJ.

Both editors wish to thank Sage acquisitions editor Jerry Westby for his enthusiastic support of this project from start to finish. Dan Gordon did an outstanding job in the copy editing. Finally, we owe a debt of gratitude to all the contributors who willingly shared their expertise and hard work with us; the people who are willing to engage in restorative practices; those who promote it; and all those who might read this book and be compelled to learn more about RJ and help advance the field in the future.

PART I

Overview: Introduction to Restorative Justice

The chapters in this section view restorative justice theory and practices yesterday as well as today. First, to provide a theoretical and historical context, we consider the contributions for this book from Howard Zehr, a pioneer of modern restorative justice. Then, in Chapter 2, we hear from another pioneer, Kay Pranis, who discusses the early adoption of restorative practices by the Minnesota Department of Corrections, a history that is not widely known. Box 2, which follows, recalls more of this history—this time from Burt Galaway, one of the founders of the Minnesota Restitution Center. While conducting research on the history of restorative justice in its contemporary form for the book, we learned that Minnesota can lay claim to having established the first victim-offender dialogue program in North America, although most writers on restorative justice trace its contemporary origins to victim-offender meetings held in Kitchener, Ontario, Canada, in 1974. The focus of both of these pioneering programs was on restitution.

A boxed reading, Box 3, is taken directly from the restorative justice website of the Iowa Department of Corrections. This selection offers a step-by-step description of the process from the point of view of the victim of crime who seeks face-to-face dialogue with the offender.

Chapter 3 describes a unique program at Bluffton University, a Mennonite college in Ohio, that consistent with pacifist traditions has integrated restorative justice principles within the criminal justice and social work curricula. The final chapter in this section by law professor David Wexler, cofounder of therapeutic jurisprudence (TJ), draws parallels between TJ (exemplified in drug and mental health courts) and restorative justice. TJ is geared more toward the needs of the offender to take responsibility for the crime while RJ focuses more on victims' needs to receive some form of reparation for the harm done to him or her. Both TJ and RJ approaches are about reconciliation and healing.

Restorative Justice: Definition and Purpose

Lorenn Walker

This introductory chapter by Lorenn Walker, which includes a contribution by restorative justice pioneer Howard Zehr, describes the basic values, purpose, and philosophy of RJ practices. The starting point is the history of this form of justice, which is now seen as an alternative to standard justice, yet has its roots in traditional settlements of disputes between warring parties. How the principles of this more informal form of justice shaped restorative justice as we know it today throughout North America is chronicled in this essay, which includes little known facts on the early role played by Zehr in the development of contemporary restorative practices.

"I came home, and someone had broken my back kitchen window. They went in my bedroom and stole my jewelry. I didn't really care about most of it, except my grandmother's wedding ring. It was too small and I never got around to getting it fitted for me," says Jane, whose home was burglarized. A few days later, Jane's 19-year-old neighbor is arrested. A web camera that Jane uses to keep an eye on her dogs while she is at work records her young neighbor taking things out of her jewelry box. When confronted by the police, the young woman quickly confesses and is arrested. Jane eventually gets her grandmother's wedding ring back, but not for many months. "Sorry, we need it for evidence," the police tell Jane.

The young woman pleads guilty in court as part of a plea bargain with the prosecutor after consulting with Jane who agrees to the sentencing terms.

Jane has known the young woman since she was 4 years old when Jane moved into the house next door. Jane and the young woman's parents are good friends. Jane knows the young woman has a drug problem. She wants her to get help, and she wants to keep her neighborhood safe.

This is the first criminal offense committed by the 19-year-old. The judge sentences her to probation for a few years and requires her to stay drug-free and maintain employment. She must also complete a residential drug treatment program as recommended by a substance abuse counselor who gave her an assessment before sentencing. The judge also suggests that the woman consider participating in a *restorative justice meeting* with a nonprofit organization that provides a facilitator who will arrange and conduct it.

The young woman, Jane, and a few of each of their family members, all participate in a restorative meeting a few weeks later. Jane explains why she wants to participate. "We live next to each other. I care about her and her parents. I can't just pretend nothing happened. I want us all to talk about what happened. Hopefully, we can move on."

The meeting takes about three hours. Everyone describes how the young woman's theft affected him or her. "It's horrible knowing someone went through my things and took my grandmother's ring. I felt trampled on, violated. It was like I didn't matter as a person to someone else, someone who I babysat for and sang happy birthday to for the last 15 years. I thought we cared about each other, loved each other, and looked out for each other. Crazy me, thinking she would protect my house. Then this. I wondered if my friendship with her parents was even over. It's been just awful," says Jane.

The young woman's mother said, "I worry it's my fault she got into drugs. I can't help thinking I was a bad parent. I worked full time when she was little. I should have stayed home with her more. And that she did it to Jane, who's been so close to us. That really hurt."

Later, the group discusses what they need to repair the harm. Jane talks about the material loss she suffered with her kitchen window broken, and also her emotional pain. Besides worrying about her friendship with the young woman's parents, she worried about her grandmother's ring while the police had it. She says she couldn't stop thinking, "If only I had gotten the ring fixed, I would have been wearing it, and it wouldn't have been stolen." Her anxiety kept her awake at night. It was hard for her to concentrate at work.

To repair the harm, Jane asked the young woman to pay the cost of repairing Jane's window and to "stay clean and sober," which she readily agreed to do. After the meeting everyone felt better and believed that they could continue being friends and neighbors. This restorative meeting, loosely based on real incidents, illustrates how restorative justice can improve the criminal justice system and justice outcomes for a community.

Restorative Justice Development

Modern restorative justice developed from experiments in the 1970s that brought people who committed crimes together with the people whom they had hurt[1] (See Box 3 by Galaway, "Reflections of a Founder," in Chapter 2). Restorative justice provided a new

---

[1]Every effort is made in this chapter to avoid using the labels "victim" and "offender," which are based on judgments about what people have experienced and done. Labels categorize people and can limit our perceptions of them. People are always more than what has happened to them and more than what they have done in the past.

focus on individuals and communities asking what people needed to heal from incidents of wrongdoing. People connected by crimes, those who committed them and those who were the targets of them, met for discussions. They talked about accountability for the crime, how people were harmed, and how the harm might be repaired. This kind of response to crime is radically different from the criminal justice system's main focus on identifying and punishing offenders.

We say *modern* restorative justice because since ancient times many indigenous cultures have continued to apply principles that embody restorative justice philosophy. Ancient Western cultures too applied restorative principles prior to the Norman Conquest about a thousand years ago when kings began representing individuals. Today, in place of kings, governments prosecute wrongdoers for the state and community, and have assumed the role of aggrieved individuals. This was a major shift in dealing with crime. Individuals no longer represented themselves, and lost "any meaningful place in the justice process" (Van Ness & Strong, 2002, p. 10). With government representing people, the individuals harmed by crime no longer had a primary role, and the focus was no longer on accountability and how the harm might be repaired.

Only the government and the people accused of committing crimes, with their lawyers and any witnesses they choose to testify, have the right to participate in criminal trials. Punishment has taken center stage away from the hurt party. Instead of considering reparations and healing for those harmed, the government punishes the convicted and collects fines for its general funds. This shift also altered personal accountability for individuals who committed crimes. Concern about how their behavior affected others shifted to defending themselves against government punishment.

The need to return to commonsense problem solving toward crime helped motivate resurgence of restorative justice (RJ). "RJ was brought back not by politicians or policymakers, but by passionate practitioners working in the voluntary and community sector in the hope of bringing balance and justice where the traditional criminal justice system failed" (Gavrielides, 2007, p. 267).

Restorative justice considers crime more holistically than the mainstream criminal justice system does. RJ recognizes that crime can cause both physical and emotional harms for people, and that crime affects different groups of people. RJ addresses any kind of harm and what may be needed to repair it. RJ gives people opportunities to heal (Zehr, 1990).

People harmed by crime include those directly targeted and hurt by the crime (e.g., a family whose house is burglarized); the loved ones of those harmed, (e.g., family members who do not live in the burglarized home who were negatively affected because their loved ones were burglarized); and the person who committed the crime, and their loved ones (e.g., the burglar and her or his loved ones). Restorative justice also provides those who caused the crime the opportunity to be accountable for their behavior, which can also be healing them[2] (Eglash, 1977).

---

[2]It can also be healing for the people harmed to have the person who committed the crime assume accountability. Many victims have reported that hearing the offender take responsibility was healing.

Since 1975, when psychologist Albert Eglash first used the term *restorative justice* (Bazemore, 1999) it has been an evolving philosophy. Eglash's use of the term *restorative justice* developed out of his work with criminal offenders, not for the concern of victims. He originally believed "restorative justice and restitution, like its two alternatives, punishment and treatment, is concerned primarily with offenders. Any benefit to victims is a bonus, gravy, but not the meat and potatoes of the process" (Eglash, 1977, p. 99). As RJ developed, it has become well-accepted that the concern for victims is a central theme in the movement (Zehr, 1990). RJ was originally only used for criminal cases while today it is recognized as useful for a wide range of situations including civil matters (Braithwaite, 2002). RJ is also expected to continue evolving (UN, 2007).

Howard Zehr is one of the world's most recognized restorative justice pioneers. In 1978, he was the director of a small halfway house for formerly incarcerated people in northern Indiana. One day the halfway house was burned down and destroyed. The nonprofit that owned the halfway house, which also employed Zehr, did not have the funds to rebuild. Instead, Zehr was asked to work with probationers by bringing them together with the people that they hurt in "victim-offender reconciliation" meetings. Today, Zehr (2011) says "The only connection with RJ and the halfway house fire is that it forced me out of my one-sided advocacy mode."

Up until this point Zehr's experience was advocating for people being prosecuted in court. Until he conducted a restorative meeting, he did not appreciate the value of bringing people harmed by crime together with those who caused it to address the injustice. Nor did he understand how crime impacted the people harmed by it, and how much they were part of the "crime equation."

The first restorative meeting Zehr facilitated was a transformative experience that completely shifted his focus. "I began then to facilitate court-referred meetings between victims and offenders, and that's when my vision changed." Not only did he become a strong advocate for restorative meetings, but he also believed strongly in "empowering and including the community" (Zehr, 2011). His first experiences with the restorative meetings set the course for the next 30 years of his professional life, and guided the important contributions he has made in restorative justice.

For the restorative meetings that took place in 1978, there were no written directions available to assist him in providing and facilitating the process. Recognizing the need for assistance and guidance, in 1980 Zehr wrote a handbook on how to facilitate meetings between victims and offenders based on his experiences. Thus began Zehr's long and prolific history of describing how restorative justice works and its rationale. He believes he first heard Eglash use the *restorative justice* term and recalls Eglash did not believe victims needed to be involved. Zehr adopted *restorative justice* to describe the work he was doing, bringing harmed people together with those who caused the harm to discuss how they were affected, to take accountability for themselves, and to address ways the harm might be repaired (Zehr, 2011).

In 1990, Zehr's seminal book on restorative justice, *Changing Lenses: A New Focus for Crime and Justice,* was published. He was surprised with the positive response that the book received (Zehr, 2011), and like the evolutionary restorative justice movement itself, Zehr's ideas about what restorative justice means today have changed since he wrote *Changing Lenses* (Zehr, 2002).

Box 1

Restorative Justice? What's That?

by Howard Zehr, Professor of Restorative Justice,
Eastern Mennonite University

Do a Google search for the phrase "restorative justice" and you will get over a million hits for a term that was virtually nonexistent 25 years ago. Ask what it means and you may get a variety of answers.

For many, it implies a meeting between victims of crime and those who have committed those crimes. A family meets with the teenagers who burglarized their home, expressing their feelings and negotiating a plan for repayment. Parents meet with the man who murdered their daughter to tell him the impact and get answers to their questions. A school principal and his family meet with the boys who exploded a pipe bomb in their front yard, narrowly missing the principal and his infant child. The family's and the neighbors' fears of a recurrence are put to rest and the boys for the first time understand the enormity of what they have done.

Restorative justice does include encounter programs for victims and offenders; today there are thousands of such programs all over the world. But restorative justice is more than an encounter, and its scope reaches far beyond the criminal justice system. Increasingly, schools are implementing restorative disciplinary processes, religious bodies are using restorative approaches to deal with wrongdoing—including clergy sexual abuse—and whole societies are considering restorative approaches to address wrongs done on a mass scale. Of growing popularity are restorative conferences or circle processes that bring groups of people together to share perspectives and concerns and collaboratively find solutions to the problems facing their families and communities.

Restorative justice emerged in the 1970s as an effort to correct some of the weaknesses of the western legal system while building on its strengths. An area of special concern has been the neglect of victims and their needs; legal justice is largely about what to do with offenders. It has also been driven by a desire to hold offenders truly accountable. Recognizing that punishment is often ineffective, restorative justice aims at helping offenders to recognize the harm they have caused and encouraging them to repair the harm, to the extent it is possible. Rather than obsessing about whether offenders get what they deserve, restorative justice focuses on repairing the harm of crime and engaging individuals and community members in the process.

It is basically common sense—the kind of lessons our parents and forebearers taught—and that has led some to call it a way of life. When a wrong has been done, it needs to be named and acknowledged. Those who have been harmed need to be able to grieve their losses, to be able to tell their stories, to have their questions answered—that is, to have the harms and needs caused by the offense addressed. They—and we—need to have those who have done wrong accept their responsibility and take steps to repair the harm to the extent it is possible.

As you might imagine with so many Google references, the usage of the term varies widely. Sometimes it is used in ways that are rather far removed from what those in the field have intended. So when you see the term, you might ask yourself these questions: Are the wrongs being acknowledged? Are the needs of those who were harmed being addressed? Is the one who committed the harm being encouraged to understand the damage and accept his or her obligation to make right the wrong? Are those involved in or affected by this being invited to be part of the "solution"? Is concern being shown for everyone involved? If the answers to these questions are "no," then even though it may have restorative elements, it isn't restorative justice.

Restorative Justice Definitions

There is no definition of restorative justice that everyone agrees with. The United Nations says

> Restorative justice is a way of responding to criminal behaviour by balancing the needs of the community, the victims and the offenders. It is an evolving concept that has given rise to different interpretation in different countries, one around which there is not always a perfect consensus (2006).

Tony Marshall, who worked for the British government, developed a restorative justice definition that is often quoted: "Restorative Justice is a process whereby all the parties with a stake in a particular offence come together to resolve collectively how to deal with the aftermath of the offence and its implications for the future" (1999, p. 5).

Carolyn Boyes-Watson, director of the Center for Restorative Justice at Suffolk University in Boston, provides this definition:

> Restorative justice is a broad term which encompasses a growing social movement to institutionalize peaceful approaches to harm, problem-solving and violations of legal and human rights. These range from international peacemaking tribunals such as the Truth and Reconciliation Commission of South Africa to innovations within our criminal justice system, schools, social services and communities.
>
> Rather than privileging the law, professionals and the state, restorative resolutions engage those who are harmed, wrongdoers and their affected communities in search of solutions that promote repair, reconciliation and the rebuilding of relationships. Restorative justice seeks to build partnerships to reestablish mutual responsibility for constructive responses to wrongdoing within our communities.
>
> Restorative approaches seek a balanced approach to the needs of the victim, wrongdoer and community through processes that preserve the safety and dignity of all (Center for Restorative Justice, 2011).

The late Elizabeth Elliot was a restorative justice professor, and codirector of the Centre for Restorative Justice at the School of Criminology, Simon Fraser University, British Columbia, and the author of *Security With Care: Restorative Justice & Healthy Societies* (2011). She believed that "restorative justice is, among other things, a problem-solving approach to conflict and wrongdoing and so invites us to bring all possibilities to the circle" (p. 47). Elliott also said, "Restorative justice processes create environments in which reflection on experiences of an event can help everyone affected to learn and grow," and "RJ processes are accountable to core values, generating questions such as, 'Was the process respectful of everyone involved? Did it include everyone who felt they needed to be there? Was the outcome fair for everyone involved?'" (pp. 104–105).

Theo Gavrielides, a London-based human rights academic and lawyer, conducted a seven-year research project studying what restorative justice meant to 40 international RJ practitioners and researchers. His arduous work culminated in a 301-page book: *Restorative Justice Theory and Practice: Addressing the Discrepancy.* Gavrielides believes "the only agreement that exists in the literature regarding RJ's concept is that there is no consensus as to its exact meaning (Daly & Imarrigeon, 1998; Harris, 1998; McCold, 1998; Sullivan, Tifft, & Cordella; 1998). The truth is that only until recently restorative theory and practice have advanced enough to create a general sense of, at least, what RJ stands for" (Gavrielides, 2007, p. 37). Further, he says: "Restorative Justice is an ethos with practical goals, among which is *to restore harm* by including affected parties in a (direct or indirect) encounter and a process of understanding through voluntary and honest dialogue" (Gavrielides, 2007). He believes that "like any practice, RJ has its own philosophical basis. Questions about what qualifies a practice to be 'restorative' should be different from . . . RJ philosophy" (Gavrielides, 2011). (See Chapter 15 of this text by Theo Gavrielides in which he discusses the role of restorative strategies in responding to clergy sexual abuse.)

Restorative Justice Terminology

As restorative justice has aged and evolved, the concepts and language used to describe it have also changed, reflecting its further development. The field of restorative justice is growing quickly, and as it does, new concepts and terms are being developed to explain and describe the field.

Ted Wachtel, an RJ educational developer, and Paul McCold, who researches and writes about RJ, popularized the term *restorative practices*. Restorative practices describe processes that embody restorative justice principles and philosophy, which may not involve crimes or even wrongdoing (Wachtel & McCold, 2003). Schools and colleges are examples of using RJ practices to help youth and adults reflect on their behavior, which can prevent crime even where there has been no crime or wrongdoing. (See Chapter 6 of this text by Margaret Thorsborne and Chapter 11 of this text by Ted Wachtel & Stacy Miller in which they discuss RJ applications by schools.)[3] Transition and planning processes for marginalized populations can also utilize restorative practices (Walker, Sakai, & Brady, 2006; Walker & Greening, 2010).

When a wrongdoing has occurred, a restorative practice asks, "Who was affected by the wrongdoing? How? What could possibly be done to repair the harm?" These questions can be asked by a facilitator of the people harmed by crime, and of those who did the harming, without the parties ever meeting. (See Chapter 5 of this text by Lorenn Walker describing how RJ practices can be used for crime victims without any participation of offenders.) Additionally, people can engage in a restorative practice without the participation of a facilitator or anyone at all (see www.apologyletter.org).

Attempting to distinguish the concept of restorative justice further, Daniel Van Ness, a former criminal lawyer and another early pioneer in the RJ movement, proposes the term *restorative living*. Van Ness proposes in his blog that when the RJ values that Zehr delineates are applied in our daily lives, we are engaging in restorative living (2011).

---

[3]That restorative practices can reduce recidivism too is important because reducing crime reduces the number of people harmed by crime.

Van Ness suggests,

> [M]y modest proposal is that we begin to use the term "restorative living" when we think of being guided by restorative values, the term "restorative practices" when we are speaking of the more limited numbers of occasions when we use collaborative encounters, and "restorative justice" when those values and practices are carried out in the context of the criminal justice system (2011).

His suggestion that we should use the term *restorative justice* only for criminal cases raises concerns. John Braithwaite, one of the most highly respected restorative justice experts in the world, commented on Van Ness' proposal. "I like restorative living and restorative practices … [but] we should also like justice as something that matters much more widely than in criminal law" (Van Ness, 2011).

Elizabeth Elliot shared Braithwaite's concern. She believed that "limiting the term 'justice' to a system would negate the idea that justice starts with each and every one of us, within a 'restorative living' context." Elliot believes "justice is too important a term to be relegated to western justice systems," which she fears could happen if we limited RJ to only criminal justice.

The discussion with Braithwaite, Elliott and others on the Van Ness blog is a good example of how the field of restorative justice is ever changing, and with more research and development it will continue changing in the future.

Regardless of people's disagreements over what is and what is not restorative justice, it is important to remember that restorative justice is concerned with people's needs and offers people opportunities for healing while the mainstream criminal justice system primarily focuses on identifying and punishing people.

Restorative Justice's Focus on People Harmed by Crime

Most restorative justice advocates and practitioners agree that more attention should be paid to the people harmed by crime. Currently the criminal justice system basically responds to crime by trying to identify the person who committed the crime, convicting them, and punishing them. Out of all the crimes known by law enforcement to have been committed in the United States, overall only 21% result in anyone ever being arrested or charged (U.S. Department of Justice, 2009). This leaves almost 80% of all reported crimes without anyone identified as accountable, and it leaves the people hurt by those crimes with little access to the justice system beyond reporting the event.[4]

After a suspect is identified and arrested, the justice system puts its resources into working for a conviction. Of the people who are charged with offenses and face trials in the United States, over 90% plead guilty without a trial (Hall, 2009). After conviction,

---

[4]Reporting an event to a police officer might be a relief for some people hurt by crime because they could express any frustration and indignation about it, but in some cities like Honolulu, reports for certain crimes including car theft are no longer made personally to police officers. Instead, car theft reports are taken over the phone, which limits assistance to people hurt by crime even further.

the criminal justice system puts more resources into punishment, which often means prison sentences. The United States continues to have the highest incarceration rates in the world (Pew, 2008).

In addition to finding the people to blame for crimes and punishing them, every state has a *crime compensation fund,* usually only for people harmed by violent crimes. The compensation funds provide money mainly for medical costs, counseling, funeral costs, lost wages and out-of-pocket losses. In 2001, about $400 million was spent on compensating harmed people (Eddy, 2003). Contrast this with the estimated $38 billion spent on incarcerating people (Executive Office of President, 2001).

What people need to heal after a crime occurs, including their material, physical, and emotional needs, is not a primary focus of the mainstream justice system. Restorative justice cares about "Who was harmed? How were they harmed? And what can be done to repair the harm?" These questions can shift the focus from only identifying and punishing people who committed crimes to concentrating on meeting people's needs for reparations and healing.

As Zehr says, when determining whether something is restorative we need to consider the principles, the values, whether the stakeholders are included, along with the other areas he outlines in *Restorative Justice in Threes.* In studying RJ and deciding for yourself what it means and what its purpose is, you can consider what Zehr suggests.

Box 2

Howard Zehr's Restorative Justice in Threes

Three *assumptions* underlie restorative justice:

- When people and relationships are harmed, needs are created
- The needs created by harms lead to obligations
- The obligation is to heal and "put right" the harms; this is a just response

Three *principles* of restorative justice reflect these assumptions: A just response . . .

- Repairs the harm caused by, and revealed by, wrongdoing (restoration)
- Encourages appropriate responsibility for addressing needs and repairing the harm (accountability)
- Involves those impacted, including the community, in the resolution (engagement)

Three underlying *values* provide the foundation:

- Respect
- Responsibility
- Relationship

Three *questions* are central to restorative justice:

- Who has been hurt?
- What are their needs?

(Continued)

(Continued)

- Who has the obligation to address the needs, to put right the harms, to restore relationships? (As opposed to, What rules were broken? Who did it? What do they deserve?)

Three *stakeholder* groups should be considered and/or involved:

- Those who have been harmed and their families
- Those who have caused harm and their families
- The relevant community

Three *aspirations* guide restorative justice: the desire to live in right relationship

- with oneself;
- with others; and
- with creation.

Critical Thinking Questions

1. What are the differences between the current mainstream criminal justice system and restorative justice? What difference would the two approaches make for someone harmed by a crime, and for someone who committed a crime?

2. How might the restorative justice movement change things by 2030 in the area of corrections, child welfare, and the courts?

References

Bazemore, G. (1999). Restorative Justice, Earned Redemption and a Communitarian Response to Crime, The Communitarian Network and the George Washington University Institute for Communitarian Policy Studies. Retrieved from http://www.gwu.edu/~ccps/Bazemore.html

Braithwaite, J. (2002). *Restorative justice and responsive regulation.* Oxford, UK: Oxford University Press.

Center for Restorative Justice. (2011). Suffolk University College of Arts & Sciences http://www.suffolk .edu/research/6953.html

Daly, K., & Imarrigeon, R. (1998). The past, present, and future of restorative justice: Some critical reflections. *Contemporary Justice Review, 1,* 21–45.

Eddy, D. (2003). State crime compensation programs: Nature and scope. National Roundtable on Victim Compensation: Exploring the Role and Future of Crime Victim Compensation, National Center for Victims of Crime.

Eglash, A. (1977). Beyond restitution: Creative restitution. In J. Hudson and B. Galaway (Eds.), *Restitution in criminal justice.* Lexington, Mass.: D.C. Heath.

Elliot, E. (2011). *Security with care: Restorative justice & healthy societies.* Nova Scotia, Canada: Fernwood Publishing.

Executive Office of the President (2001). Drug treatment in the criminal justice system, Office of National Drug Control Policy. Retrieved from http://www.whitehousedrugpolicy.gov/publications/factsht/ treatment/index.html

Gavrielides, T. (2007). *Restorative justice theory and practice: Addressing the discrepancy.* Helsinki, Finland: European Institute for Crime Prevention and Control affiliated with the United Nations. Retrieved from http://www.heuni.fi/uploads/8oiteshk6w.pdf

Gavrielides, T. (2011). Online comments to Van Ness' Restorative terminology: A modest proposal, *Restorative Justice Online.* Retrieved from http://restorativejustice.org/RJOB/restorative-terminology-a-modest-proposal

Hall, D. (2009). *Criminal law and procedure.* Lexington, KY: Delmar Publishing.

Harris, K. (1998). Reflections of a Skeptical Dreamer: Some Dilemmas in Restorative Justice Theory and Practice, *Contemporary Justice Review* 1:57–69.

Marshall, T. (1999) *Restorative Justice: An Overview.* London, UK: Home Office.

McCold, P. (1998). Restorative justice: Variations on a theme, In L. Walgrave (Ed.), *Restorative justice for juveniles: Potentialities, risks and problems for research.* Leuven, Belgium: Leuven University Press.

McCold, P., & Wachtel, T. (2003). In pursuit of paradigm: A theory of restorative justice, *Paper presented at the XIII World Congress of Criminology, 10-15 August 2003, Rio de Janeiro.* Retrieved from http://www.realjustice.org/articles.html?articleId=424

Pew Center on the States (2008). One in 100: Behind bars in America 2008. Retrieved from http://www.pewcenteronthestates.org/report_detail.aspx?id=35904

Sullivan, D., Tifft, L., & Cordella, P. (1998). The Phenomenon of Restorative Justice: Some Introductory Remarks, *Contemporary Justice Review* 1(1): 7–20.

U.S. Department of Justice (2009). Federal Bureau of Investigation, Criminal Justice Information Services Division, *Crime in the United States 2009, Percent of Offenses Table 25 Cleared by Arrest or Exceptional Means.* Retrieved from http://www2.fbi.gov/ucr/cius2009/data/table_25.html

United Nations, Office on Drugs and Crime (2006). *Handbook on restorative justice programmes.* United Nations: New York.

Van Ness, D. (2011). Restorative terminology: A modest proposal, RJONLINE BLOG, Restorative Justice Online. Retrieved from http://www.restorativejustice.org/RJOB/restorative-terminology-a-modest-proposal#comments

Van Ness, D., & Strong, K. (2002). *Restoring justice.* Cincinnati, OH: Anderson Publishing Co.

Walker, L., Sakai, T., & Brady, K. (2006). Restorative circles: A reentry planning process for Hawaii inmates, *Federal Probation Journal, 70*(1). Retrieved from http://www.uscourts.gov/uscourts/FederalCourts/PPS/Fedprob/2006-06/index.html

Walker, L., & Greening, R. (2010). Huikahi restorative circles: A public health approach for reentry planning, *Federal Probation Journal, 74*(1). Retrieved from: http://www.uscourts.gov/uscourts/FederalCourts/PPS/Fedprob/2010-06/06_restorative_circles.html

Zehr, H. (1990). *Changing lenses: A new focus for crime.* Scottdale, Pa.: Herald Press.

Zehr, H. (2002). *The little book of restorative justice.* Intercourse, Pa.: Good Books.

Zehr, H. (2011). Personal correspondence with Lorenn Walker May 22, 2011.

2

Reflections From a Descendant of the Minnesota Restitution Center (MRC)

Kay Pranis, former Restorative Justice Planner,
Minnesota Department of Corrections (1994–2003)

A consultant for the National Institute of Corrections and the National Institute of Justice, Kay Pranis has received many awards for her work in restorative justice and peacemaking, the latest being the 2001 American Probation and Parole Association's Sam Houston State University Award. Pranis is the author of numerous articles and book chapters. Her most recent book, The Little Book of Circle Processes, *describes the working of peacemaking circles in a broad range of contexts.*

I went to work for the Minnesota Department of Corrections in early 1994 in a brand-new position that we titled *restorative justice planner*. It was the first government position in the United States focused on restorative justice. I occasionally heard references to the Restitution Center, but did not connect that directly to the work I was doing.

I was very surprised to recently learn from Joe Hudson that the original Restitution Center (which began its victim-offender dialoguing in 1972) had included face-to-face meetings between victims and offenders to determine restitution. I had heard about the Restitution Center, but not about these face-to-face meetings. This was startling new information! That realization prompted several reflections for me.

The first idea that came was that there was a connection, unconscious perhaps, but nevertheless a connection between that project and the creation of a restorative justice position in the Department of Corrections 20 years later. John McLagan, who created the position I held at the Department of Corrections and was my supervisor, was the last director of the Restitution Center. By the time he joined the center, the face-to-face meetings were no longer being held. So that core element of a restorative framework was not part of his experience there. The focus was on restitution but not on victim involvement. John continued to work on restitution even after the center was closed. John was part of a cohort in the Department of Corrections who got degrees in social work and worked with Joe Hudson.

John McLaglan was not familiar with the concept of restorative justice in the 1980s, but he is a social worker at heart. He was oriented toward restitution and meaningful community service for offenders. I believe it was this orientation that resulted in his openness to the idea of restorative justice when it presented itself to him in the early 1990s. This orientation was partly who he is and partly his experience at the Restitution Center. John is the link from the Restitution Center to the creation of the position of restorative justice planner.

Change moves in nonlinear ways. Though John was not familiar with restorative justice and he was not part of the face-to-face meetings at the Restitution Center, I believe that it was no accident that John is the one who created the position of restorative justice planner at Minnesota Department of Corrections (MN DOC). I believe that one of the outcomes of the Minnesota Restitution Center initiative was the leadership of MN DOC in the restorative justice movement in the 1990s.

The creation of the position at MN DOC was one of the most important developments in the restorative justice movement in the 1990s because it gave government legitimacy to the movement. Before that happened, restorative justice was the interest of churches and small nonprofits. It was not something that governments got involved in. Because of the positive reputation of the MN DOC, restorative justice immediately became a legitimate government interest. The creation of that position changed the profile of restorative justice in the United States.

Like most good ideas, restorative justice has more than one source. The MRC was an effort from within the criminal justice system to implement criminal justice reform based on principles later identified as restorative justice. The Victim-Offender Reconciliation Program (VORP) movement with its roots in Mennonite churches and its restorative justice articulation by Howard Zehr was an external effort to influence criminal justice reform. The creation of the restorative justice position at MN DOC based on Zehr's vision and nestled in the heart of the corrections bureaucracy brought those two streams together creating a momentum for the movement that rippled across the United States.

The task force that developed the concept of the restorative justice position at MN DOC in 1993 was composed primarily of probation officers who specialized in restitution and community service. That ripe ground for planting the seeds of restorative justice was a result of the work that was piloted by the MRC.

At a recent training in Alberta, Canada, I spoke about the loss of numerous restorative justice programs as a result of budget cuts in the first decade of the 21st century.

I noted that after that contraction we now see an expansion of restorative justice programs and that they seem to me to be more deeply rooted than the early flurry of programs. A training participant who is a farmer suggested that a useful metaphor here is that of winter wheat. It comes up in the fall, dies above ground during the winter cold and then comes back strong in the spring. He said that if the winter is not cold enough to kill it above ground, it does not do well in the spring. This metaphor seems to describe very aptly what happened with the MRC. It appeared to die but the roots still had life that fed the growing disciplines of restitution and community service that became the seedbed for the full restorative philosophy within the corrections system.

I find this a cautionary tale about our ability to really know the impact of any particular initiative. And a cautionary tale about our tendency to want to tell a symbolic story as the origin of an important idea—our tendency to want to create singular heroes when life is much more complex than that. Change is not the work of singular heroes, but of many working together. That does not diminish the importance, for instance, of the Elmira, Ontario, story but reminds us that the wisdom exists everywhere and may emerge in nonlinear ways in multiple settings. And that I find an encouraging lesson!

It's always humbling to realize that you had ancestors who had the same wonderful ideas you have before you were born! That is metaphoric, of course—I was born before 1971, but I was not birthed in the criminal justice field until 1988. I honor Joe Hudson and Burt Galaway and those who worked with them who were trying to implement principles that I later got to promote on a full-time basis. My work at the MN DOC was hugely gratifying and deeply purposeful, and it was built on the foundation they helped create. [To learn more of this early history, see Hudson, J., & Galaway, B. (1974), Undoing the wrong: The Minnesota Restitution Center, *Social Work, 19*(3), 313–318. To see what the Minnesota Department of Corrections is doing today to advance restorative strategies, go to http://www.doc.state.mn.us/rj/links.htm]

Box 3

Reflections From a Founder of the Minnesota Restitution Center

Burt Galaway

Tracing the history of the Minnesota Restitution Center brought the editors of this book to Burt Galaway, one of the original founders of this early program. Galaway graciously agreed to recall this history and to set the record straight on which of the modern victim-offender restitution programs came first. Dr. Galaway is retired from professorships in social work at the University of Manitoba and the University of Minnesota. He is an internationally recognized author and researcher on specialist foster-family care, restorative justice, restitution, crime victim-offender dialogue, community service sentences, and spouse battering.

(Continued)

(Continued)

I joined the faculty of the University of Minnesota School of Social Work in 1970 and soon met Joe Hudson who was also a member of the faculty. We both had an interest and background in corrections and believed strongly that incarceration was overused. We had many discussions about alternatives to incarceration and were keenly aware and concerned that alleged alternatives often widened the net rather than replaced institutions.

Two events occurred in the early 1970s that were instrumental for establishing the Minnesota Restitution Center (MRC). The federal Law Enforcement Assistance Administration (LEAA) had been created in 1967; initially, this federal program focused on assisting local law enforcement primarily by providing grants for hardware. By the early 1970s, LEAA was under political pressure to provide support for corrections, especially community corrections; the agency responded by providing grants to state and local governments for halfway houses and other community correction's programs. Secondly, Wendell Anderson, a new Minnesota governor, had campaigned on a pledge to reform government, including prisons and corrections. Anderson recruited David Fogel from California as commissioner of corrections. Fogel had a reputation as a prison reformer. He was a creative and forward-looking commissioner. As it turned out, he was a little too forward-looking even for relatively progressive Minnesota!

Joe was doing his doctoral research at the Minnesota Department of Corrections and had met Fogel. I had been thinking about restitution for some time and was concerned that in social work and corrections there was reluctance to ask clients, both offenders and others, to take responsibility for their actions and engage in activities to better their communities. We arranged a meeting with Fogel and pitched out ideas to him. He was very receptive; the availability of LEAA funding provided an available funding source. We wrote a grant, with Fogel's support, to fund a residential community corrections center for adult male property offenders who would be diverted from the Minnesota State Prison to the center. Programming would center on restitution with the offenders and victims meeting for purposes of negotiating the amount and form of restitution. The grant was awarded. The MRC was located in leased space in the Minneapolis YMCA. The first resident was admitted in October 1972.

Joe served as the first director of the MRC and I was responsible for the research. We were concerned that MRC not admit offenders who might otherwise have been placed on probation; diverting from prison was central to our mission. Therefore, in cooperation with the Minnesota Adult Corrections Commission (parole board), we devised a series of criteria that were applied to each new admission to the Minnesota State Prison. Inmates who met the criteria went into an eligible pool from which we randomly drew two groups—those to be offered the opportunity to participate in the program of the MRC as an alternative to remaining in prison and a second, comparison group. Parole and restitution plans were prepared with the men selected for the MRC.

The plans were presented to the Adult Corrections Commission with a recommendation for parole in the fourth month after admission. Restitution and parole plans were developed during these four months; meetings were held at the prison between the offender and his victims for purposes of negotiating a restitution agreement that was presented to the ACC and, if approved, became a part of the offender's parole plan. The ACC would not agree in advance to parole randomly selected offenders who presented a parole plan and restitution agreement; they did, however, honor the spirit of the design. In the first 18 months of MRC operation, the ACC paroled all but one inmate for whom we could develop a parole plan and restitution agreement.

In 1973, Joe Hudson resigned as the MRC director to accept a faculty position at the University of Minnesota, Duluth; I was named director of the MRC. David Fogel resigned as Commissioner of Corrections in January 1973; Fogel was under heavy pressure from prison staff, the legislature, and the public because of his reforms and a series of prison escapes that were often attributed to the reforms. Ken Schoen, a Minnesota native, was named commissioner of corrections to replace Fogel. Schoen was also a reformer but more low key and gradual than Fogel; he did not have a commitment to the MRC.

A father-son team (the Freemens) had been operating a large-scale fencing operation and were arrested and convicted in 1973. They were purchasing stolen goods from an unknown number of burglars and shipping many of the items out of state for sale. They were high-profile offenders; their arrests and convictions were followed with considerable publicity. Both met the criteria for inclusion in the restitution group, and one was randomly selected to be offered the opportunity to participate in the MRC. Schoen asked me not to prepare a restitution parole plan for Freeman. I explained that this would be inconsistent with our policies and procedures, would be singling this man out for special treatment, and that the public safety was protected by the ACC, which would make the decision about parole to the MRC. I then received a direct order from Schoen not to prepare a restitution parole plan for Freeman and not to take any recommendation for parole to the ACC. I indicated that I could not follow this order because it would be wrong to single out an inmate for treatment inconsistent with our policy and procedures and that the ACC was the appropriate body to decide the public safety issue. I was then summarily fired on January 9, 1974, from the position of director of the MRC.

I sued the Department of Corrections and staff including Schoen in U.S. District Court in Minnesota (Galaway v. Lawson), alleging that I was dismissed because of my efforts to protect the constitutional rights of an inmate and asking for damages. I lost the case because the judge (Ross) ruled that my actions were motivated by a desire to protect the research design rather than the rights of an inmate. I received funds from a professional association to appeal the decision to the U.S. Court of Appeals, Eighth Circuit, but that court upheld Judge Ross's decision.

The Minnesota Department of Corrections closed the MRC in 1976 and reallocated staff to the Restitution Unit that was created to enhance and encourage more diverse use of restitution. I decided not to pursue the legal matter further and, after three months' unemployment, secured a faculty position at the University of Minnesota, Duluth. The balance of my career has been spent in academic settings, teaching and doing research. Occasionally, I wonder if my decision regarding Freeman grew out of inappropriate stubbornness or was an appropriate effort to treat inmates fairly and consistent with established policy and procedure.

Publications That Described These Early Developments

Galaway, B., & Hudson, J. (1972). *Restitution and rehabilitation: Some central issues. Crime and delinquency, 18*(4), 403–410.

Galaway, B., & Hudson, J. (1974). Undoing the wrong: The Minnesota restitution center. *Social Work, 19*(3), 313–318.

Galaway, B., & Hudson, J. (1977). *The use of restitution. Crime & delinquency, 23*(1), 57–67.

Heinz, J., Galaway, B., & Hudson, J. (1976), Restitution or parole: A follow-up study of adult offenders. *Social Service Review, 50*(1), 148–156.

Critical Thinking Questions

1. What do we learn from these early pioneers about an event in the history of restorative justice that has not made it to the history books on restorative justice?

2. Check out the website for restorative strategies offered today by the Minnesota Department of Corrections—what did you find out about its programming?

3. Now that you are familiar with the basics of RJ, consider the cover design, which was, as is the usual case, not chosen by the writers of the book. To what extent do the two chairs represent RJ? How might they be considered misleading?

3

Preparing Students of Criminal Justice for Restorative Justice Practice

Rudi Kauffman and Heather Koontz

This firsthand account by faculty at Bluffton University, a Mennonite school, describes how students are introduced to the restorative principles and practices at a university in which restorative justice serves as a bridge between departments of criminal justice and social work. Rudi Kauffman and Heather Koontz are assistant professors of restorative justice and social work respectively. Both are graduates of Bluffton University.

Studying, teaching, and applying restorative justice in America today offer a range of challenges and opportunities. Depending on the context, "restorative justice" takes on dramatically different meanings. Among victims, it may be received as a welcome opportunity to become involved in the process or rejected as overly lenient with offenders. In political decision-making, it can be seen as a means of saving money on incarceration or an added cost in a system that is already stretched. Different emphases provide widely varying applications. Is restorative justice solely about meeting the victim's needs, or does it require that the offender be spared violent retribution? Should it accept legal definitions of victims and offenders or is an offender anyone who offends regardless of the law?

The variation that comes from different perspectives and practices is often magnified in the diverse environments found in the American criminal justice system. Factors including position in the system (law enforcement, corrections, etc.); the population (juvenile, adult programs, etc.); and cultural influences (related to geographic region, dominant religious influences, etc.) alter the reception and implementation of restorative justice principles. One might find that juvenile corrections facilities in suburban eastern Pennsylvania are welcoming or even active in implementing restorative justice while an adult corrections facility or the police force in the same town are suspicious of the idea.

This chapter focuses on restorative justice education at Bluffton University, a small, Christian Midwestern liberal arts school. The program has a close relationship with the sociology and psychology program and extensive student and faculty overlap with the social work major. Students and faculty explore the real world value of restorative justice in the context of the U.S. criminal justice system.

The chapter provides three vignettes that illustrate common tensions expressed by Bluffton students. Although not diametrically opposed, the tensions between restorative justice and the assumptions of the criminal justice field can be expressed as tensions between procedural and substantive justice, rules-oriented and relationship-oriented justice, and pain allocation and right-making responses to injustice.

Vignette No. 1: "Everyone Speaks Gun . . ."

While exploring options for a field placement, I was speaking with a law enforcement officer. I had asked many of the standard questions about intern oversight and likely experiences of students when a theme emerged around the wide range of people that an intern was likely to meet. The officer noted that the biggest changes in the population he served were recent and tied to immigration.

He noted that he was coming in contact with more languages and "strange ideas of what's normal." Wondering a bit about how my student would fit in and be shaped by the environment, I asked if language training was necessary or desirable for the internship. I was told, "Everyone speaks gun."

This certainly got my attention; however, it illustrates an underlying assumption about the nature of justice. Clearly, the officer intended to communicate that he was able to overcome a range of challenges with force or a show of force. I would speculate that he saw justice as an extension of the law—something that could be created and maintained by force.

The views expressed here by a potential field supervisor are consistent with the assumptions of many students entering careers in criminal justice who often see it as powerful. From the symbolism of the badge and the power of a gun, both societal and student expectations are reinforced by these expectations, and by the tools and nature of the job. "Everyone speaks gun" more honestly means "everyone understands gun." This idea of justice does not require a deep understanding of the other—if one knows the rules and knows that they were violated, all that remains to be done is forcing the guilty party into submission.

This understanding provides tensions at a number of points with restorative justice leading to a range of teaching and learning opportunities. For those working and teaching in the field, the assumptions of justice that this makes serve as a valuable starting point for a conversation. The idea that justice can come through imposing power invites questions about the students' own experiences with such situations. Have life experiences proven this to be effective? What works? What does not work? How have you responded when somebody used force to "correct" you, whether you were speeding, picking on a sibling, or cheating on a test?

Ideally, such questions lead to honest responses. Some students undoubtedly have seen positive uses of dominance and power but can acknowledge the dangers. Others have likely seen examples where the short-term efficacy of being forced into a "just" outcome leads to powerful injustices over time. The discussion opens the door to questions about tension between rules-oriented and relationship-oriented justice.

Such conversations also offer opportunities for the teachers and practitioners. The stories and situations that are disclosed offer insights into the assumptions of others within restorative frameworks. In the broadest terms, many people experience a world in which violence and abuse grew from positions of power. In some instances, they experienced real relief only in situations where a greater power confronted their tormentor while in others, no relief has come, but the hope is that power might have made the difference. The stories are unique, usually painful, and almost always valuable in contextualizing, refining, and recreating one's own understanding of justice.

The first foundational step of developing an understanding of restorative justice in the criminal justice context at Bluffton is identifying one's own assumptions about how justice works and what justice looks like. Doing this through personal stories has the residual value of strengthening relationships within the class and between the teacher and student. Ideally, these discussions lead to a place where there is room to consider the real implications of both rules-based justice and relationship-based justice.

Vignette No. 2: Justice in the news, "Where is justice?" Versus "Justice has been done . . ."

In my classes, we start each period by discussing issues in the news and on campus. The focus is on ideas of justice with particular attention to the underlying assumptions of the media and various parties. Two examples of national stories that brought out some interesting discussion are presented here.

The first example comes from the fall of 2009 when award-winning director Roman Polanski was arrested in Switzerland at the request of the United States. The arrest was made in connection with a crime that Polanski had pleaded "guilty" to during his 1977 trial. The charges were related to the rape of a young girl. As the case reemerged, the victim publicly requested that it be dropped. There was substantial public outcry for a harsher response as well as some expressions of support for Polanski. The class really wrestled with the full spectrum of responses.

Students seeking more robust sanctions cited a range of ideas. Within the restorative context, they suggested more robust sanctions were necessary because of their own status as victims because they too were members of the community and Polanski had not made things right with them. Some openly called for revenge while others asserted that his extreme wealth and celebrity were the obvious sources of his lenient treatment, making it inherently unjust.

On the other side, students seeking more lenient treatment noted the victim's public forgiveness, the long period of apparent nonrecidivism, and the good that Polanski had brought to the world that would have been lost with extended incarceration. A broad range of other thoughts and ideas developed around these and other core arguments

The second case is from May 1, 2011. Following the shooting of Osama bin Laden in Pakistan, U.S. President Barack Obama said that "justice has been done." In spontaneous gatherings in New York and Washington, DC, the same phrase was repeated. Within the class, there were certainly those who agreed while others questioned the celebration of death or expressed a desire to see a process that involved the courts and formal sentencing. Broadly, however, in a younger class (predominantly sophomores) the underlying assumption was that there was justice in Osama bin Laden's death.

These cases represent widely different experiences, and the brief summary does not include all the experiences and ideas that entered the discussion. Even so, the cases illustrate a clear step in restorative justice pedagogy. As students learn to express their desire for justice and offer rationales, the opportunities grow for students of criminal justice to become champions of a more complete concept of justice. In these cases, students were considering critical distinctions and were exposed to honest discussion of what justice should be instead of simple debates about the meaning and application of law.

A variety of themes and tensions grow out of the discussions. Most prevalent among students who are just beginning to engage with the ideas of restorative justice is the distinction between justice and revenge. While one need not condemn or prioritize one concept over the other by acknowledging the distinction, there is a clear preference within the program to focus on justice rather than revenge. Indeed, responding to crime with revenge addresses very different objectives than those espoused by the criminal justice field. Revenge is reactive and affords no protection to the population. In the restorative context, revenge may be introduced by the victim as a need or desire for restoration to occur. If one accepts bin Laden's victimhood, the act of revenge against the United States might be considered an attempt for justice, while those who view the United States as the victim of bin Laden's actions might see the American demand for war as justified revenge. This problematic acceptance of violence illustrates the core problem that arises when accepting revenge as a piece of justice—new victims are created by new acts of revenge in the name of justice.

Invariably, these discussions raise questions about how procedural justice and substantive justice relate. While students express their desire for justice to be related to the outcomes of their actions, concern about the inconsistencies that arise from treating each case individually becomes a central theme. In short, as students try to decide how to handle Polanski or bin Laden, the desire for procedural justice grows out of pragmatic desire for the act of rendering justice itself to be fair, consistent, and evenhanded. These conversations lead in various directions. Ultimately they provide opportunities for aspiring criminal justice professionals to think critically about a variety of foundational assumptions including the problems and benefits of focusing on procedural justice.

Vignette No. 3: To choose justice or self-determination . . .

When Crystal entered her last semester of her senior year, she expected that her internship would be challenging in many ways. She felt academically prepared; after all, she had studied ethical dilemmas, oppressed populations, and the importance of social and economic justice for the past four years and maintained a 3.98 GPA. Nevertheless, she did not anticipate the reality of conflict between social work values in working with clients.

While completing an intake assessment in the mental health agency, she encountered a 50-year-old clinically depressed white male client who responded to a recommendation for pharmacological treatment by adamantly rejecting a referral to the local medical clinic because the primary physician "is colored." Crystal interrupted the assessment process and consulted with her field instructor who took over the case. She observed how the instructor skillfully stayed client-centered and only focused on how to get the client's need met for medication and did not address the client's racist remark about the physician.

She decided this was an issue to write about in her field journal. She said that her initial reaction was to educate the client about how his words were oppressive and offensive and did not understand how the field instructor could ignore these harmful comments. She wrote in her reflection, "How do we end this type of discrimination and promote equality, when at the same time, we have to respect all people's values even when they are socially oppressing?" She was questioning how to balance justice and self-determination . . . how to meet the requirements of the rules while aspiring to a sense of relational justice.

At Bluffton, the social work program offers a critical perspective to the criminal justice major. Four required courses within the major are taught by professors with social worker licensure. Many criminal justice majors also pursue majors and licensure in social work. This leads to an interesting set of challenges and outstanding opportunities.

A number of recurring questions can be drawn from these types of experiences: How can one meet the requirements of a system while still prioritizing an understanding of justice that goes beyond following the rules? Are there professional values that are incompatible with their understanding of justice? Such questions are important to developing a functional sense of restorative justice.

As in restorative dialogue, growth and understanding rarely leads to "positions" so much as an identification of "issues." Choosing how to respond in these types of challenging situations is a process that grows out of clear and thoughtful purpose ("issue") rather than rigid statements about what a person will "never" or "always" do ("position"). For these reasons, we encourage students to consider the purpose and value of the rules and of challenging the rules. The goal is not to create orthodox practitioners of restorative justice, but to help the students develop an understanding of what restorative justice looks like in their lives. This can be a painful and life-altering experience. Some students will find themselves incapable of serving in law enforcement settings because they cannot in good faith enforce drug laws, carry a gun, or accept the rules-oriented understanding of justice. Others will embrace a career path after discovering that the tensions they feel between their understandings of justice and the law's requirement can be dealt with in ways that energize them and bring about meaningful change to individuals or systems.

Throughout this discernment process, Bluffton strives to provide students with opportunities to experience and critically analyze the impact of career choices on their ability to be effective proponents of justice. By its very nature, restorative justice precludes forcing external standards on what justice must look like; however, introspective consideration tends to make those pursuing careers in justice more aware and engaged in the systems and choices that define their professions.

Critical Thinking Questions

1. In what ways are the concepts of "crime" and "justice" related? What makes them different? Develop an example of (1) an unjust crime, (2) a just crime, (3) legal injustice, and (4) legal justice. How do you deal with the various cases you have described? How does your community deal with each? How does our country deal with each?

2. Consider each of the three stories. How would you have conducted yourself if you were the instructor in each setting? How do you respond to the statement, "Everyone speaks gun"? How do you reply when you hear another person speaking about "justice" in a way that you find immoral or unacceptable? How do you respond when someone is comfortable using language and expressing views that hurt other people?

4

Restorative Justice and Therapeutic Jurisprudence: All in the Family

David Wexler

Therapeutic Jurisprudence, often abbreviated as 'TJ', is an attempt to humanize the law by incorporating insights from psychology, criminology, and social work into the law and its administration. It sees the law as a dynamic social force that affects the emotional well-being of people. To TJ, the "law" consists of legal rules, legal procedures, and the roles of legal actors (judges, lawyers, and social workers) working in a legal context.

Practitioners today draw on TJ principles to set up therapeutic courts, such as drug courts and mental health courts (see Substance Abuse and Mental Health Services Administration [SAMHSA], 2009). Mental health courts provide intensive supervision by probation officers and a team of mental health professionals. Courts are being set up as well for veterans whose offenses are associated with war-related trauma. The following chapter, written by co-founder and scholar of therapeutic jurisprudence, contemplates the connection between the philosophy of therapeutic jurisprudence and restorative justice. David Wexler is professor of law and director, International Network on Therapeutic Jurisprudence, University of Puerto Rico, and distinguished research professor of law emeritus, University of Arizona. The author may best be contacted at david Bwexler@yahoo.com.

In a chapter of a forthcoming book, prepared for an Organization of American States project on drug treatment courts (DTCs) and therapeutic jurisprudence, Western Australia Magistrate Michael King and I wrote that "DTCs and TJ are close cousins, but they are not identical twins" (Wexler & King, in press). Exactly the same might be said about restorative justice (RJ) and therapeutic jurisprudence. Indeed, there is a palpable movement in the justice system, known in the United States as the "comprehensive law movement" and in Australia as "non-adversarial justice," in which "law and legal practice may be more humane, therapeutic, beneficial, humanistic, healing, restorative, curative, collaborative, and comprehensive" (Daicoff, 2000).

Restorative justice and therapeutic jurisprudence are key "vectors" within that movement, as are a number of other practices and processes, such as problem-solving courts (such as DTCs), preventive law, collaborative law, and more. The vectors are obviously different from each other, and yet they share certain characteristics relating to the promotion of human well-being (Daicoff, 2000).

My late colleague Bruce Winick "has aptly compared the vectors to a family and their common features to family resemblances—that is, some members are tall, some are short, some are brown-haired, and some are blonde, but all have similar noses and eye color" (cited by Daicoff, 2000, p. 471). As Susan Daicoff put it, "each vector is a distinct, independent entity with its own individuality, yet all the vectors are clearly related," that is, part of a larger family" (p. 471).

Without doubt, RJ and TJ each has a distinct, independent identity and individuality. Traditionally, RJ developed outside the law, or as an alternative to the legal process. TJ, by contrast, looks at the therapeutic and anti-therapeutic consequences of the law itself—rules of law, legal processes, and the roles (practices and techniques) of legal actors, such as lawyers, judges, and others who work within a legal context.

Despite their distinct identities, many of the vectors of the comprehensive law movement are beginning to interact. TJ has played a major role in relating to other vectors. Examples are DTCs and TJ (Winick & Wexler, 2002), TJ and preventive law (Patry, Wexler, Stolle & Tomkin, 1998), TJ and procedural justice (Wexler, 2008a).

TJ and RJ are also beginning to interact (Scheff, 1998; Schopp, 1998; Braithwaite, 2002). First of all, some use the term *RJ* in a very loose and imprecise (perhaps even inaccurate) way—to refer principally to a system of justice not anchored to a backward-looking, retributive, punitive model (Mail and Guardian, 2010). RJ in that loose sense is of course completely compatible with TJ and its rehabilitative agenda (Wexler & King, in press; King, 2009).

Moreover, even in its more technical sense, RJ is of immense importance to TJ. One cannot, for example, hold himself or herself out as a TJ lawyer without knowing of existing RJ programs, and trying, on appropriate occasions, to resolve a client's case through the use of procedures such as victim-offender dialoguing and the like. Also, a bit of RJ/TJ "blurring" is beginning to occur as proposals emerge regarding fuller victim participation in legal proceedings (Bibas, 2001; Wexler, 2008b; Erez, Kilchling, & Wemmers, 2011).

Finally, we are beginning to realize that TJ may learn from RJ and vice versa. Recently, for example, I used an article on modified restorative circles by this book's co-editor Lorenn Walker to prepare a TJ piece regarding a proposed "reentry moot court" for incarcerated persons readying for a parole hearing (Wexler, 2010a). A further example of RJ influencing TJ is Nicky McWilliam's recent study of school conflict resolution and peer intervention. McWilliam suggests that findings from the school bystander intervention project could well assist the development of legal processes, thereby contributing to the development of TJ (McWilliam, 2010). And the learning process is surely bidirectional, where TJ scholarship and practice can contribute to the development of RJ. Obviously, for example, the substance of Magistrate King's definitive judicial bench book on TJ and "solution-focused" judging (King, 2009) would provide excellent guidance to those involved in facilitating RJ processes. It is evident, then, that those in RJ and in TJ would enjoy and profit from frequent "family reunions."

As a take-away from this initial family reunion, let me suggest that RJ students and practitioners interested in learning more about TJ begin by reading a comprehensive and up-to-date introductory essay (Wexler, 2010b) and familiarizing themselves with the website (and comprehensive bibliography) of the International Network on Therapeutic Jurisprudence at www.therapeuticjurisprudence.org (where one can also join a useful and non-burdensome listserv) and the impressive TJ Facebook page, a fully international and interdisciplinary resource where many articles and documents of interest are constantly posted, www.facebook.com/TherapeuticJurisprudence. I look forward to interacting with many of you in the future.

Critical Thinking Questions

1. What is therapeutic jurisdiction? Give some examples from the Internet.

2. What are some major differences between RJ and TJ? How do specialized courts such as drug courts and mental health courts hold the possibility of incorporating RJ principles?

References

Bibas, S. (2001). Judicial fact-finding and sentence enhancements in a world of guilty pleas. *Yale Law Journal, 110,* 1097.

Braithwaite, J. (2002). Restorative justice and therapeutic jurisprudence, *Criminal Law Bulletin, 38*(2), 244.

Daicoff, S. (2000). The role of therapeutic jurisprudence within the comprehensive law movement. In D. P. Stolle, D. B. Wexler, & B. J. Winick (Eds.), *Practicing therapeutic jurisprudence: Law as a helping profession* (pp. 45–471). Durham, NC: Carolina Academic Press.

Erez, E., Kilchling, M., & Wemmers, J. (Eds., 2011). *Therapeutic jurisprudence and victim participation in justice. International perspectives.* Durham, NC: Carolina Academic Press.

King, M. S. (2009). *Solution-focused judging bench book.* Available at http://www.aija.org.au/Solution%20 Focused%20BB/SFJ%20BB.pdf

Mail and Guardian online (2010, November 20). Retrieved from http://www.mg.co.za/article/2010 -11-20-shiceka-calls-for-restorative-justice

McWilliam, N. J. (2010). A school peer mediation program as a context for exploring therapeutic jurisprudence (TJ): Can a peer mediation program inform the law? *International Journal of Law and Psychiatry*. Available online at http://ssrn.com/abstract=1694577

Patry, M. W., Wexler, D. B., Stolle, D. P., & Tomkins, A. J. (1998). Better legal counseling through empirical research: Identifying psycholegal soft spots and strategies. *California Western Law Review, 34*, 439–455

Scheff, T. J. (1990). Community conferences: Shame and anger in therapeutic jurisprudence. *Revista Juridica de la Universidad de Puerto Rico* (Law *9:(59)*1, 1–23.

Schopp, R. F. (1998). Integrating Restorative Justice and Therapeutic Jurisprudence7 *Revista Juridica de la Universidad de Puerto Rico* (Law), *67(3)*, 665.

Substance Abuse and Mental Health Services Administration[SAMHSA]. (2009). Treatment as an alternative to jail for people with mental illness. *SAMHSA News, 17*(2), 1–4.

Wexler, D. B. (2008a). Adding color to the White Paper: Time for a robust reciprocal relationship between procedural justice and therapeutic jurisprudence, *Court Review, 44*(78). Available online at http://ssrn.com/abstract=1131768

Wexler, D. B. (2008b). Crime victims, law students, and therapeutic jurisprudence training. In D. B. Wexler (Ed.), *Rehabilitating lawyers: Principles of therapeutic jurisprudence for criminal law practice*, (pp. 323–326). Durham, NC: Carolina Academic Press.

Wexler, D. B. (2010a). Retooling reintegration: A reentry moot court. Available online at http://ssrn.com/abstract=1526626

Wexler, D. B. (2010b, November 10). Therapeutic jurisprudence and its application to criminal justice research and development. *Irish Probation Journal, 7*, p. 94, 2010; Arizona Legal Studies Discussion Paper No. 10-20. Available at SSRN: http://ssrn.com/abstract=1628804

Wexler, D. B., & King, M. S. (in press). Promoting societal and juridical receptivity to rehabilitation: The role of therapeutic jurisprudence. Available online at http://ssrn.com/abstract=1722278

Winick, B. & Wexler, D. B. (2002). Drug treatment court: Therapeutic jurisprudence applied. *Touro Law Review, 18*, 479–485.

PART II

Prevention Programs and Community Practice

The beauty of restorative justice as you will see in this section is its flexibility. Once advocates have mastered the basic principles—RJ after all is a new way of thinking about wrongdoing and victimization—they can promote and design innovative programming for use in a wide range of situations. Chapter 5 by Lorenn Walker shows an adaptation of restorative principles for healing work with crime victims in cases where the offender may not have been caught or identified. Chapters 6 and 7 by Margaret Thorsborne of Australia and Dennis Wong of Hong Kong, respectively, discuss anti-bullying programming in the school systems where they live. Both writers are pioneers who have done much to advance the cause of prevention of harm done to youth by each other or by the system. Similarly, Ida Hydle reviews the history of child welfare programming in Norway and shows how it has progressed over time to increasingly protect the human rights of children in trouble with the law. She also describes innovations in the use of restorative concepts.

A personal narrative written by Lorenn Walker describes her experience as a participant in a restorative conference, not as facilitator but as a parent. This is the subject of Chapter 9. We also hear details of actual conferencing in Gale Burford's description in the following chapter of Family Group Conferencing sessions that took place in Vermont. Included in this chapter is Box 4, in which Deputy County Attorney Mary E. White describes how restorative justice principles guide the treatment of juveniles in Yuma County, Arizona. Finally, Ted Wachtel and Stacey Miller describe the use of restorative circles in university residence halls in Chapter 11.

5

Restorative Justice for Victims Without Offender Participation

Lorenn Walker

RJ is commonly thought of only applying to cases where there is an identified offender, yet 70% of all crime in the United States goes without any arrests made. This Hawai'i study shows the benefits of applying RJ for victims where there is no meeting or involvement of the offender. This chapter is reprinted from Walker, L. (2004, February 10). Restorative practices. E Forum, which is available at http://www.iirp.org/library/lwalker04.html.

Introduction

"Shut up or I'll kill you!" shouted the man as he shoved the hard barrel of a 9 mm handgun into the young woman's stomach. She was a store clerk. The robber wanted her to open the store safe. "I don't have the whole combination," she sobbed. "Where's your purse?" he demanded. He took the $32 out of her wallet along with her car keys. Then he wrapped duct tape around her mouth, hands and feet. He left her facedown on the ground and ran from the store. Until she was rescued and untied by a coworker about an hour later, she imagined him returning and shooting her. She kept thinking about her two young children, whose father was already gone, and what they would do without their mother.

The robber stole her car, which ran out of gas a few miles from the store. The police found the car and impounded it. She was stunned when she had to pay $92 for towing and storage fees to get her car back. Her boss later reimbursed her.

The robber was apprehended in another holdup. She was subpoenaed to testify at his trial. She waited outside the courtroom for an hour and a half while she was taunted and threatened by the robber's family. Although she was afraid, she still testified.

Her experience in court was brief and painful. The robber's lawyer acted like she had done something wrong and was lying. "Isn't it true you never saw his teeth clearly? You don't even know if he had gold caps on this teeth or not, do you?" he sneered, raising his eyebrows at the jury. She left the courtroom feeling dreadful and dirty. She longed for a hot shower.

Ten years later the woman was still haunted by the experience. Why did the robber pick her store to rob that day? Why did she risk her life and lie to him about not having the combination to the safe? What would her children have done if she had been killed? What happened to the robber after the trial? Was he convicted or acquitted? She had talked only briefly with her husband about the experience, and remained deeply troubled by it.

The woman later learned about the experimental restorative justice program reported in this paper. The program provided two trained facilitators who came and met with her at her home. For the first time she had a detailed conversation about the effects that the crime had had on her life. Six months after this restorative process, she reported, "It helped me a lot. I used to think about the robbery all the time." The conversation "helped me to not worry about it anymore." Today, she is working toward a bachelor's degree in criminal justice.

Program Development

The Hawai'i Friends of Justice and Civic Education (Hawai'i Friends) collaborated with the International Institute for Restorative Practices (IIRP) on this project, beginning in June 2002. At a meeting in August 2002 and through subsequent e-mail exchanges, IIRP staff assisted in designing the restorative processes, and in planning how to obtain cooperation from government and other agencies and how to engage the public.

In addition, a group interested in victim services in Honolulu, including representatives from the Honolulu Police Department, the state Department of the Attorney General, the U.S. attorney general's offices, the City and County of Honolulu Prosecutor's Office, Mothers Against Drunk Driving (MADD), Kapiolani Sex Abuse Treatment Center, Community Alliance on Prisons, and the state Crime Victim Compensation Commission helped develop and guide this experimental program through a series of three meetings, beginning in September 2002.

Restorative Justice

Restorative justice is a response to crime that considers the needs of victims, offenders and the community (Zehr, 2002). While the modern restorative justice movement began in the 1970s, some believe that "restorative justice has been the dominant model of criminal justice throughout most of human history for perhaps all the world's peoples" (Braithwaite, 2002). Restorative justice in Europe was largely abandoned at the time of the Norman Conquest (Van Ness, 1986). However, many indigenous cultures worldwide have never stopped using it (Braithwaite, 2002 and Zehr, 2002).

The general goal of modern restorative justice is to create a process for reconciliation between defendants who accept responsibility for their wrongdoing, their victims, and their community, family, and friends who are affected by the crimes (Zehr, 1990). Usually, restorative justice happens after a defendant has admitted guilt, and if the victim agrees to participate in a restorative process, it brings both parties together. There are many situations, however, where a shared victim and offender process is not possible but where a restorative response can provide important benefits for the victim or offender, even without the other's presence.

Some complain that a shortcoming of restorative justice is its failure to address the needs of victims when they do not meet with offenders (Roche, 2003). However, there are many reasons why meetings between victims and offenders are not possible. First, in most criminal cases the offenders are unknown. Less than 20 percent of all crime results in an arrest (FBI, 2003). Therefore, even if victims wanted to meet with offenders in a restorative process, often no offender is ever identified and arrested, making such a meeting impossible.

Secondly, many offenders fail to take responsibility for their crimes. Although over 90% of all charged defendants eventually admit that they committed a crime, by means of a plea bargain (Hall, 1996), many maintain that they were not responsible for the crime. Restorative justice meetings between victims and offenders are about potential reconciliation. Meetings with victims and offenders, when offenders deny responsibility, usually create further hardship to victims, although under certain conditions these meetings may have some benefit (Walker, 2002).

Finally, many victims simply do not want to meet with the offenders. Eight restorative justice programs collected data on the percentage of victims unwilling to meet with offenders (Kerner, Marks, & Schreckling, 1992; Moore & McDonald, 1994; Maxwell & Morris, 1996; McCold & Wachtel, 1998; Strang, 2000; Trimboli, 2000; Braithwaite, 2002; and Hoyle, 2002). Analysis of these studies showed that an average of 47 percent of victims, when offered the opportunity to participate in a restorative process with the offenders, declined the invitation.

Howard Zehr, a recognized leader of the modern restorative justice movement has written

> In a restorative system, services would start immediately after a crime to address victim needs and to involve the victims, regardless of whether an offender is apprehended. Thus victim assistance, while it cannot be seen as fully restorative, is an important component of a restorative system and should be seen at least as partially restorative (2002, p. 55–56).

John Braithwaite, a well-known Australian criminologist and proponent of restorative justice, agrees that providing a restorative response for victims not meeting with offenders can assist them and should be pursued even without the offender's participation (personal correspondence, November and December, 2003). Indeed, "partially restorative" processes can be beneficial for anyone who participates.

Partially Restorative Practices

There are ranges of restorative justice practices, from "fully restorative" to "mostly restorative" to "partially restorative" (McCold & Wachtel, 2002). The main criterion for determining where a particular practice fits in the restorative gauge is based on *who participates* in the process. A fully restorative practice includes the participation of all direct stakeholders: the victim, the offender, their families and friends. A restorative practice with only the victim or offender is a "partially restorative" practice. For reconciliation purposes, a partially restorative practice is not as ideal as a fully restorative practice but still offers important benefits.

While offenders have the opportunity to participate in restorative programs without victim participation, usually victims do not. Although there are counseling, compensation, and support-group programs for victims of particular types of crimes, such as sexual abuse, drunk driving, and violent crimes, most crime victims are on their own to meet their needs, both materially and psychologically. Ironically, our justice system provides more resources for criminal offenders than for the people they harm.

The National Center for Victims of Crime (NCVC) has undertaken the Parallel Justice project, which seeks to "revolutionize our response to crime victims" (NCVC, 2003). Parallel Justice is being conducted at four sites in the United States, with the aim of assisting crime victims in a variety of ways, including "establishing nonadversarial forums where victims have an opportunity to explain what happened to them, what the impact on their lives was, and what resources they need to get their lives on track." The experimental restorative justice program reported in this paper coincides with the goal of the Parallel Justice project.

INFLUENCES AND RELATED THINKING

The work of many individuals was applied in developing this restorative practice, including Howard Zehr, John Braithwaite, Kay Pranis, Paul McCold, Ted Wachtel, and Daniel Van Ness.

Terry O'Connell, an Australian who is largely responsible for introducing restorative conferencing to the American criminal justice system (Pranis, 1998; Wachtel, 1997), and Insoo Kim Berg, a cofounder of solution-focused brief therapy (Nichols & Schwartz, 2001), were consulted in the development of the questions that form the general outline of the practice.

Solution-focused brief therapy (SFBT) was originally developed by Insoo Kim Berg and Steve de Shazer "as a quiet revolt against the prevailing view of what is helpful to people with problems of living" (Berg & Steiner, 2003). SFBT represents a radical departure from traditional psychological therapy. "In SFBT the therapist's role is more like a facilitator than a counselor" (De Jong & Berg, 2002). SFBT empowers people to solve their own problems, which is consistent with restorative justice.

In a more general way, others who have dealt with surviving trauma and suffering, and whose thinking is consistent with the goal of restorative justice, have influenced the project. Viktor Frankl, who suffered in Nazi concentration camps has written, "Life ultimately means taking responsibility to find the right answer to its problems and to fulfill the tasks, which it constantly sets for each individual" (Frankl, 1984, p. 85). The Dalai Lama, Tibet's exiled leader, advises that "our confidence and self-reliance can grow and our courage become strengthened as a result of suffering." This, he says, can be achieved by "examining it, analyzing it, determining its causes, and finding out how to deal with them" (The Dalai Lama; 1999, p. 140).

A restorative response can provide crime victims with an effective method for finding meaning from their suffering, as it did for the artist who created something beautiful out of garbage. He told his story when he participated in this restorative pilot program.

The Creation of the *Shattered Heart*

"What are you doing!" the man yelled. He had just returned home and found a stranger in his house rummaging through some desk drawers. The apparent thief turned around and made a wailing sound as he moved his lips. He was deaf and mute. He grabbed a piece of paper on the desk and scribbled out a message "Can you help me? I was robbed of all my money. I'm hungry. I need a clean shirt." He was disheveled and looked desperate, but he was also young and seemed innocent. The man decided to help him. He gave him clean clothes, some food and let him sleep on his couch for the night. The intruder told him his name.

It was 1975 and the helpful man was 26 years old. He was an artist who had just received his master's degree in fine arts from the University of Hawaii. He had struggled himself in life and the intruder seemed harmless. It was natural for him to be kind.

Later that night, the artist woke up choking on smoke billowing up from the bottom story of his house. The place was on fire. He rushed downstairs, looking for the intruder, but he was gone. The roar of sirens got louder. As he ran out of his house, two fire trucks screeched into his driveway. But it was too late. His house went up in flames. All his artwork was gone, work that he had spent years on. His home and all his belongings were destroyed. The firefighters said the fire had been started by arson.

Later, at the police station, wrapped in a blanket, the artist gave a statement to the police. He told them about the intruder, who must have started the fire. But the artist was arrested. A man with the same name as the intruder's had been found dead earlier that day. The artist was no longer an arson victim but a murder suspect. After spending hours at the police station, the artist was able to convince the police that his story was true. The police finally recognized the intruder as the suspect in a string of other crimes. The artist was released.

The artist not only lost his home that night, he also lost his job. Some of his employer's property that had been stored in his house was destroyed in the fire. "How could you be so stupid as to help some criminal? You're too stupid to work for me," said his boss when she fired him.

Losing everything that grim night put the artist on a path that led to a successful career 25 years later. Because he had no money to buy art supplies, he was forced to become creative with what he could find for free to make his art. He found his supplies in the garbage. Over the years, he developed high-level *assemblage* art skills. One type of garbage he found, and still works with today, is broken glass.

The artist has a studio in downtown Honolulu. His shattered hearts are popular art pieces. These stunning three-dimensional hearts are made from broken pieces of colored glass glued together. Shattered hearts are in art galleries and museums and are collected by other artists and individuals.

After meeting for several hours as a participant in this restorative project, the artist said, "Looking back on it, losing everything turned out to be a good thing. It was important for me as an artist. If I hadn't lost my house, my job and all my work that night, I wouldn't have gotten into the work I do now," he said.

Description of Practice

The restorative practice developed for this project simply gives victims an opportunity to tell their stories in a small group setting. They can talk about how they have been affected by the crime and what might assist them in repairing the harm.

The idea for this practice was conceived of by the program coordinator, herself the victim of a violent crime 27 years ago. She recognized the need to provide a forum and small group setting like this for victims, without offenders' participation. Her cofacilitator in the project is also a former crime victim who recognized the need for this program. Their combined experience in therapy, public health and the law provided them with the ideal background to develop the practice.

Working as two facilitators together in the cases gave them the opportunity to discuss the practice, its effectiveness for victims and ways to improve it. While two facilitators are not necessary to conduct restorative practices, in this case having cofacilitators provided a serendipitous effect. Working together and discussing the cases of other victims gave the facilitators the opportunity to reaffirm how their own suffering, resulting from the crimes committed against them, made their lives more meaningful.

An eventual goal of the pilot program is that the crime victims who participate in the program become facilitators of the practice and also benefit from this service role. Having prior crime victims cofacilitate the practice can provide a positive benefit for them, as well as for the other victims they are assisting. Several victims that participated in the pilot have indicated an interest in becoming facilitators themselves in the future.

When the practice includes only the victim and the facilitators it is called a *restorative conversation* and when the victim brings one or more supporters to the meeting it is called a *circle-of-care.*

Before the restorative event, a facilitator talks with victims about what to expect in the meeting, which is held at a place and time convenient for them. The facilitator asks victims if they want to bring supporters with them to the meeting. Most of the victims in this project chose to meet alone with the facilitators. Most meetings were held at the victims' homes.

Victims are asked a series of open-ended questions, presented below. The questions are not followed in every case. The list of questions is still a work in progress. The initial questions address the issue of how the victims have coped with the aftermath of the crime:

- How have you managed to get through this so far?
- Who or what has been most helpful in dealing with this terrible situation?

Subsequent questions facilitators may use to help the victims tell their stories:

- What happened?
- How has the crime or crisis affected you?
- What has been the hardest thing about what happened?
- How have others who are close to you been affected?
- How have they responded?
- What would you want those responsible for what happened to you to know about your experience?
- What is needed to help you deal with some of your hurt and pain?
- How might others help?
- What things can you do that might also help?
- What can others learn from your experience?
- Can you think of anyone else who also has experienced the same or a similar event?
- How have others dealt with the same or similar crises or crimes?
- What other crises or crimes have you experienced in the past?
- How did you deal with those crimes or crises in the past?

A written plan may be developed as a result of the meeting. The plan states the goal or goals the victim may develop as a result of the meeting. After the initial meeting, the victims are offered the option of additional meetings. Most victims in this project chose to meet only once.

CASES REFERRED

Sixteen crime victims have participated in the program to date and three are scheduled for future meetings. Four victims received services over the telephone and did not need to meet personally. Crimes included harassment, assault, attempted rape, robbery, arson, negligent homicide, fraud, burglary, and car theft. The length of time from the occurrence of the date of the crime to the date of participation in the program varied from a crime that occurred one week earlier to two cases that involved crimes that occurred 20 years before.

Most restorative conversation meetings lasted about 90 minutes. One restorative conversation, with a victim traumatized by a death that occurred the month before, lasted well over three hours.

Another restorative conversation with a victim led to holding a formal *restorative conference* with the offender and other key stakeholders. A group of 10 participants, including supporters for both the victim and offender, met and came to an agreement about how to reconcile the harmful crime. In another case where the victim expressed a strong desire to meet with the offender, it was ultimately decided that it was best not to contact the offender, who had denied sexual abuse for many years. The victim in that case, however, benefited from two restorative conversations with the facilitators.

Over 500 brochures were distributed by several of the collaborators (MADD and the Crime Compensation Commission) and to three hospital emergency rooms and a mental health clinic, but only one of the 16 victims who participated learned of the program this way. Most cases were referred to the program by word of mouth through one of the two facilitators or through a collaborating organization. A short newspaper article describing the program provided five victims with information about the program.

PARTICIPANT SATISFACTION WITH PROGRAM

The victims surveyed about their participation indicated high levels of satisfaction with the practice. Many indicated that the practice greatly surpassed their expectations of what it might accomplish. "Thank you so much! I never thought this could have been so helpful!" said one victim as she hugged the facilitator.

Some of the things that the victims found most useful:

- "I could tell my story and be listened to and look for positive outcomes."
- "Realizing that my own reactions (or nonreactions) are my strength."
- "Closure. Identifying things that we can do."

Goals

- Continue the pilot program for 12 more months. Work to recruit and train victim participants to become facilitators themselves in the program.
- Work with the City and County of Honolulu Prosecutor's Office, which plans to select negligent homicide cases that will not be prosecuted and refer them to MADD, which may then refer them to this program.
- Continue working with the other Honolulu collaborators in distributing the brochures, including the police department, which has resisted referring crime victims to the program for "liability reasons." This is unfortunate because the police are the ideal outlet for informing victims about the program.
- Continue collecting and telling the stories of victims who want to share them with others about the benefits of a restorative approach to crime.

- Finally, remember that it took over 2,000 years to create our current criminal justice system, and recognize that it may take some time to return to restorative justice.

Critical Thinking Questions

1. What experiences have you, or someone else you know, had being harmed by wrongdoing? What were your needs as someone directly harmed? What were your needs if any of your loved ones were harmed by wrongdoing? Were your needs met by the criminal justice system if it was involved?

2. What difference does it make for the community if crime victims who do not know who harmed them have an opportunity to engage in a restorative process? What kind of message does it send the community if victim needs are ignored? What is the message if victim needs are addressed?

References

Berg, I., & Steiner, T. (2003). *Children's solution work.* New York, NY: W. W. Norton.

Braithwaite, J. (2002). *Restorative justice and responsible regulation.* New York, NY: Oxford University Press.

Dalai Lama. (1999). *Ethics for the new millennium.* New York, NY: Riverhead Books.

De Jong, P., & Berg, I. (2002). *Interviewing for solutions.* Pacific Grove, CA: Wadsworth.

De Shazer, S. (2003). *"Don't think, but observe;" What is the importance of the work of Ludwig Wittgenstein for solution-focused brief therapy?* Retrieved from http://www.brief-therapy.org/steve_thoughts.htm

FBI. (2003). *Crime in the United States, 2002.* Washington, DC: FBI, U.S. Department of Justice.

Frankl, V. (1984). *Man's search for meaning.* New York, NY: Simon & Schuster.

Hall, D. (1996). *Criminal law and procedure.* New York, NY: Delmar Publishers.

Hoyle, C. (2002). *Securing restorative justice for the "non-participating" victim.* In C. Hoyle and R. Young, (Eds.), *New visions of crime victims.* Oxford, UK: Hart Publishing.

Kerner, H., Marks, E., & Schreckling, J. (1992). Implementation and acceptance of victim-offender mediation programs in the Federal Republic of Germany: A survey of criminal justice institutions. In H. Messmer and H.-U. Otto (Eds.), *Restorative justice on trial: Pitfalls and potentials of victim-offender mediation: International research perspectives.* Dordrecht, Netherlands: Kluwer Academic.

Maxwell, G., & Morris, A. (1996). Research on family group conferences with young offenders in New Zealand. In J. Hudson, A. Morris, G. Maxwell, & B. Galaway (Eds.), *Family group conferences: Perspectives on policy and practice.* Monsey, NY: Criminal Justice Press, p. 88–110.

McCold, P., & Wachtel, T. (2002). Restorative justice theory validation. In E. Weitekamp and H-J. Kerner (Eds.), *Restorative justice: Theoretical foundations* (pp. 110–142). Devon, UK: Willan Publishing.

McCold, P., & Wachtel, B. (1998). Restorative policing experiment: The Bethlehem police family group conferencing project community service foundation. Pipersville, PA. Retrieved from http://www.restorativepractices.org/Pages/bethlehem.html

Moore, D. B., & O'Connell, T. (1994). Family conferencing in Wagga Wagga: A communitarian model of justice. In C. Alder & J. Wundersitz (Eds.), *Family conferencing and juvenile justice: The way forward or misplaced optimism?* (pp. 45–86). Canberra, Australia: Australian Institute of Criminology.

National Center for Victims of Crime [NCVC], Parallel Justice program. (2003). Retrieved from www.ncvc.org

Nichols, M., & Schwartz, R. (2001). *Family therapy*. Boston: Allyn & Bacon.

Pranis, K. (1998). *Conferencing and the community*. Retrieved from http://www.realjustice.org/articles .html?articleId=478

Roche, D. (2003). *Accountability in restorative justice*. New York, NY: Oxford University Press.

Strang, H. (2000). *Victim participation in a restorative justice process: The Canberra reintegrative shaming experiments*. Unpublished PhD thesis, Australian National University.

Trimboli, L. (2000). *An evaluation of the NSW youth justice conferencing scheme*. Sydney, Australia: New South Wales Bureau of Crime Statistics and Research.

Van Ness, D. (1986). *Crime and its victims*. Downers Grove, IL: Inter Varsity Press.

Wachtel, T. (1997). *Real justice*. Pipersville, PA: The Piper's Press.

Walker, L. (2002). Conferencing: A new approach for juvenile justice in Honolulu, *Federal Probation, 66*(1), 38–43.

Zehr, H. (1990). *Changing lenses*. Scottdale, PA: Herald Press.

Zehr, H. (2002). *The little book of restorative justice*. Intercourse, PA: Good Books.

6

A Story of the Emergence of Restorative Practice in Schools in Australia and New Zealand: Reflect, Repair, Reconnect

Margaret Thorsborne

Margaret Thorsborne, the managing director of Transformative Justice Australia (Queensland), is a pioneering RJ school specialist who has practiced in the field for over 20 years. In the following autobiographical and historical sketch, she discusses initiatives from Australia and other countries where bullying and other misbehavior of youth is dealt with restoratively. She also describes projects from the UK, New Zealand and Canada.

I will begin the story of the osmosis of restorative justice into schools with an Australian flavor, because I am more familiar with these perspectives, and because I was intimately involved in the early experiments and still am, much to my ongoing delight and excitement. I want to state up front that I cannot, with any degree of accuracy, report on the detail of developments in schools in the Northern Hemisphere, although I think the developments Down Under have, happily, contributed to the emergence of a whole raft of restorative thinking and practices in schools the world over. I hope that readers in these places can access sources that will give an accurate account of local history. But this story about the emergence of restorative "discipline" is also a story of convergent evolution. That is, schools in all parts of the world have been reaching the same conclusions about the exercise of power and authority and the use of punitive measures to manage student misbehavior—that is, realizing that young people these days are very different and old, more traditional ways of discipline are no longer anywhere near adequate.

I would also like to emphasize the model developed in Australia is not the "right" model, but one of many developed, searching for the same outcomes of acceptance of responsibility, reflection, repair, and reconnection. These sorts of stories always have a beginning somewhere. And this is our story.

In the early 1990s, I was in residence as a school counselor at Maroochydore State High School, on the Sunshine Coast, Queensland, Australia. Another counseling colleague of mine, Mary Hyndman, and I were tasked by the guidance division in our state education department to develop a whole-of-school approach to the prevention of bullying, an ongoing challenge for schools worldwide. We were confident that we could devise effective responses for low-to-medium-level bullying based on common sense and the experience of such writers as Olweus (1993) and Maines and Robinson (1992), but were keen to find some way to handle more serious cases. In these cases we knew somehow that we needed to bring together not just the children involved as victims and wrongdoers, but their respective families. How could we do this in a way that was both safe and effective, and put an end to the behavior and the suffering?

At about that time, it came to our attention that the New South Wales (NSW) Australia police, in the regional city of Wagga Wagga, had adapted the New Zealand Family Group Conference process into a form of restorative cautioning to divert young offenders away from court (Moore, 1995). To us, it sounded like the answer to our prayers in our search for a formal yet safe process for our serious cases of bullying. My first conference in 1994, done with fingers crossed and little training, was convened to deal with a serious assault after a school dance. The victim, a 16-year-old student, was so traumatized by the assault that he refused to come back to school. The conference was attended by this young man, his parents and the other boys responsible, together with members of their families and senior managers. When I look back on that early effort, I can run a truck through the technical holes in the process, but it did the trick and all four students were integrated back safely into the school community with no further conflict arising between the boys. The parents were both delighted and relieved by the positive outcomes.

The process held huge appeal to a significant number of schools across our state of Queensland, and federal and state funding was obtained to run a 12-month project to assess the effectiveness of this process in high school settings (Queensland Department of Education, 1996). While the trials were successful, when the funding dried up, schools simply snapped back to the old ways of doing things—that is, using traditional, punitive responses such as suspension and exclusion to deal with serious incidents. Heartbreaking, really, for those of us closely involved, but incredibly naïve of us to think that we could expect a state department of education would realize the potential of, and continue to pour funds into, such an initiative!

What we also didn't realize at the time was that an effective process for dealing with "high end" incidents of bullying, theft, violence, vandalism, environmental damage, persistent disruption, and disobedience, etc., could only influence outcomes for a very small proportion of the school population—a few students and their families, and fewer staff and school administrators. The capacity, then, of this initiative to influence and create culture change within an ultra-authoritarian system was very limited. We did not realize what was needed for whole-scale organizational change—the changing of hearts and minds.

In 1998, the Restorative Justice Unit of the NSW police were invited by Robyn Hutchinson, the progressive principal of a small inner-Sydney disadvantaged school (Lewisham Primary School), to assist in the transformation of the school and its community into a safer place for learning and gathering. Over a 12-month period, all school staff were introduced to the philosophy and basic practice of questioning students around the impact (harm) of their behavior on others and relationships. The dialogue had an emphasis on making things right between the affected parties. The questions evolved from the highly structured and scripted Wagga model of restorative "conferencing",[1] the same process that had been adopted by Queensland schools. Lewisham Primary School reported that their suspension rates halved and there were fewer reports of disciplinary responses in classrooms and playgrounds (O'Connell and Ritchie, 2001). This was quite possibly the first attempt, at least in Australia, at a whole-of-school approach to using restorative justice processes.

At about the same time, two restorative revolutions were occurring over the Tasman Sea that separates New Zealand (NZ) from Australia. One was the migration of the model developed in Queensland schools, thanks to the gathering of delegates at international conferences and the increasingly close networks among educators because of the Internet. Word of mouth is very powerful. The second was the development of a narrative[2] approach in a conferencing model, the Hui Whakatika, by the University of Waikato School of Education in the regional city of Hamilton in the North Island, New Zealand (The Restorative Practices Development Team, 2003). While this latter approach was somewhat procedurally different from the Australian model, the outcomes for individual students, their families and their school communities were similar.

At the same time, the New Zealand Ministry of Education was concerned with the over-representation of Maori and Pacifica students in school suspension and attendance data and began to pressure and support schools to improve this data with the adoption of a range of programs, including restorative practices. As New Zealand schools became more familiar with the conference process and its philosophy, they too developed a kind of restorative dialogue known locally as the restorative "chat." This allowed the philosophy and practice of the formal conference process to be adapted and pushed down into, as a less formal response, classrooms, corridors, and playgrounds. And in another case of convergent evolution, these adaptations were also appearing in schools across all Australian states. It does appear that when good practitioners grasp the fundamentals

---

[1]The "scripted" restorative conference process has found its way into many countries and criminal justice and education systems, including the United Kingdom, United States, Canada, Europe, and New Zealand.

[2]Based on a Narrative Therapy approach, a community of care is drawn around a student experiencing trouble; the problem is separated from the person and an alternate strength-based identity is developed for that young person, along with a plan to support the young person to change.

of something, then creativity can find ways of using the ideas in different settings. What teachers now report about the regular use of such restorative problem-solving is that relationships between teacher and student have improved and there are fewer disciplinary issues. Teacher stress is reduced along with their blood pressure!

Meanwhile, the whole idea of using what is essentially a youth justice process in a school setting took hold in the United States and in the United Kingdom. In the UK, the use of circles to develop social capital and a positive environment for learning in classrooms meant that there was fertile soil for the introduction of restorative interventions in response to wrongdoing. Circles adapted from First Nations practice have long been used in Canadian and American schools (Pranis, 2006), to build social capital and solve problems, so again it has been no stretch to embed the restorative philosophy. Programs around conflict resolution, peacemaking, and nonviolent communication have a long history in schools with the skilling of young people to become peer group facilitators in order to de-escalate playground and classroom conflict. One issue that has become obvious with these incredibly hopeful programs is the fact that a *limited number of staff* is involved in the training and support of the student facilitators—not enough staff involved to create the behavior changes among adults necessary for culture change.

So why has it been such a struggle for schools to take up the philosophy and practice of RJ, when it is clearly such a good idea? *Because the RJ approach challenges our basic assumptions about the best way to raise children.* I was raised in a family that was strict as well as warm and loving. My parents had been raised to believe, in their *own* families of origin, that "sparing the rod would spoil the child," that "children should be seen and not heard," and that children should do as they were told. In other words, for generations and centuries, it was completely acceptable for the adult to have complete authority, power, and control over children. They were not regarded as equals in any sense, indeed, in earlier times were regarded as goods to be sold, bartered, enslaved, and even killed. Children had no voice. Their needs were secondary to that of the adult. They took no part in decision making that might affect their lives. Raising a child was, in some ways, and still is for some, regarded as a burden.[3]

This authoritarian approach to child-rearing can be best illustrated using Wachtel and McCold's Social Discipline Window (2001). The upper lefthand quadrant in the Johari window is the space and place of high pressure (rigidity around rules and limits) but offers little support and scaffolding for the wrongdoer and, as it turns out, for those harmed, as well. The teacher, parent and wider community believe that rule-breaking must be punished, so that the child (and others) learns the lesson and won't do it again (deterrence).

This black-and-white thinking means that punishment for wrongdoing is the *only* option. *Not* to punish means the child has not been held accountable ("they have got away with it"), and if that is done in a context of rescuing and protecting the child from the consequences of their wrongdoing, then the parent or teacher is being *permissive*. In this rigid thinking, there is no room for any other approach. Alfie Kohn, in his book *Beyond Discipline: From Compliance to Community*, so aptly writes that there are many

---

[3] *Parenting for a Peaceful World* (Robin Grille, 2005) is a critical review of the history of childhood and of our social evolution to more democratic and emotionally intelligent ways to raise children.

of us who still believe that "trying to get to the bottom of a problem is just a fancy version of doing nothing" (2006, p. 31).

The alternative (besides doing *nothing at all* in response to wrongdoing) is to employ a different kind of accountability. Genuine accountability, as described by Howard Zehr in his wonderfully brief *Little Book of Restorative Justice* (2002), means a face-to-face encounter. The people responsible are held accountable directly to those they have harmed. They must take responsibility for this harm and be part of a process in which all affected help decide how to repair the harm. The victim and the wrongdoer both have a say in what's needed to fix things. This democratic approach is a far cry from a system where adults decide outcomes based on retributive thinking. And it is a huge challenge for a generation of classroom teachers and school administrators who firmly believe that compliance in a classroom must be achieved for learning to occur—compliance in this sense therefore becomes *an end in itself.*

The Limitations of Punishment

What is the research currently saying about the use of punitive measures? The overuse of exclusionary practice (stand-down,[4] suspensions, exclusions) in response to serious wrongdoing has been shown to discriminate against students already at highest risk (minority groups are overrepresented in the data), much like prison populations in every country have similar overrepresentation of minority groups (Skiba, Simmons, Staudinger, Rausch, Dow, & Feggins; 2003). The practice of incapacitating a student by sending them home has blossomed in recent decades as schools have pulled back from the use of the cane (Slee, 1995). While some school administrators and teachers believe that sending wrongdoers away from the school is good for other learners, there is little proof that the practice actually does improve educational outcomes for those left behind (Skiba et al., 2003). It certainly disconnects those already at risk from engaging in an education that might in fact save them from a life of crime.

Kohn (2006, p. 28) suggests that increasing levels of punishment actually teach a kind of selfishness in the wrongdoer, as they harden their thinking about the authority figure who is punishing them; and fail to understand anything about the impact of their behavior on others. As a mother of two young men, I would have hoped that whatever the school was moved to do in response to any wrongdoing, that they might, in the future, be more thoughtful about their own behavior and its impact on *others* rather than the consequences for themselves. I remember after several days to-ing and fro-ing to the high school when one of our boys was in Year 8 (13 years old) and had been in trouble for hassling others in class (he thought he was being cool), I asked him at the final meeting at the school what had been the worst of it for him. He replied "Hurting you, Mum." I knew at that point that we were getting somewhere. I have always hoped that they understand that there is nothing we do or don't do that doesn't have an impact on others, and if we make a mistake, we have to fix it.

---

[4]*Stand-down* is a New Zealand term for the more widely used term "suspension" where a young person is sent home in response to a serious misdemeanor, usually limited to a maximum of five consecutive days.

Both he and his brother are turning into fine young men, thoughtful of others and learning about empathy and compassion, and what helps relationships stay healthy.

I have a very strong belief that both school and family *share the responsibility for raising children*, and that we can and must reach a shared understanding about the best and most effective way to do this. What a powerful partnership this could be, and what a challenge to achieve!

A Vision for Something Different

The question, I think, for schools to address in their vision for their students and the wider school community is, "What sort of *people* do we want them to be? How do we want them to be able to relate to others? What sort of parent, employer, employee, friend, life partner will they be? What attitudes do we want to influence? What skills do they need? What does all that mean for how we manage our relationships with them in the school? What does this mean for the way we manage the disciplinary issues that will inevitably arise? What is the culture we want to create so these outcomes about character and skills can emerge? What does this mean for our priorities in the classroom?

The uptake of the restorative philosophy and its continuum of practice from formal to informal process has already contributed to the acquisition of life attitudes and skills such as empathy, compassion, kindness, responsibility to self and others, honesty, and integrity. But to a certain extent it is, in its responsiveness, still the *ambulance at the bottom of the cliff*. It is not enough to be able to hold people accountable, have them understand the harm they have done, and repair relationships, within a continuum of care and support. We have to work explicitly to *create* the culture of care, to build a sense of community where the well-being of individuals and groups in classrooms and playgrounds matters *first* to the adults in the school and then to the young people in their care. We have to deliberately develop social capital with a relational approach to pedagogy. This becomes *the fence at the top of the cliff*. Young people learn best when they feel safe with each other, with the task, and with their teacher. They learn best when their families feel connected to the school, where the school has reached out to engage with them in imaginative ways, instead of blaming the family for not sharing their views around the values of education. Where the pathology of the situation is not parked at the feet of students or their families, but a more holistic and blame-free approach is taken to problem solving.

Teachers are, first and foremost, in the business of relationships. Children these days are somewhat more emancipated than we were. They no longer automatically respond with obedience when we tell them to do something. They question the rules and the whys and wherefores. They have found their voice and expect to be heard. If we continue to respond in ways that are informed by our own authoritarian past when children had no voice, then we risk the loss of engagement. Without this, we have lost our learners. On the other hand, if we allow young people to rule the classroom environment so that they can do what they like when they like, then this permissiveness risks a loss of respect by the learner and the loss of care for others. Again, we have risked losing engagement. I think that our discipline policies need a change of language to reflect this more modern view of the place of the child and that we need to move away from terms like "behavior" management to "relationship" management. I am encouraged when I see school policies titled Care and Responsibility Policy or Care and Respect Policy. What really matters though is how the policy comes to life in our hands.

Whole-of-School Approach—Managing the Culture Change

In all the years I have been involved in the training of school staff in the range of restorative practices, I have always emphasized that the adults in the school community are the ones who must take the lead and change their behavior first. We must model what we want. Only then will we see a change in the way young people treat each other, their teachers, and their own learning. This of course is very challenging for some, especially those who still are firmly entrenched in an authoritarian, retributive paradigm.

It has become increasingly clear to us involved in this culture change and social evolution that the change will not happen by accident, just because it's a good idea. The change process of aligning people and practice with a restorative philosophy is a complex one and will not be detailed here in this chapter.[5] It is worth making comment here though about some of the critical success factors that will make the change a real possibility.

First and foremost is the willingness and capacity for the school leadership/ administration team to lead the change process and to be walking, talking models of how they want the staff and students to behave. Those of you familiar with school settings know how easy or difficult it might be to get buy-in from this group of senior people—is their leadership style congruent with the relational approach, or are they themselves still steeped in authoritarian practice?

Blood and Thorsborne (2005, 2006) have suggested that this change process will probably take at least three years for implementation, with ongoing attention beyond this to issues of maintenance. There will always be new children, new parents, new leadership and new staff to be inducted and skilled into the restorative philosophy and practice.

There has to be passion to drive the process of implementation, and it is beyond the capacity of one person in a school to do this. We suggest that it will need a *team* of people. Careful selection of the team is vital, and thought needs to be given to the ways in which the parent/community and student voices might be heard in the decisions about structures, protocols, and policy.

Organizational change of this extent will need very careful strategic planning to achieve the vision of a relationship-centered school. Key planning areas seem to be, but are not limited to, systems, policy development, learning, and growth (usually referred

---

[5]"The Challenge of Culture Change" (Blood & Thorsborne, 2005) and "Overcoming Resistance" (Blood & Thorsborne, 2007) are two papers addressing organizational change and can be found at www.thorsborne .com.au and www.circlespeak.com.au

to as professional development—PD) and resourcing issues. Particular care will need to be taken around the issue of PD. Skill acquisition is not simply a matter of providing a day here and there for staff, hoping they "get it." Adults do not acquire skills by injection! Any PD provided must be hung off the school's strategic plan, be in the service of the school vision, and linked to people's professional goals. Values that reflect the restorative paradigm must become explicit and equally important for adult behavior as they are for young people.

Coaching and mentoring should play a part in developing these news skills, and will work best when systems of accountability are in place in any performance development/management program. The same approach for developing behavior change in the student population must to be applied to the adults in the school—that is, a combination of pressure and support. This is, in fact, one of the hardest aspects of implementation. How do we hold each other accountable for our behavior? Restoratively, of course, but easier said than done, and beyond the scope of this chapter to address in detail.[6] A careful communication strategy will also need to be developed in order to keep the stakeholders in the change process abreast of developments and to maximize engagement and buy-in.

If careful planning to achieve a values-based vision of the school led by school administrators who lead by example is not undertaken, then all that we can expect in a school is isolated pockets of good practice that are not joined up into a comprehensive whole.

Conclusion

Does this sound overwhelming? For some, yes. Especially for people looking for a quick fix. But with careful planning, committed school leadership and a clear vision for a school where young people and adults can live in peaceful community together, it is indeed possible. It goes back to the central question. How do we want our young people to *be*? What skills are needed by young people to participate in such an approach? Are we prepared to modify our own behaviors? Is the school committed to prioritizing the developmental education around social and emotional competencies needed so that young people can learn how to be together? Can this be achieved with the increasing pressure of curriculum imperatives and national standards that seem to be dogging the education agenda? We strongly believe so. Learning outcomes are best achieved when equal attention is given to relationships and pedagogy. Young people learn best when they feel safe and respected and the curriculum is relevant and engaging. Teachers perform at their best when they too feel safe and respected and are supported to achieve their professional best. If *relationship* is at the heart of our efforts to educate our young people, then it makes perfect sense to explore the possibilities of a restorative approach.

---

[6]These areas are addressed in advanced workshops being provided in Australia and New Zealand called "Leading Restoratively." Course materials for these workshops are currently being incorporated in an implementation manual by Blood and Thorsborne (in press).

Critical Thinking Questions

1. What outcomes would a restorative school seek in the wake of wrongdoing by a student? How would these be different from a traditional, retributive school?

2. What are the critical factors that will ensure the successful uptake of the restorative philosophy across a whole school community?

References

Blood, P., & Thorsborne, M. (2005). *The challenge of culture change: Embedding restorative practice in schools.* Sixth International Conference on Conferencing, Circles and other Restorative Practices: "Building a global alliance for restorative practices and family empowerment." Sydney, Australia, March 3–5, 2005.

Blood, P., & Thorsborne, M. (2006). *Overcoming resistance to whole-school uptake of restorative practices.* International Institute of Restorative Practices: "The Next Step: Developing Restorative Communities, Part 2" Conference. Bethlehem, PA, October 18–20, 2006.

Kohn, A. (2006). *Beyond discipline: From compliance to community* (2nd ed.). Alexandria, VA: Association for Supervision and Curriculum Development.

Maines, B., and Robinson, G. (1992). *The no blame approach.* Bristol, UK: Lame Duck Publishing.

Moore, D. B. (1995). *A new initiative in juvenile justice.* Wagga Wagga, Australia: Centre for Rural Social Research (with L. Forsythe).

O'Connell, T., & Ritchie, J. (2001). Restorative justice and the need for restorative environments. In H. B. Strang & J. Braithwaite, *Bureaucracies and corporations: Restorative justice and civil society* (pp. 156–158). Cambridge, UK: Cambridge University Press.

Olweus, D. (1993). *Bullying at school. What we know and what we can do.* Oxford, UK: Blackwell.

Pranis, K. (2006). *The little book of circle processes.* Intercourse, PA: Good Books.

Queensland Department of Education. (1996). *Community accountability conferencing: Trial report.* Brisbane, Australia: Department of Education.

Skiba, R., Simmons, A., Staudinger, L, Rausch, M., Dow, G., & Feggins, R. (2003). *Consistent removal: Contributions of school discipline to the school-prison pipeline.* School to Prison Pipeline Conference: Harvard Civil Rights Project, May 16–17, 2003.

Slee, R. (1995). *Changing theories and practices of discipline.* London, England: The Falmer Press.

The Restorative Practices Development Team. (2003). Developing restorative practices in schools: A resource. School of Education, University of Waikato, Hamilton, New Zealand.

Wachtel, T., & McCold, P. (2001). Restorative justice in everyday life. In J. Braithwaite & H. Strang (Eds.), *Restorative justice in civil society* (pp. 117–122). New York, NY: Cambridge University Press.

Zehr, H. (2002). *The little book of restorative justice.* Intercourse, PA: Good Books.

7

Restorative Justice for Juvenile Delinquents in Hong Kong and China[1]

Dennis S. W. Wong

This chapter is written by Dennis Wong, associate professor, Department of Applied Social Studies, at the City University of Hong Kong. Wong is the foremost restorative justice organizer in Hong Kong. In the following paper he describes the use of restorative strategies to help children deal with conflict and bullying in the Hong Kong school system. Dennis Wong has done a great deal of advocacy work in the area of juvenile justice reform as well. He teaches restorative strategies he learned in trainings in the United States and adapted to workshops for individuals working in the school system in Hong Kong. Note the Chinese cultural values that are expressed in this essay, among them the value of filial piety, inner-directedness, and the expression of social disapproval for wrongs done. Although we editors do not generally condone the concept of integrative shaming, this concept is central to Dennis Wong's work in the prevention of juvenile delinquency and therefore to this chapter.

It is no secret that the juvenile justice system is far from perfect. Sending juvenile offenders to court and then to custody is definitely not an ultimate solution for resolving juvenile crimes. Increasingly, more scholars have begun to understand that children from deprived family and social backgrounds are pulled into delinquency in

[1] **Acknowledgment:** The Research Grants Council of the Hong Kong Special Administrative Region in China provided a grant to support this piece of work (CityU 148809).

various ways (Gelsthorpe & Morris, 1994; Pratt, 1985; Rutherford, 1986; Tutt, 1982). There has also been an awareness of the ineffectiveness of juvenile incarceration in reducing delinquent behavior. What is needed is a more balanced strategy such as a restorative justice approach to hold delinquents accountable while rehabilitating them and building supports in the community for them and their families (Bazemore and Umbreit, 1997; 2001; Braithwaite, 1989; Johnstone, 2002; Zehr, 1990, 2002).

Over the past 25 years, I have tried, as both a social work practitioner and as an academic, to find answers to two questions. My first question is, "Are there ways of holding badly behaving young people accountable to victims for offending and anti-social behavior, while at the same time leaving them the opportunity to be rehabilitated?" Given that restorative justice is widely considered to be a balanced strategy, then, my second question is, "How can it be implemented?"

In this chapter, I first describe how it was that I became interested in the study of juvenile delinquency and restorative justice. Then, I will share with readers my experience of advocating the use of RJ for juvenile delinquents in Hong Kong. Finally, I highlight recent RJ development in mainland China. Throughout this chapter, I discuss the extent to which restorative initiatives are likely to be consistent with traditional Chinese cultural values and the challenges that we are facing ahead.

Personal Discourse and Interest in RJ

My first experience of practicing RJ, unwittingly, came about when I was very young and on the verge of delinquency myself. I was born in a working-class family with five siblings in the late 1950s in Hong Kong, a British colony. My father was a porter, and my mother was a cleaning lady in the same building. At primary school, my classmates were also from working-class families. When we were 11 to 12, we occasionally shop-lifted snacks from a shopkeeper who sold ice cream and snacks from his motorcycle. My friends and I used foul language and sometimes were truant to go out gambling.

To the Chinese teenager, the growing-up experiences of engaging in unruly behavior is a process in which one is torn between two Chinese salient values, "filial piety (respect for parents)" and "gang brotherhood." It was not until my first year in high school that, with the help of a pastor and some Christian brothers and sisters in church, I became aware of the importance of education and planning for a future career. Advised by my pastor, I took the lead in restoring my relationship with my parents and siblings, then with my teachers, and, finally, with the motorcycle ice cream shopkeeper. To recover from the guilt of hurting others and to show my repentance, I wrote letters of apology to parents and teachers. Most important of all, I tried to make amends to the motorcycle shopkeeper by buying five or more ice creams even though I did not intend to eat them all. By doing so, I felt much better—as if I had repaired the harm I had done. In hindsight, I now see these actions as examples of restorative justice.

I worked as a youth worker for a year before getting into a college to study social work. After graduation, I became a social worker and committed myself to delinquent youth work and eventually became the superintendent of a boy's home. In those years,

I tried my best to empower youths to restore their relationships with their family members, school teachers and the community.

One of the roles I played was to resolve conflicts as a mediator between antagonistic gangs. Those contacts gave me valuable insights into the pathways to juvenile delinquency and made a solid foundation for my later studies on delinquency and restorative justice. Studying for a master's degree in the UK in 1985–86, I was guided by my awareness of the detrimental effects of negative labeling. Reflecting on my experience with the kids on streets when I was a social worker, I believed that some youths in trouble who were labeled as such by criminal justice personnel would go the way of no return under a retributive justice system. I further believed that punishment alone is not effective in changing human behavior, and additionally, that it is disruptive to community harmony.

Restorative Practices Are Compatible With Chinese Culture

In 1989, I became a lecturer at a Hong Kong university and developed a theoretical model to explain the onset and continuation of delinquency. For my Ph.D. thesis, I interviewed a total of 63 male youngsters, half of whom had committed juvenile offenses (Wong, 1996; 2001a). For children who became delinquents and later got into crime, the early negative shaming practices seemed to play a major role in putting them on that path.

When a child gets into trouble, a key protective factor is forgiveness. Forgiveness is the central theme of reintegrative shaming practices (Braithwaite, 1989; Braithwaite and Mugford, 1994). Reintegrative shaming as defined by Braithwaite involves the adults in a child's life showing tolerance and acceptance together with appropriate social disapproval of delinquency. Mutual respect between adults and children, or older and younger people in general, can act as a preventive device in "saving face"—something which is very important in Chinese culture.

To prevent the onset of delinquency, we need to cultivate the adolescent's filial piety towards parents or mutual respect between adults and youngsters in the form of "respect with love." In this way, adolescents will be socialized or resocialized as inner-directed people whose values will effectively prevent them from engaging in law-breaking behavior.

A restorative justice approach deserves consideration as it emphasizes the concept of Chinese collective responsibility towards crime control (interdependency) and is consistent with the values of forgiveness, interpersonal harmony, and the centrality of family, which are at the heart of Chinese culture (Wong, 2001a).

ADVOCATING RJ IN HONG KONG

Since 1996, I have advocated for reform of the juvenile justice system to allow family group conferencing (FGC) to be used for holding delinquents accountable while at the same time reintegrating them into the community (see Maxwell & Morris, 1993;

Maxwell, Robertson, Morris & Cunningham, 2004). When I failed to get the media coverage I needed to spread the word, I reorientated my work toward advocacy of the use of restorative practices outside the judicial system. This involved training social workers to facilitate restorative conferences or victim-offender dialogue so that youths in trouble with the law might have the chance to repair the harm they caused to victims and the community. Sometimes we helped children move to a better home situation when they were not getting the support they needed.

Today, I work with a team of social workers who conduct victim-offender conferencing for juveniles involved in minor crimes. The forum for the dialogue is a voluntary one. The social workers work in a "juvenile self-strengthening team" of a nongovernmental organization (NGO). Clients who have committed minor crimes are placed under the Police Superintendent Discretionary Scheme. The scheme provides community support services to those who are diverted from prosecution to the police cautioning project. Major TV coverage was provided to the workings of this project, including documentation of a restorative conference that I conducted. This was the first restorative conference that ever appeared in a TV program (*Wednesday Report*, Hong Kong TVB, July, 21, 1999). From then on, more and more restorative conferences have taken place, and more people have heard of the term "*fuk he*" (restoration).

SCHOOL BULLYING, BLAME APPROACH AND RESTORATIVE PRACTICES

Hong Kong is a highly competitive society in all aspects—politically, economically, and academically. The schools have been putting a lot of emphasis on boosting academic results instead of personality development. School bullying has been dismissed as mere "bullying games," and teachers do not have the time or skill to deal with them (Olweus, 1993). If teachers do intervene, a blaming and admonishing approach is commonly adopted. In 1997, when a skinny 14-year-old boy, Luk, was tortured to death and burned as a result of group bullying, people became aware of the detrimental effect of bullying. (Four offenders, 1999). Thirteen teenagers were convicted and sentenced.

The process by which school bullying is learned is circular: a victim becomes a bully and, in turn, creates more victims and more bullies (Cowie, 2000; Olweus, 1993). As teenagers enmesh themselves in bullying subcultures, they become insensitive to others' feelings.

Therefore, instead of harsh disciplinary action, we favor the restorative practices of facilitation and of mending broken relationships in tackling bullying. After joining the First International Forum on Initiatives for Safe School in South Korea in June 1999, I became aware of the importance of evidence-based intervention strategies. I obtained several research grants to continue research on the impact of restorative practices and, in particular, to experiment with anti-bullying programs.

My associates and I conducted the first comprehensive survey on school bullying in Hong Kong and published the results (Wong, Lok, Lo and Ma, 2002). This study of a sample of 7,025 Chinese primary schoolchildren found that over half of the sample had witnessed physical bullying and social exclusion in the past six months. About a quarter (24%) reported that they had physically bullied another child during the preceding six months. Nearly a third (32%) reported that they had been the victims of physical bullying at some time. The prevalence of school bullying was particularly high in senior primary school classes. These figures of physical bullying reflect a relatively high prevalence of school violence compared with those found in the United States and United Kingdom (also see Wong, 2004; Wong, Lo, Lo and Ma, 2008).

WHOLE-SCHOOL RESTORATIVE APPROACH FOR TACKLING SCHOOL BULLYING

Few schools in Hong Kong were aware of the use of a whole-school restorative approach for tackling or preventing the problem of bullying. As part of our research, we worked with a group of teachers and social workers to try out the first "whole-school restorative approach" in Hong Kong for tackling school bullying problems from 2000 to 2002. The objectives of the project were to create a peaceful and happy learning culture among pupils; to decrease the number of bullying incidents; and to enhance pupils' intrapersonal as well as interpersonal skills. At the beginning of the academic year, our team used the orientation weeks to provide information to parents about prevalence and causes of bullying. We publicly invited parents to join in the anti-bullying movement in order to respond to the problem of bullying proactively and restoratively. The program also effectively told parents that the school is taking bullying very seriously while at the same time adopting a restorative approach to actual instances of bullying rather than relying on punishment or exclusion.

In the second month, we had organized a staff development day for the school principal, teachers, and social worker staff of the school. During this training workshop, a clear message was passed to the teachers: "Bullying can grow to become very serious or it can be nipped in the bud" (Sullivan, 2000). At the end of the workshop, participants were asked to plan policies and procedures for counseling bullies, assisting victims and educating bystanders in their school. They were also encouraged to run a series of peace education curricula for students. After the staff development day, the school authority decided to set aside 90 minutes of class time each week to run a peace education course for all children of junior high age. In this way, each student will receive a total of 21 hours peace education in the academic year. The program consists of four major parts: self-understanding, emotional control, problem-solving skills, and interpersonal communication skills.

In summary, our works have developed a framework which integrated restorative justice theory and whole-school approach (Braithwaite, Ahmed, Morrison, & Reinhart, 2003; Hopkins, 2004; Morrison, 2007) for tackling school bullying. Aside from publishing research results, we have published a number of academic articles, research monographs and text-books in the field of RJ and school bullying and at least five sets of restorative practice packages for social workers and teachers (Wong, 2004; Wong, Cheng, Ngan and Ma, 2007; Wong & Lee, 2005; Wong & Lo, 2002; Wong, Lo, Lo and Ma, 2008). We also trained a number of social work students to provide RJ in schools and promote restorative practices. Three of these students eventually became key staff of the Centre for Restoration of Human Relationships described below.

CENTRE FOR RESTORATION OF HUMAN RELATIONSHIPS

In August 2000, with the support from a group of dedicated school principals, social workers and social work scholars, I set up the Centre for Restoration of Human Relationships, a voluntary organization committed to promoting harmony in human relationships. The center has been actively involved with restorative practices in schools, providing professional support in conflict resolution and other activities such as publications, seminars, and workshops related to restoring harmony in human relationships. With limited resources, the center was run by three part-time staff in its first year of service. As the chairperson of the center, I frequently went to schools to conduct conferences when there were serious conflicts between students, and this also provided an opportunity to demonstrate the relevant skills for running a conference to teachers. To help teachers and facilitators to grasp the ideas of restorative justice, the Centre for Restoration has translated the Victim-Offender Conferencing Manual (Mediation Services, 2001) into Chinese (Wong, Lee, & Tsang, 2004).

Following attendance in conference facilitation in Pennsylvania provided by Ted Wachtel of the International Institute for Restorative Practices (IIRP), the center signed a contract with the IIRP. This contract allows the center to conduct conference facilitator training in Hong Kong, Taiwan, Macau, and mainland China. Today, over 1,500 persons (mostly social workers and teachers) have been trained, and more and more professionals have come to understand the user-friendly Real Justice Approach[2] (O'Connell, Wachtel, & Wachtel, 1999; Wachtel, 1997). Over the past five years, the center has been providing formal RJ training to government officials as well as staff of NGOs in both Macau and Taiwan. The center has also been brought to the attention of scholars and officials in mainland China who are interested in such an approach to handling juvenile delinquency (Wong & Mok, 2011).

RJ AND JUVENILE JUSTICE IN CHINA: THE WAY AHEAD

An earlier project commissioned by the Government of Hong Kong investigated alternative measures for treating juvenile offenders (Lo, Wong, & Maxwell, 2003; Lo, Maxwell, & Wong, 2006). The research team identified six jurisdictions globally that represented a variety of alternative practices in their juvenile justice system as the samples of the study. They were England and Wales, Singapore, Canada, Belgium, New Zealand, and Australia. A seminar in 2002 brought experts from these countries to Hong Kong and enabled relevant government officials and others involved in working in the area of juvenile justice to hear and discuss the experience of these various jurisdictions. In submitting our report and recommendations to the Hong Kong Government, we proposed a number of pre-court restorative options including the use of family group conferences for developing restorative plans to respond to juvenile offending. Despite all these endeavors, there has so far been no positive formal

---

[2]The conference protocols are as follows: have the offenders talk about what happened, what they were thinking and who was affected, followed by the victims and supporters, and finally, the offenders' family and supporters. The focus is then on how to make things right.

feedback from the government indicating intent to reform the juvenile justice system in line with restorative principles.

Unlike its counterpart in Hong Kong, the governments in Macau and Taiwan have formally incorporated restorative justice into the existing juvenile justice system. The Department of Social Rehabilitation of the Legal Affairs Bureau is the agency responsible for implementing restorative practices and working in close partnership with juvenile court judges. Since the implementation of restorative options in 2007, nine restorative conferences have been conducted. The Legal Affairs Bureau has recently formulated a set of follow-up policies to keep improving the use of conferences.

Another promising development is that with the increasing academic interactions among Hong Kong, mainland China, and overseas countries, criminologists and legal professionals in mainland China are becoming more aware of the modernized and up-to-date juvenile justice philosophies and policies adopted around the world. Recently, I have participated in a number of regional conferences on juvenile justice where ideas of restorative justice have been shared and discussed among mainland China, Hong Kong, Macau and Taiwan. During these events, seeds related to restorative justice might be planted that will have an influence on mainland Chinese scholars (Wong & Mok, 2011, p. 29).

While we are trying our very best to promote the use of RJ in Greater China, I am fully aware that RJ may not work well if the government does not uphold the basic principles on the use of RJ in criminal matters as set forth in Article 15 of UN Economic and Social Council Resolution 2002/12. We have to make sure therefore that RJ is implemented in an open, fair, and just manner. Prospects of adoption are good, however, because RJ practices were being used in communist China long before the concept was articulated in the Western world. The Chinese preference for this form of conferencing is deeply rooted in Confucian philosophy, which sees social conflict as disrupting the natural order of life.

To sum up, in mainland China, Van Ness's idea about building a RJ city[3] seems at present to be a dream, especially to those who have experienced more than 40 years of the informal, unregulated, and often arbitrary and unfair social control system currently operating in communist China. There is certainly a need for a more inclusive form of RJ in Hong Kong, and perhaps this is within the realm of possibility as Hong Kong is a more open and judicially based international region than the mainland.

Critical Thinking Questions

1. Discuss the uses of restorative justice as a balanced strategy that can help in situations of school bullying.

2. Discuss what you learned about how RJ philosophy is a good fit for work with juveniles in Hong Kong and China.

---

[3]RJ City is a research and design project to conceive what a jurisdiction might look like that responded to all crimes, criminals, and victims as restoratively as possible. It is a project of the PFI Centre for Justice and Reconciliation (see www.restorativejustice.org).

References

Bazemore, G., & Umbreit, M. (1997). *Balanced and restorative justice for juveniles: A framework for juvenile justice in the 21st century.* St. Paul, MN: Center for Restorative Justice and Peacemaking.

Bazemore, G., & Umbreit, M. (2001). *A comparison of four restorative conferencing models (Juvenile Justice Bulletin).* Washington, DC: Department of Justice, Office of Juvenile Justice and Delinquency Prevention.

Braithwaite, J. (1989). *Crime, shame and reintegration.* Cambridge, UK: Cambridge University Press.

Braithwaite, V., Ahmed, E., Morrison, B., & Reinhart, M. (2003). Researching the prospects for restorative justice practice in schools: The life at school survey 1996–1999. In L. Walgrave (Ed.), *Repositioning restorative justice* (pp. 169–190). Cullompton, UK: Willan Publishing.

Braithwaite, J., & Mugford, S. (1994). Conditions for a successful reintegration ceremony. *British Journal of Criminology, 34*(2), 139–171.

Cowie, H. (2000). Bystanding or standing by: Gender issues in coping with bullying in English schools. *Aggressive Behavior, 26,* 85–97.

Four offenders were sentenced to life imprisonment (1999, January 31). *Apple Daily,* p. A2 [in Chinese].

Gelsthorpe, L., & Morris, A. (1994). Juvenile justice 1945–1992. In M. Maguire, R. Morgan, & R. Reiner (Eds.), *The Oxford Handbook of Criminology,* pp. 949–993. Oxford, England: Clarendon Press.

Hopkins, B. (2004). *Just schools: A whole school approach to restorative justice.* London, England, and New York, NY: Jessica Kingsley.

Johnstone, G. (2002). *Restorative justice: Ideas, values, debates.* Cullompton, UK: Willan Publishing.

Lo, T. W., Maxwell, G. M., and Wong, D. S. W. (2006). Diversion from youth courts in five Asia Pacific jurisdictions: Welfare or restorative solutions. *International Journal of Offender Therapy and Comparative Criminology, 50*(1), 5–20.

Lo, T. W., Wong, D. S. W., & Maxwell, G. M. (Eds.). (2003). *Measures alternative to prosecution for handling unruly children and young persons: Overseas experiences and options for Hong Kong,* Research report from Youth Studies Net at City University of Hong Kong to Security Bureau of Hong Kong Government of SAR. Hong Kong: Youth Studies Net at City University of Hong Kong.

Maxwell, G. M., and Morris, A. (1993). *Family victims and culture: Youth justice in New Zealand.* Wellington, NZ: Institute of Criminology, Victoria University of Wellington.

Maxwell, G. M., Robertson, J., Morris, A., & Cunningham, C. (2004). *Achieving effective outcomes in youth justice.* Wellington, NZ: Ministry of Social Development.

Mediation Services (2001). *Victim offender mediation deepening our practice manual.* Manitoba: Mediation Services in Canada.

Morrison, B. (2007). Schools and restorative justice. In G. Johnstone and D. W. Van Ness (Eds.), *Handbook of Restorative Justice* (pp. 325–350). Cullompton, UK: Willan Publishing.

O'Connell, T., Wachtel, B., & Wachtel, T. (1999). *Conferencing handbook. The new real justice training manual.* Pipersville, PA: The Piper's Press.

Olweus, D. (1993). *Bullying at school: What we know and what we can do.* Oxford, England: Blackwell.

Pratt, J. (1985). Juvenile justice, Social work and social control: The need for positive thinking. *British Journal of Social Work, 15.* 1–24.

Roland, E. (2000). Bullying in school: three national innovations in Norwegian schools in 15 years. *Aggressive Behavior, 26,*135–43.

Rutherford, A. (1986). *Growing out of crime: Society and young people in trouble.* Harmondsworth, UK: Penguin.

Sullivan, K. (2000). *The anti-bullying handbook.* Auckland, NZ: Oxford University Press.

Tutt, N. (1982). Justice and welfare. *Social Work Today, 14* (7), pp. 6–10.

Van Ness, D. W. (2004, July). *Creating a restorative system: Update on RJ City*. Restorative Justice Online. Retrieved from www.restorativejustice.org

Wachtel, T. (1997). *Real justice*. Pipersville, PA: The Piper's Press.

Wong, D. S. W. (1996). *Paths to delinquency: Implications for juvenile justice in Hong Kong and China*. PhD thesis submitted to University of Bristol, U.K.

Wong, D. S. W. (2001a). Pathways to delinquency in Hong Kong and Guangzhou (South China). *International Journal of Adolescence and Youth, 10*(1&2), 91–115.

Wong, D. S. W. (2001b). Changes in juvenile justice in China. *Youth and Society, 32*(4), 492–509.

Wong, D. S. W. (2004). School bullying and tackling strategies in Hong Kong. *International Journal of Offender Therapy and Comparative Criminology 48*(5), 537–553.

Wong, D. S. W., Lee, M. F., & Tsang, S. Y. (2004). *Victim offender mediation manual*. Hong Kong: Breakthrough.

Wong, D. S. W., & Lee, S. S. T. (2005). Strategies for tackling school bullying: A whole-school approach. In W.L. Lee (Ed.), *Working with youth-at-risk in Hong Kong* (pp. 39–52). Hong Kong: Hong Kong University Press.

Wong, D. S. W., & Lo, T. W. (2002). School bullying in secondary schools: Teachers' perceptions and tackling strategies. *Educational Research Journal, 17*(2), 253–272.

Wong, D. S. W., Lok, D. P. P., Lo, T. W., & Ma, S. K. (2002). *A study of school bullying in primary schools in Hong Kong*. Hong Kong: Department of Applied Social Studies [in Chinese].

Wong, D. S. W., Lo, D. P. P., Lo, T. W., & Ma, S. K. (2008). School bullying among Hong Kong Chinese primary school children. *Youth and Society, 40*(1), 35–54.

Wong, D. S. W., & Mok, L. W. Y. (2011). Restorative justice and practices in China. *British Journal of Community Justice, 8*(3), 23–35.

Wong, D. S. W., Ngan, R., Cheng, C., & Ma, S. (2007). *The effectiveness of restorative whole-school approach in tackling bullying in secondary schools*. Hong Kong: City University of Hong Kong.

Zehr, H. (1990). *Changing lenses: A new focus of crime and justice*. Scottdale, PA: Herald Press.

Zehr, H. (2002). *The little book of restorative justice*. Intercourse, PA: Good Books.

8

Youth Justice and Restorative Justice in Norway

Ida Hydle

Ida Hydle, MD, is a senior researcher at the Norwegian Institute for Research on Child Development, Welfare, and Aging (NOVA) and professor at the Center for Peace Studies, University of Tromsø, Norway. Her contribution takes us through major historical developments in Norway, the country that is ranked as No. 1 on the United Nations Human Development Index.

At the request of the editors of this text, Hydle *is translating* the Konfliktrådet *as the* Conflict Council *instead of the standard translation,* Mediation Services. *We prefer this translation to reflect the fact that increasingly the actual practice is based on dialogue and conferencing rather than negotiation between disputing parties, as the term* mediation *implies.*

In this chapter, I examine some historical traits of Norwegian Youth Justice, especially from the 19th century onward and with an emphasis on the past two decades. This investigation will be based upon a particular societal perspective and consider the question: How can we provide justice for youth who get into trouble in today's society? A partial answer comes in the form of restorative justice as a recent innovation that is regarded as a tool to avoid many of the problems of the traditional criminal justice system.

The major task of this chapter is defining what is considered crime or juvenile delinquency within the Norwegian context. For comparison purposes: Norway has one of the highest incomes per capita in the world, has 4.5 million inhabitants, 12 years of

Source: From "Hidden Juvenile Justice System in Norway: A Journey Back in Time," K. van Wormer. *Federal Probation 54* (1), 57–61, March 1990.

obligatory state paid schooling, has been a modern welfare state for the last four or five decades and has one of the lowest crime rates in Europe.

Youth or juvenile justice is not a term in Norwegian language; neither does *one* such public body exist, to take care of juveniles committing crimes, but *two*: The criminal justice system, which is for everybody over the age of 15, and the Child Protective Services, which is for everybody under the age of 18 (although recently extending its care-taking services in some cases to the age of 23). The interrelationship between the two bodies emerges as a partly unexplored and contested complex of ideologies, knowledge fields and practices.

Secondly, we need to face and analyze the Norwegian child protective and crime control policies. How have the Norwegian medico-legal frames for the handling of this case been constructed? What contemporary governing principles by the Norwegian state may be traced in the case and how did they emerge throughout the last centuries and, with a closer look, throughout the last two decades?

Thirdly, we will explore some of the practices of the established services and the professionals working with juvenile delinquents. In my investigation, I will shed light on the changes in the formation of the jurisdiction of the Norwegian state and its more or less visible traits and consequences concerning youth and justice.

My perspective and position are influenced by my background as a medical doctor and social anthropologist, having conducted research and pondered such phenomena as "truth," "deviance," "normality," "crime," and "violence" for decades.

History of Juvenile Justice in Norway

The Norwegian nation state saw close relations between the emerging medical, legal, and national economical science fields with the aim to build a strong state, based upon a law-abiding, healthy, and educated population (Neumann & Sending, 2003).

A significant struggle has emerged throughout the era from the end of the 18th century through the 20th century, namely the struggle of the believers of education against the believers of punishment. The literary historian Yngvar Ustvedt (2000) has documented from the end of the 18th century the cruel conditions under which young offenders over the age of 10 suffered in Norway. The ideological struggle between the educationalists and those of a punitive mind-set does, however, seem to have gelled into one. The sensational aspect of this history of systematic cruelty against very young, mostly poor and sick boys is not that it existed but that the poor, illegal, and state-acknowledged conditions were brought to light decade after decade from various sources (parents, teachers, the boys themselves by disturbed behavior, fires, suicides, or runaways), without any significant change up till the 1970s. It is especially note-worthy that despite the emerging manifestations of a comprehensive welfare system, there were some groups that were systematically left out, such as the "bad" boys, the "traveling people," and mentally retarded and poor people.

The history of Norwegian "school homes" is horrifying reading. It concerns prison-like conditions with overfilled sleeping halls, miserable food, and the most monstrous punishment methods, where whipping until bleeding was an everyday occurrence for the most trivial error. But worst of all was perhaps how the torture was mixed with religiosity, how the belief in the whip and the belief in Jesus went hand in hand in the education of the children. Two remarkable women stood up through decades as significant defenders for the rights of these children, the journalist and author Gerd Benneche (see Benneche, 1967, 1979) and the rector of school of social work in Oslo, Gerd Hagen (2001).

The Norwegian history of the fates of "bad" (and mostly poor) boys up to the 1980s is a sad history of a particular but significant part of the development of Norwegian social conditions in the broader sense. This history is part of the basis upon which present-day ideologies, knowledge, and practices rest. My aim here is to refer with a broad pencil to some features in this history up to the past two decades.

Norwegian "Youth Justice"

There never was and has up till now not been an institution called "Youth Justice" in Norway (or in the Nordic countries as a whole) in the legal sense of the term. There are no *juvenile courts, juvenile judges*, or *juvenile prisons*. This is now changing. The criminal legal procedure has in principle been the same for everybody above the age of 15. Criminal court proceedings are the strictest of all rituals in Norwegian society. And the ritual starts long before the opening of the case. When somebody offends against the criminal code and the police start the investigation, a long chain of strictly formalized events are set in motion.

Legislation and the administration of justice have long-standing traditions in Norway. As the well-known 12th-century quotation from the code of the Frostating jurisdiction puts it: "Our country shall be built on law and not by lawlessness laid waste" (Winsvold 1996, p. 1). The current criminal procedure including the jury system in cases before the Court of Appeal was founded by the Criminal Procedure Act of 1887, although some legal changes have taken place lately. A fundamental change was implemented in 1995 concerning the appeals system.

It should be noted that Norway was one of the first countries in the world to forbid by law the hitting, smacking, or clipping, etc., of children, (and there is even a law that requires municipalities to organize music education for children, although not in the Criminal Procedure Act). A key principle of the Norwegian legal system is that the politicians in the parliament (Storting) pass most laws as opposed to common law as in Britain, although there are examples of legal rules based upon judge-made law as well.

If a person is less than 18 and the crime sufficiently serious, the police *shall* report to the Child Protective Services (CPS), but this is not always the case, depending upon internal routines, personnel, and priorities at police headquarters. The CPS in such cases was until recently a public body at the county level, a child welfare committee, the so-called *barnevernsnemnda*, consisting of a legal professional (as the head), another professional (often social worker), and one local, politically appointed lay person, according to rules of court.

Now this has changed, with a composition of the *nemnd* more like an ordinary court. The legal head has to be an experienced judge and the others are professional child protective workers. The child or parents may be assisted by a lawyer at the expense of the *nemnd*. Moreover, during recent years, more than 70 municipalities have had a trial project with the restorative justice model of *Family Group Conferencing*, much like the practice in New Zealand and Australia and increasingly in other countries (Falck, 2006). Here one tries to come to a common decision without force or pain that everybody can live with.

The CPS may, if necessary, take responsibility for children and move them to a foster home or an open or closed institution. Such moves may be coercive; if the child or child's parents refuse, i.e., the police evidence is turned over to the CPS, not for prosecution, but for *treatment*. Older teenagers who commit serious crimes may be tried in ordinary courts of law and sentenced to prison. For the year 2004, 61 children were sentenced to ordinary prison as custodian prisoners, some of them in total isolation, while their cases were under police investigation (Storberget, 2004). During the last years, Norwegian justice authorities have tried to omit such sentencing, by introducing restorative justice in a new way, called *ungdomsstormøte* (youth conference) and *ungdomsplan* (youth plan). This was first launched as trial projects in five cities. The projects were then evaluated on a scientific basis (2009), and are now (2011) proposed from the government as a permanent institution of the criminal law, administered by the courts and Norwegian Conflict Council Service (a general description of this service will follow later in the chapter). If this is accepted by the parliament, the courts are now proposed *to sentence* a young offender to a *youth conference* and a *youth plan*, coordinated by a *youth coordinator* in the NMS, *instead of prison*.

There is a clear difference between this new way of handling youth crime in the NMS and the other dialogue and conferencing services in the NMS: A youth conference and the youth plan will be according to a court *sentence* and along a strict scheme listed in the criminal law. Until now, cases handled by the NMS are based upon voluntary participation by the parties at conflict, whether that be in criminal or civil cases. In the youth conference, offenders and parents also have to agree to the participation and to its purpose. Some of the other participants in the youth conference are representatives from the police and the probation service. The youth coordinator may also call upon representatives from the school, the child welfare department, the health care office, etc. It remains to be seen whether this proposal to the parliament will be accepted and implemented into Norwegian criminal law. And interestingly, in the same period where this new kind of restorative justice invention has been planned, there has been built a new kind of prison, called *ungdomstiltak etter straffegjennomføringsloven*, "youth institution according to the law of criminal procedure" (author's translation), planned to hold 10 young people between 15 and 18.

In an article from 1990 called "The Hidden Juvenile Justice System in Norway: A Journey Back in Time," the American social work researcher Katherine van Wormer described her fieldwork from a juvenile justice context:

> Norway is the model: Ask about health, childcare, social equality, and Norway leads the world. Ask about juvenile justice and much of the world leads Norway. As a practicing social worker in Norway, I set out to discover progressive treatment of children in trouble by a progressive country. My journey at first led me nowhere, for I was told there was no

mechanism for controlling young lawbreakers' behavior. This system was so progressive that there was no system at all. Then some social workers from the "social office" introduced me to a world hidden from public view, to a process that is punitive, arbitrary, and an instrument of social control. It is a process that has largely gone unexamined, either by foreign or native observers" (1990, p. 57).

Van Wormer's concern was with the legal protection of children within the CPS: "The concern [of the CPS] is not with evidence about the crimes but, rather, with appropriate treatment for the child" (1990, p. 58). She questioned the "treatment" practice of the CPS as being a hidden punitive practice not exposed to democratic, judicial control: "The condition of being a child, as a former Supreme Court justice once stated, 'does not justify a kangaroo court.' The condition of being a child does not justify years of confinement where an adult, for the same offense, would receive a suspended sentence, if anything at all" (1990, p. 60).

Thus, in current Norwegian legal practice young people are to a certain extent *supposedly* treated differently from adults. There are complex reasons and explanations for this double-bind situation. First of all, the views upon age limits concerning "children," "adolescents" or "youth," and "adult" have changed during the past two centuries, caused by changes both in ideologies and practices. Currently the age of criminal liability is 15. It was raised from 14 in 1990 and there is a constant political pressure from right-wing and populist party politicians to reinstall the age of 14 again. Secondly, there have been shifting strategies concerning the definitions and practices of punishment versus treatment and education, and there certainly is a mixture of the three, especially related to children and adolescent persons not complying with the "normal." Like van Wormer, Norwegian sociologists have described how the CPS handles the coercive means in "youth justice" (Falck 1998, 1999).

Van Wormer claimed that the statute in the Norwegian Constitution of 1814, "No one can be punished except after a judgment at law," does not apply to the handling of Norwegian children committing criminal acts: "By conceiving of the loss of freedom for a child as treatment rather than punishment, the right of habeas corpus is circumvented," she maintained. The problem is that even if the child is tried in an ordinary court the case is then turned over to the *barnevernsnemnd*. Thus, the child may in reality be tried twice by two different legal bodies. "The system of justice for children accused of crimes or behavioral problems is therefore often very harsh in Norway. This is in sharp contrast to the criminal justice system in general, which is strikingly lenient. . . . Social workers helped bring about this system in the first place. The system which set out to prevent child abuse had now become a key instrument of child abuse" (1990, p. 60). At the end of the article, van Wormer advised abolition of the *barnevernsnemnda* altogether and the introduction of an independent juvenile or family court.

What has happened with this juvenile justice system after 1990? First of all van Wormer described a system and also its practicing bodies and actors (she did fieldwork) from the 1980s. Secondly, did van Wormer's investigation have some relevance or even parallels described by Norwegians? The answer is yes, and thus the system has changed to a more just and safe system for children and parents, and new projects are invented in order to strengthen their roles in the decision process. And there are some researchers and practitioners, such as Falck, who have pointed to the same problems as van Wormer. My concern is to trace such shifts in this child protective and crime preventive policy and investigate whether they are related to other societal changes in governance, i.e., to find possible governmental instruments.

1. The new problem-oriented investigations procedures by the police from 2000

The Ministry of Justice's part of the plan of action for fighting criminality among children and juveniles delineates the following tasks for the police:

- To use restorative justice as a supplement or an alternative to punishment
- To develop the so-called "police cautioning" (a structured tool for the police to talk with young people and their parents about risk behavior related to criminality)[1]
- To use "youth contracts" as an alternative to incarceration

In signing a youth contract, the young person agrees with his or her parents on the one side and the police and the municipality on the other to carry out specific activities such as restitution/compensation for the harm done and restorative facilitation—in addition to the continuing of education, work, drug abuse treatment, etc.

Special measures for young persons in prison include a tight relationship to probation and aftercare services (*Kriminalomsorg i frihet*), normally cooperating with the parent(s), CPS and the school authorities. The prison rules normally open up for young persons to stay in so-called "open" prisons, which include schooling, preferably close to the inmate's home.

The police, in short, seem to have changed from taking a traditionally past-oriented approach to a future-oriented approach towards criminality, i.e., emphasizing *risk* as the entry to prevention in what the police call "proactive and problem oriented police work and situational prevention."

2. The use of dialogue as part of the criminal justice process from 1991

The National Conflict Council (NCC) has its legal basis in the separate Act on Mediation, passed in 1991. The act, regulations stipulated by Royal Decree, and particular paragraphs in the Criminal Code and the Circular Letter of the Director General of Public Prosecution make up the legal basis of the restorative and reconciliation services. The NCC is available for free in all Norwegian municipalities. The NCC coordinators are trained as social workers, probation officers, teachers, etc., and the facilitators are local lay people, representing the community.

---

[1]The problem with this is that the police use the "cautioning" to register personal data in order to work "proactively." Another problem is the way in which this conversation is structured.

Victim-offender conferencing has been generally available as part of the public conflict resolution service since 1994. More and more, family group conferencing is merging into the ordinary intervention services. In addition, school restorative strategies that partly can be defined as a criminal preventive measure, is partly available in primary school, and is now also spreading in secondary school.

The NCC may be regarded as a hybrid between criminal and civil justice. Although constructed and existing as a legal provision under the Criminal Legal Act, it serves as the rationale for dispute resolution in both criminal and civil cases. And it certainly breaches with fundamental criminal legal ideas, such as objective facts, guilt, and punishment. The aim of the NCC is to bring the disputant parties together in order for them to express emotions and narrate the act or case of dispute once more in order to come to a common conclusion on their own premises, whatever that may be. Thus, they are their own problem-solvers without the help of experts on legal or criminal or youth matters. In cases of juvenile delinquency of a minor nature, as determined by the police, the agreement between the parties may cause the police to withdraw the legal claim. Thus, juveniles may solve their problems by good conduct, i.e., self-governance.

Criminologist Sturla Falck warns of an unintended consequence of restorative justice: The use of the NMS does not prejudice the right of the state to prosecute alleged offenders. This might open "the way for twofold criminal prosecution for the same offence" (Falck, 2004, p. 8).

My own research interests lie in this field of restorative justice as a new and possibly more democratic solution to the contemporary credibility problems of the criminal justice system. The linguist Ingrid Hasund and I worked on a research project called Conflict Regimes based upon a trial project launched by the Ministry of Justice, restorative justice "as supplement to punishment in serious cases of violence" (Hydle 2004; Hydle & Hasund 2004, 2007). Our findings show that parties in dispute may reach a considerable degree of satisfaction and improvement in self-esteem and vitality. The dialogues that they develop during meetings may change their views upon themselves and others. This seems to have happened even in prisons so far according to trial projects.[2] There is reason to believe that NMS used in prison may improve the possibilities for a successful rehabilitation, i.e., the NMS may function as a supplementary punishment for some, and for others it may be a way to improve their living conditions on their own premises.

3. The implementation of the UN Convention on the Rights of the Child

The UN children's rights convention, enacted in 1990, is particularly relevant for our discussion with regard to Articles 25 and 37, which give children "who have been placed by the competent authorities for the purposes of care, protection or treatment of his or her physical or mental health, to a periodic review of the treatment ... ensures that no child shall be subjected to torture or other cruel, inhuman or degrading treatment or

---

[2]It needs follow-up research, however.

punishment. . . . or deprived of his or her liberty unlawfully or arbitrarily. The arrest, detention or imprisonment of a child shall be in conformity with the law and shall be used only as a measure of last resort and for the shortest appropriate period of time." Article 40 "recognizes the right of every child alleged as, accused of, or recognized as having infringed the penal law to have the normal legal guarantee, such as presumed innocence until proven guilty according to law; to be informed promptly and directly of the charges against him or her, to have the matter determined without delay by a competent, independent and impartial authority or judicial body in a fair hearing according to law, in the presence of legal or other appropriate assistance . . . to have the free assistance of an interpreter, to have his or her privacy fully respected at all stages of the proceedings" (UN, 2000).

These articles emphasize the rights of the child as an individual with certain claims on the state. The Norwegian legal provisions for the CPS as well as the criminal justice system have both during the last decade been adjusted to the UN convention. In a thorough investigation and analysis of CPS, the experts came to the same conclusion as van Wormer (NOU 2000, p.12). This formed the basis for the recent reforms.

Future Trends

In this chapter my aim has been to trace the changes in governmental tasks and principles constructed during the last two decades in Norwegian juvenile justice practices. Such practices include medical practices—psychiatric measures, schooling, child protective care, and police practices, as well as criminal legal procedures and punitive procedures—or rather, the lack of such practices. I have here emphasized just a few of these measures, procedures, and practices. One issue that needs more emphasis in particular is the intersection between the CPS, the prison services, and the psychiatric care for juveniles. The Child Care Expert Committee (NOU 2000, p. 12) describes this intersection as particularly problematic in Norway; the case which I have described in the beginning of the chapter may have served as a general and typical example.

How did the emphasis on "criminal act" shift into "risk of criminal act," and in what practices may this shift be observed? In general, and especially within certain state policy practices such as medical care, education, immigration policy or poverty policy (Sending, 2003), we may trace the contemporary Norwegian "reform-state" emerging from the nation-state in the 19th century, through the intermediary "planning-state" in the 20th century (Neumann & Sending, 2003). New public management and risk control are supposed to be forceful tools for guiding the population in the reform-state—or rather, that individuals govern themselves. There are important tasks ahead for researchers as well as for policy planners in order to draw careful social, cultural and political charts of juvenile justice. Practices should be followed carefully in order to evaluate the foreseen as well as unforeseen consequences of reforms. Such reforms, as well as the results thereof, should be seen against the perspective of the UN convention on children's rights as a new cornerstone in the Norwegian society.[3]

The punitive, treatment-oriented, and educational caring practices have emerged to dominate during different periods in the 20th century, especially with regard to those practices called crime prevention, deviance prevention, or sickness prevention. The ideologies of punishment were overthrown by pedagogical ideas. The professionals were first and foremost concerned with the pedagogical treatment of *the criminal within the person*. The focus upon crime control is to a certain extent displaced *from* the state's punishment of the deviant *to* what every single citizen may do in order to free himself or herself from criminality. Today, offenders are offered within prison walls courses in managing stress, violence, and unacceptable sexual desires as well as courses in self-recognition. Correspondingly, the focus within medical fields is displaced *from* hygiene, where the categories are bacteria, virus and contamination, *to* risk, where the categories are lifestyle, predispositions, and genes. These strands of thought are spreading to other societal sectors, e.g. the criminal justice system or the psychiatric system, where one kind of therapy is a bed and a more-or-less locked room along with the administration of narcoleptics or sedatives or both. (I watched the prison guards distribute such medications every night to their young and healthy—but diagnosed-as-sick inmates.)

Today, there is a steady increase in prisons and in the numbers of inmates, particularly among the young, that is disturbing. The incarceration of youths and their exclusion from society is an effective exclusion from developing and leading a self-reliant life with work and income, a decent place to live, a family, and a social life. The question is, will the trends toward restorative justice practices help to reconcile offenders, victims, and the community? Will these new hybrids between punishment and restorative justice have the effect of helping more troubled youth to remain within the community rather than being excluded from it? And will the different services aiming at helping young people at risk, become well-coordinated and goal-oriented by the new institution created within the Norwegian Conflict Council services?

---

[3]One such trend may serve as an example: there are current efforts in the use of dialogue between the parties in cases on honor-related violence, e.g. forced marriages, extreme control of teenagers, and so-called religious marriages among new citizens to Norway from the Middle East, North Africa, and some Asian countries. Here Norwegian authorities deliberately use "dialogue" because of this problematic connotation of mediation. There have been two murder cases of young women in the last years, one in Sweden and one in Denmark, and several court cases in the Nordic countries against fathers, brothers, uncles, and some female family members who have forced their young children (mostly girls but also boys) to marry against their will. The aim has been said to save the honor of the family (and to uphold different kinds of relations and obligations: religious, economic, political, clan ... with the home country). These cases emerge as endless tragedies, involving people in very difficult life situations, on both sides of the country's borders. One term, "bride dumping" or "groom dumping," contains stories of young girls and boys being sent to Norway or from Norway to the "home country" without any consent of the two who are planned to be married, being told adventurous stories about the future, only to be "dumped" with the family in law (without the partner), left in shame and with small chances of getting back with an intact future in the country they came from. The Norwegian governmental authorities are now evaluating the current practices of the police, the child welfare department *barnevernet*, the Konfliktråd, the family counselors, the mental health services, the Red Cross, the women's shelters etc., to see if and how they try to establish dialogue between the young girls (mostly) and their family members.

Critical Thinking Questions

1. In what ways did Norway make changes in their child welfare system which previously handled cases involving youths in trouble with the law to comply with requirements of the UN Convention on the Rights of the Child?

2. What could restorative justice practices offer to Norwegian children who have gotten into trouble?

References

Benneche, G. (1967). *Rettssikkerheten i barnevernet* (The legal protection in the Child Care Services, author's translation). Oslo, Norway: Universitetsforlaget.

Benneche, G. (1979). *Taushet: vern eller maktmiddel* (Silence: Care or tool of coercion, author's translation). Oslo, Norway: Institutt for Journalistikk.

Falck, S. (1998, January). Juvenile delinquency in Norway. Three papers on sanctions, alternatives, age of criminal responsibility and crime trends. *NOVA Skriftserie* (Norwegian Social Research, report).

Falck, S. (1999). *Barnevernet mellom hjelp, straff og hjelpeløshet* (The child protective services between aid, punishment and helplessness, author's translation). Kopenhagen: Scandinavian Research Council for Criminology.

Falck, S. (2004, October 14–16). *Restorative justice: A giant leap or just another tool for the criminal justice system?* Paper presented at the European Forum for victim-offender mediation and restorative justice. 3rd biannual conference: Restorative justice in Europe, Budapest, Hungary.

Falck, S. (2006). Hva er det med familieråd? Samlerapport fra prosjektet: Nasjonal satsing for utprøving og evaluering av familieråd i Norge. NOVA Rapport 18/06. Oslo, Norway: NOVA.

Hagen, G. (2001). *Barnevernets historie: om makt og avmakt i det 20. århundre* (The history of the Child Care Services, on power and powerlessness in the 20th century, my translation). Oslo, Norway: Acribe Forlag.

Hydle, I. (2004). *Prosjektet megling i voldssaker ved konfliktrådet for Hordaland.* Evalueringsrapport, Høgskolen i Agder.

Hydle, I., & Hasund, K. (2004). Evaluating a Norwegian Restorative Justice project: Mediation as supplement to punishment in serious violence cases. *Newsletter of the European Forum for Victim-Offender Mediation and Restorative Justice.* Retrieved from http://www.euforumrj.org/html/news .newsletter.asp

Hydle, I., & Hasund, K. (2007). *Ansikt til ansikt. Konfliktrådsmegling mellom gjerningsperson og offer i voldssaker* (Face to face. Victim-offender-resolution in cases of violence). Oslo, Norway: Cappelen Akademisk Forlag.

Neumann, I., & Sending, O. J. (2003). *Regjering i Norge* (*Government in Norway*, author's translation). Oslo, Norway: PAX forlag.

NOU (Norwegian Official Report). (2000). *Barnevernet i Norge: Tilstandsvurderinger, nye perspektiver og forslag til reformer* (Child Protective Services in Norway: Asessments, new perspectives and reform proposals, author's translation).

Sending, O. J. (2003). Fattigdom og politisk rasjonalitet (Poverty and political rationality, author's translation). In I. Neumann & O. J. Sending, (Eds.), *Regjering i Norge* (*Government in Norway*, author's translation) (p. 157–172). Oslo, Norway: PAX Forlag.

Storberget, K. (2004, December 28). Barn i fengsel (Children in prison, author's translation). *Dagbladet,* p. 42.

United Nations [UN]. (2000). United Nations Convention on the Rights of the Child. Adopted by the General Assembly, 1989. New York, NY: UN. Retrieved from http://www.unhchr.ch/html/menu3/b/k2crc.htm.

Ustvedt, Y. (2000). Djeveløya I Oslofjorden. Hitorien om Bastøy og andre straffeanstalter for slemme gutter (The history of Bastöy and other penal institutions for misbehaving boys, author's translation.)

van Wormer, K. (1990). The hidden juvenile justice system in Norway: A journey back in time. *Federal Probation, 54*(1), 57–61.

Winsvold, L. (1996, July). *The courts and the administration of justice in Norway.* Information produced for the Ministry of Foreign Affairs. *Nytt for Norge*, UDA138.

9

Beyond Policy: Conferencing on Student Misbehavior

Lorenn Walker

*In this personal description of her experience as a parent in a restorative confer-
ence, when her 14-year-old son was assaulted in a Hawai'i public school, Walker
shows how the process is viewed from the inside. This paper was originally
published in* Principal Leadership, 1(7) *March 2001. Available at http://www
.lorennwalker.com/articles/student_article.html*

Aconferencing approach to student discipline not only addresses the infraction
but also decreases repeat offenses.

I answered the phone and heard the vice principal of my son's high school saying,
"Mrs. Walker, I have Trent in my office. He's all right, but he's been hit in the head by
another student." I felt a quick wave of nausea and asked, "Does he need a doctor?
Should I come and get him?"

"No, he saw the health aide, and he seems fine, just shook up," responded the vice
principal reassuringly. When he told me that "it was Victor who hit Trent," my mind
flashed to an earlier image of the two boys about 10 years before. They were in their
soccer uniforms scrambling for goals down a grassy field. They played together on the
same soccer teams for a few years. Although they were friendlier in those days, Victor
tended to get physical quickly when things didn't go his way.

I convinced the vice principal not to call the police and I pleaded with him not to
suspend Victor. "Kicking him out of school will just make him angrier with Trent.

Besides, he needs to be in school," I argued. But the vice principal insisted he must follow "policies" and suspended Victor for three days. Although Trent seemed fine when I saw him later that day, my nerves were a wreck. I couldn't stop worrying about what could happen to him after Victor came back to school.

When this incident occurred, I happened to be coordinating a restorative justice research project for juvenile offenders. I am a former trial lawyer turned public health educator. I went to law school because I wanted to help people solve problems. After being a trial lawyer, however, I realized adversarial processes mostly perpetuate problems and do not solve them. When I studied public health, and the health education approach to helping people solve problems, I learned that empowering people to solve their own problems is the most effective way to help them. This concept applies to conflict resolution, where victims and offenders are best served by participating in a problem-solving process.

We know that participatory education is more effective than the lecture format for learning (Tharp & Gallimore, 1988). The same is true for dealing with student misbehavior. Instead of a teacher or principal simply telling an offending student that their behavior was wrong and asking them why they acted badly, it is more effective to have students participate in a process where they can personally experience the consequences of their behavior and then participate in problem solving to try and repair the harm that their wrongdoing caused. This process begins with getting the offender to consider who was affected by their misbehavior, how they have been affected, and finally, strategizing about what can be done to make things right. Conferencing is such a process.

The Conferencing Process

Conferencing is a group conflict resolution process that focuses on repairing relationships when offenders admit wrongdoing. Victims, offenders, and the affected community, including the victims' and offenders' families and friends, participate in conferences. The process is mainly based on ideas from indigenous people including the Maoris of New Zealand. Many other cultures including Hawaiian, Native American and Native Canadian have similar conflict resolution practices (Maxwell, 1996; Shook, 1985; Schiff, 1998; & Stuart, 1996).

Conferencing is a restorative justice practice. Restorative justice is an "alternative approach to criminal justice" that began evolving about 15 years ago in response to the ineffectiveness of our current justice system (Pranis, 1996). Our current system is based primarily on retributive values where "crime is a violation of the state, defined by lawbreaking and guilt. Justice determines blame and administers pain in a contest between the offender and the state directed by systematic rules" (Zehr, 1990). In contrast, restorative justice is based on the principle that "crime is a violation of people and relationships. It creates obligations to make things right. Justice involves the victims, the offender, and the community in a search for solutions which promote repair, reconciliation, and reassurance" (Zehr, 1990). Of interest to principals is that student re-offending significantly decreases after conferencing is introduced at schools (Cameron & Thorsborne, 1999).

When Victor hit Trent, we were conferencing similar cases through a federally funded diversion project for the Honolulu Police Department. Juvenile offenders who admitted wrongdoing were having their cases diverted to conferences instead of going through the usual police and court interventions. I realized that we needed a conference as well. Our high school principal was familiar with conferences and readily agreed that the school would participate. One of the conference facilitators from our police project, who lived in our neighborhood, volunteered to convene and facilitate the conference. He contacted Victor's dad, who also agreed to attend the conference along with the boy.

A REAL JUSTICE CONFERENCE

We used the Real Justice conference model for our police project and for Victor and Trent's conference. Several conference models have developed, including family group conferencing, community conferencing, family group decision making, and Real Justice conferencing.

Real Justice conference participants sit in a circle. Participants include victims, offenders, supporters (family and friends) of the victims and offenders, and other members of the affected community, which is often a school when incidents happen on campus or involve students. The conferences are facilitated by a neutral third party who does not participate in decision making and who uses a script that provides a series of open-ended questions to ask each of the participants.

There are basically four phases to a Real Justice conference (O'Connell, Wachtel, & Wachtel, 1999). First, offenders describe what they did, explain what they were thinking at the time and since, and whom they think has been affected by their misbehavior. Secondly, the other individuals in the group discuss how they have been affected by the offender's wrongdoing. Thirdly, the group discusses and then decides what can be done to repair the harm caused by the misbehavior to make things right. Finally, a written agreement is entered that all participants sign, and the conference ends with the participants having refreshments together—a ceremonial breaking of bread.

Victor and Trent's conference was held about two weeks after the incident. Although the high school principal agreed to participate, no one from the school was available the day of the conference. Luckily our neighborhood elementary school, which both boys attended, has a flexible and caring staff. With only 15 minutes' advance request, the vice principal of the elementary school (who was also familiar with conferencing) agreed to participate and hold it at her school.

The facilitator of Victor and Trent's conference began the process by explaining that its purpose was "to discuss the way people have been affected by the wrongdoing" and "to try and find ways to repair the harm." He explained that the conference was voluntary, but if Victor did not participate the case could be referred to the police. Victor spoke next admitting that he had "slapped" Trent on the face and explained that he meant it as a joke. He said he was surprised that Trent cried. Next Trent, my husband, and I described how we were affected by Victor's behavior, e.g., Trent said it hurt, I said I was worried about Trent getting hurt again and that Victor would get in more serious trouble in the future.

Next Victor's father spoke. What he said surprised my husband and me. Before the conference, we thought that he was an unconcerned parent, but we learned the opposite.

He shared his worries about Victor and told us what he was doing to try and influence him not to fight. The conference also made Victor's father aware of our concerns and situation. While he thought we were born privileged, he learned that I was a high school dropout who experienced the juvenile justice system myself as a youthful offender. The conference was an opportunity for all of us to learn about each other and connect our experiences with each other. From this process we built better relationships and ended up with compassion for one another. It was a remarkable experience.

The vice principal of the elementary school was there as a supporter for Victor (since we already had two people for Trent and Victor only had his father), but she actually supported both boys because the dynamics of the conference group process often encourage participants to support one another. The vice principal told us how she'd known Victor and Trent since they were third graders and how much she cared for them both. She said she wanted Victor to learn to control his impulsiveness. She said that Trent needed to understand his feelings more and not just verbally attack others when he was hurt. She and I both got teary-eyed when she said that she was proud of both boys for coming back to the elementary school and working on solving their problems in a constructive way.

After we'd all discussed how we'd been affected by Victor's hitting Trent, we collectively decided what could be done to "promote repair, reconciliation, and reassurance." Our agreement was simple. We decided that Victor would not hit others and Trent would think about how he felt when his feelings were hurt and work on articulating his feelings instead of insulting whoever hurt him. The facilitator prepared a written agreement that we all signed. The group then shared some cake, cookies, and juice together. The vice principal hugged everyone, Victor's father and I hugged each other, and my husband and he shook hands. Community was built that day as a result of the conference. It has been over six months since the incident, and Trent and Victor have had no more problems.

CONFERENCING PROVIDES AN OPPORTUNITY TO LEARN FROM BAD BEHAVIOR

Conferencing is a powerful learning strategy. First, by taking responsibility for their behavior, offenders recognize that they are in control of their actions, which is the foundation for developing self-efficacy and effective learning (Bandura, 1977). In Real Justice conferences, offenders speak first, admitting their bad behavior. Secondly, by hearing from the true community affected and harmed by their wrongdoing (not just a third party explaining how others have been affected, e.g., a judge or principal), offenders have the opportunity to develop empathy, which is an important quality for preventing repeat offenses especially for youth (Goldstein & Pentz, 1984). In Real Justice conferences the victims personally tell offenders how they have been harmfully affected. Thirdly, because the group uses consensus in decision making, moral development is more likely than what results from autocratic decision making (Kohlberg, 1964, 1969). In Real Justice conferences, all participants agree on what can be done to repair the harm.

Finally, offenders experience reintegrative shame at conferences (Braithwaite, 1989). Reintegrative shame is more effective for changing behavior than stigmatizing shame which is when an offender is distinguished for his or her bad nature, e.g. the offender holds a sign "I am a cheat." Stigmatizing shame also puts the offender outside the group. In contrast, conferences focus on the offender's bad behavior; not one's bad essence or nature and offenders are surrounded by supporters. These aspects of a conference allow the offender to continue as an accepted member of the community after the group processes the effects of the bad behavior. Continued membership in the group makes it more likely that the offender will conform to the community's standards in the future. This communitarianism element of the conference is necessary for preventing repeat offenses (Braithwaite, 1989).

Conclusion

Conferencing is a public health approach to wrongdoing that meets the needs of victims, offenders, their families, friends and schools. It can become a school's standard conflict resolution practice when an offender admits misbehavior. It is a process that can teach empathy and problem-solving skills. Additionally, it teaches that those most affected by wrongdoing can come together in a positive way to work toward repairing harm. This aspect of conferencing leaves participants feeling hopeful and optimistic. Optimism is vital for individuals to develop coping skills and resiliency (Seligman, 1996). Conferencing is a powerful process that can build relationships and community out of wrongdoing—it is something that can strengthen schools.

2012 Postscript: After the conference Trent and Victor had no more conflicts. Sadly, in 2005, Victor was shot and killed when he was 19 years old by another youth in an altercation. He would have been 26 in 2012, and his family still grieves today for the terrible loss.

Critical Thinking Questions

1. What experiences have you had either directly or indirectly with bullying or other forms of harsh antagonism by others toward you or someone else you know in school? How might restorative justice have helped in those situations both in the short and long term?

2. What do you think "peacemaking skills" are? How do youth learn these skills? How does a restorative response to bullying compare to "zero tolerance" and other harsh punishments for teaching youth how to get along with others?

References

Bandura, A. (1977). Self-efficacy: Toward a unifying theory of behavioral change. *Psychological Review, 84*, 191–215.

Braithwaite, J. (1989). *Crime, shame and reintegration.* New York, N.Y.: Cambridge University Press.

Cameron, L., & Thorsborne, M. (1999). Restorative justice and school discipline: Mutually exclusive? Retrieved from http://www.realjustice.org/Pages/schooldisc.html

Goldstein, A. and Pentz, M. (1984). Psychological skill training and the aggressive adolescent. *School Psychology Review, 13,* 311–323.

Kohlberg, L. (1964). Development of moral character and moral ideology. In M. L. Hoffman & L. W. Hoffman (Eds.), *Review of child development research* (Vol. I). New York, N.Y.: Russell Sage Foundation.

Kohlberg, L. (1969). Stage and sequence: The cognitive-developmental approach to socialization. In D. Goslin. (Ed.), *Handbook of socialization theory and research*. Chicago, IL: Rand McNally.

Maxwell, G. (1996). *Restorative justice: A Maori perspective.* Wellington, NZ: The New Zealand Maori Council.

O'Connell, Terry, Wachtel. B., & Wachtel, T. (1999). *Conferencing handbook.* Pipersville, PA: The Piper's Press.

Pranis, K. (1996). A state initiative toward restorative justice: The Minnesota experience. In B. Galaway and J. Hudson (Eds.), *Restorative justice: International perspectives* (pp. 493–504). Monsey, NY: Criminal Justice Press (pp. 493–504).

Schiff, M. (1998). Restorative justice interventions for juvenile offenders: A research agenda for the next decade. *Western Criminology Review, 1*(1). Retrieved from http://wrc.sonoma.edu/vlnl/schiff.html.

Seligman, M. (1996). *The optimistic child.* New York, NY: HarperPerennial.

Shook, E. V. (1985). Ho'oponopono: Contemporary uses of a Hawaiian problem-solving process. Honolulu: University of Hawaii Press.

Tharp, R., & Gallimore, R. (1988). *Rousing minds to life.* New York, NY: Cambridge University Press.

Zehr, H., (1990). *Changing lenses.* Scottdale, PA: Herald Press.

10

Family Group Conferences in Youth Justice and Child Welfare in Vermont

Gale Burford

Professor of Social Work at the University of Vermont Gale Burford was a pioneer in the promotion of restorative justice strategies in the Canadian justice system and the author of numerous chapters and books in the field. Vermont is a state that like Minnesota has been at the forefront of the restorative justice movement, especially with regard to juveniles. This chapter takes us right into the child welfare system where Family Group Conferencing according to the New Zealand model is being actively applied. Gale Burford with coeditor Joe Hudson published one of the best known books on family group conferencing. Because it also deals with restorative initiatives for young people, we editors have placed Box 4: Restorative Justice in Yuma County, Arizona, by Mary E. White at the end of the chapter.

"When you think about it, why *wouldn't* extended family and friends be included in planning for a family?" (Comment by social worker after attending a family group conference for the first time)

Indeed. Why *wouldn't* the extended family and friends be included when there are decisions to be made that might have lifetime consequences for young persons and their families?

This chapter shows through interviews with young people and adults who have participated in family meetings in Vermont some of the possibilities that are opened up for the expression of emotion, repair, and restoration when the extended family is brought to the table. These are possibilities, open spaces if you will (Morris & Burford, 2009), that tend to get closed off when things travel down the usual pathways of legal and individualized assessments and interventions. The examples come from data being collected for an evaluation of Vermont's efforts to transform their services in child protection and youth justice.[1] The intention of the chapter is not to teach about how family group conferences (FGC) and other family engagement practices work but to identify by example some of the ways bringing the family to the forefront welcomes the language of emotions and the engagement of the people most affected in youth justice and child protection matters with professionals rather than shuts it down. We start with an example from Vermont.

Question: How did it feel to be there with your sisters and your [family] as a group?

Answer: Good.

Question: I mean, that isn't something that happens very often I imagine.

Answer: No. It was the first time I saw my grandmother in seven years.

The exchange above is from an interview with a teen after her family attended a family group conference, that is, a meeting attended by extended family members and professionals to make decisions about her and her siblings.

In Vermont, child welfare and youth justice are administered together under a central human services agency. This arrangement is known to have advantages and disadvantages. Some argue that youthful offenders are treated less punitively than when juveniles are administered separately or under an adult corrections agency. Others argue that this can overemphasize the protection needs of the child and fail to hold young people accountable for their behavior. The state has been committed to the use of Balanced and Restorative Justice (BARJ) principles (Bazemore & Umbreit, 1998) for several years mainly through the use of diversion programs. More recently, the state has passed enabling legislation requiring the infusion of restorative justice principles in all aspects of juvenile justice (Marsh & Piper, 2009) including that the Department for Children and Families must "actively engage families in case planning, and solicit and integrate the input of the child, the child's family, relatives and other persons with a significant relationship to the child" (Juvenile Proceedings Act Title 33, Chapters 51–51, Section 5121).

When Young People and Families Are Involved in Multiple Systems

For good reason, cross- or dual-jurisdiction youth, that is, those who are being caught up in multiple systems like child welfare and youth justice, have increasingly become the focus of attention in the United States (Burford, 2005; Pennell, Shapiro & Spigner,

---

[1]Burford, G. (principal investigator), Evaluation of Vermont Department for Children and Families Family Services Division Practice Transformation, Institutional Review Board CHRBS 06-115 (2011).

2011; Tuell, 2003). The interest derives from recognition of how quickly family members and others in the informal network of relationships can be alienated. As legal and multiple professional protocols and assessments come into play, pathways back to family and community can close down. Research suggests this is true for many parents trying to get needed mental health services for their children and young people in child welfare and youth justice (Ashby, 2003). Additionally, mothers in domestic violence relationships who both want to protect their children and do not want to leave their abuser can be simultaneously blamed (Keeling & van Wormer, in press) and unable to get services they need as abused women (Goodmark, 2009). Extended family members who have no legal standing are shut out of legal proceedings and confidential professional processes but are increasingly turned to as the use of kinship placement grows, sometimes with consequences for themselves (Day & Bazemore, 2011).

Pennell, Shapiro, and Spigner (2011) point out that young people often become highly alienated from their families, communities, and helpers and age out of the system without connections and pro-social or age-appropriate developmental assets. Family engagement and restorative justice practices are seen as ways to foster these connections and bring balance to the professional and legal decision-making processes (American Humane Association, 2009, 2010; Maxwell, Kingi, Robertson, & Morris, 2004; Walker, 2005) and put children's and family rights in the forefront (Pennell, Burford, Connolly, & Morris, 2011).

While FGC can be used in a variety of situations where the family's leadership is desirable, including when the family thinks so, the youth justice child welfare interface poses a particularly challenging set of opportunities for situations that seem to have their origins in family conflicts that are spilling out into schools and neighborhoods.

Many teens do not like the idea when it is first presented to them of involving their extended relations. Some simply cannot believe these relatives could possibly want to be involved. Others cringe at the thought of a relative finding out what they did. Sometimes, family members are the same way. If they see the behavior as better left alone, relatives will balk at participation, often feeling they have no influence. When the offense has been serious, however, relatives almost never fail to understand a role for themselves and offer to participate. The following quote sums up best the view of young people and families about when to have a meeting:

> I think it [FGC] should happen before a child is placed in custody, depending on the circumstances of course. I mean, if some kid is stabbing people then no, but if it's just like, whatever, they should definitely look into that *before* making any decisions (Vermont teen in post-FGC interview).

What follows are three examples of the ways in which bringing the family to the table opens space for emotions, restoration, and healing.

EXAMPLE 1: THE ICE BREAKER

After a physical altercation that resulted in her daughter storming out of the house and heading in the direction of an adult male's house where she feared her daughter often went to use drugs and more, June said she "came to the end of my rope." She called the police. Not for the first time, either. And the police were not the only ones she had called in the past trying to get help on her terms to manage her daughter's behavior. June had ended a relationship with her own boyfriend when she realized she could not manage the conflict between the two of them. She tried to get help from the school to deal with her daughter's truancy. In June's view, she was trying to protect her daughter and keep her from getting into "trouble." She was trying to be "a good mother."

On the day in question, one thing led to another in the space of a few hours. The police took her daughter into custody, contacted youth justice, and the daughter was admitted to a foster care placement. The matter was referred to a local agency to try and get a family group conference together. Within days, a coordinator contacted June and her daughter separately and explained to them what was being proposed: that a group of their family members and anyone else they would like to be present would come to a family group conference. June did not like the idea. She was still reeling from the incident, and to top it off, her daughter had been "given a cell phone in that foster home" and was using it to phone her younger sister and tell her about the new clothes she had gotten in the foster home. June was furious. She felt everyone including the foster parents and the school representatives were all trying to make her look like a "bad parent." Things got worse. When asked who she would like to have come to the conference, June's daughter wanted her father, whom she had not seen or had any contact with in years to be there. This was out of the question as far as June was concerned. He had not contributed anything by way of support and his behavior while they were in the marriage toward June and the children was proof enough that he was not a fit parent.

The coordinator employed all the skills of shuttle diplomacy, respect, patience, and reassurance. Stories that June's daughter was attending school regularly and generally being a "model citizen" only served to make June feel that no one was willing to side with her. Other family members and friends offered to come and help out. It helped when her daughter told the coordinator that she wanted "to go home." A conference was finally held. In addition to June's family members locally, her ex-husband, his wife, and their children came to the conference from another city. A surprise occurred early: It turned out that the foster mother always gives young people in her home a cell phone because she wants to know where they are all the time "on her watch." This seemingly little thing broke the ice between them. And to top it off, it had been the juvenile justice social worker who had suggested the foster mother get some clothing and not phone June because June was so angry. At the meeting, June could see that it would be better if she allowed father and daughter to establish a relationship. And she saw that she had other family members who wanted to support her. June and the foster mother teamed up to supervise the daughter. A plan was made for the daughter to visit during the summer break with her father and get to know him and her half-siblings. June's daughter moved back home after the meeting. In an interview held several weeks after the conference, June's daughter had this to say:

Question: Is there anything else that you want to say, that you want people to know about your experience?

Answer: It's not as bad as I thought it was going to be.

Question: What isn't as bad?

Answer: The meeting. I thought it was just gonna be conflict. Even though we did argue, it broke the ice a lot, so it kind of resolved something. Like we weren't afraid to talk. 'Cause we were kind of confused about what we were fighting about, and it all came out at the meeting.

Question: Can you say more about that?

Answer: Just how we felt. We didn't ever talk about . . . we never sat down and talked about how we feel and when we did, like kind of when me and my family were meeting, like we all knew each other was aggravated and sad and just pissed off about the whole situation. So at the end of the meeting we just calmed everything down, and it broke the ice, and we talked for a while after that.

When asked about the result of the meeting, the school representative and the police officer were in agreement that the meeting helped because they were all communicating. The police officer observed that he and June and June's daughter now greet each other by name and talk in a friendly way when they see each other out in the community.

EXAMPLE 2: REBUILDING

Kristin had a lot of fence-mending to do with people in the community, including the school district where she returned after being in a series of foster homes and finally a residential group placement outside the community. But the hardest part was facing her family. In her interview, she talked about how hard it was to have her extended family learn the details of her negative behaviors. Yet she knew that if a rather large contingent of family had not come to her conference, the recommendations of the professionals for her to stay in group care probably would have prevailed. When she was asked what advice she would give to anyone else coming to a family group conference she said

> Maybe just keep it to a minimum of a few people. Well, actually, no, that's really not a good idea, because if I hadn't had all those people there, it probably wouldn't have happened in the way that it did, so no, I don't really have any advice on that. [Teen after her family's FGC brought her out of residential group care.]

Kristin's story is all too familiar. Her behavior had been escalating from truancy to disruptive behavior at school and home and staying out with friends whenever she felt like it. Her mother refused any mention of help from relatives, most of whom felt it was the mother's own psychiatric challenges that were part of the problem in managing things at home. When Kristin was finally taken into foster care as an "unmanageable" child, she reacted with further disruptive behavior and running away. Thus began a pattern of reactivity on Kristin's part that was met each time with higher penalties. She went through a string of foster homes. She heard about FGC from a peer who had one and had gone home. She asked for one for herself out of desperation. She was afraid she would end up in the system until she turned 18. At the family meeting, the social worker saw and encountered a large, interested group of family who wanted to be helpful and involved. Some of their initiatives had previously been rejected by the mother, who felt her problems were none of their business, and some had been rejected by the cloak of confidentiality put up by professionals. Others said they simply didn't know the full extent of what was happening to their family member, and although they knew things weren't right, they felt they had no right to insinuate themselves unless they were asked. Just seeing them all at the meeting was emotional enough for Kristin, but on top of it all, they wanted her back. They felt it was not right that she had gone into the system in the first place. The social worker agreed, and a plan was set in place for her to move back to the community. As is often the case, professionals had never "seen" the family together, especially on terms where they could put their best foot forward as a family group, and had no idea there were so many interested people in her life. Confidence in the family was raised. Confidence in the professional system was raised.

EXAMPLE 3: MAPPING THE SPREAD OF EMOTIONS: "FOLLOW THE FEELINGS"

A conference coordinator is preparing an officer to attend his first-ever conference. The officer had been called to the scene where a young man had gone on an angry public rampage, threatening anyone who was around, breaking windows and anything else he could get his hands on. When the officers arrived, the boy was still angry, threatening, and resisting being taken into custody. The coordinator perceives the officer to be skeptical about the idea of a family meeting. He has had dealings with this family and does not see what good could come out of attending and describing the incident to them. She asks the officer how the incident affected him. She already knew when she asked the question that in order to take the boy into custody the officer had to chase the boy down, tackle him, disarm him of a piece of metal that he had been swinging, and hold him down until his partner could catch up and they could get the boy in the car. The officer allows that the boy was "a tough kid for his age and size," but sticks to statements like "it was nothing," "had to be done," and "all in a day's work" to respond to the question. He is "glad" the boy was not injured and adds that he is probably "a pretty good kid" but the family has a lot of problems. Being somewhat acquainted with the officer and his wife, the coordinator explained later that she felt it was appropriate when she asked, "What was it like to go home after a day like that?" The officer acknowledges that his wife had a lot to say about the scratches he had on his face, his broken glasses, bruises on his ankles and back, the buttons torn off his shirt and the fact that the boy had spit in his face. He says that "while she was sewing the buttons on my shirt" she was talking, and not for the first time, about him being "young now" and a "new officer in good shape" but raised her feelings about what it would be like for him and her in a few years if he was still having to chase people down the street. The coordinator asks if the officer would be comfortable sharing any part of that story at the conference. She explains how conferences work and why she thinks it might be good if the young person and his family fully understand the impact of the boy's actions on others, including those whose property had been damaged. She even asks if his wife might be willing to attend. The officer decides that he will say briefly what happened including the damages to private property and to the police car and how he dislikes having to be "physical" with young people. He regretted that there seemed to have been no other way to manage the situation. At the actual conference, once the officer saw that the family members were very concerned about the boy's behavior and problems he had been having, the officer felt comfortable saying even more about the events of the arrest and how he felt afterward. He acknowledged to the group how upsetting the event was to his wife. Some family members acknowledged knowing his wife and her family, as they are all from the same area, and expressed regret to the officer. The coordinator felt it was a turning point in the conference.

For an example from Arizona, see Box 4, which follows. The county described, which is in southwest Arizona, is working closely with children in trouble with the law. Mary White, the deputy county attorney, describes the process by which her office works closely with juveniles and their families to keep them in their home communities while closely monitoring their progress.

Box 4

Restorative Justice in Yuma County, Arizona

Mary E. White

Overview

From January 2005 to the present, restorative justice has been applied in Yuma, Arizona, in a form called Community Justice Boards. This program relies upon community volunteers who work with first offender juveniles and their families. If appropriate, the victim of a crime may also be a part of the process. The program is a partnership between prosecutors (Yuma County Attorney Jon Smith) and Juvenile Court. First offenders are screened and referred to our boards by Juvenile Court diversion officers.

Cases referred are misdemeanors such as shoplifting, simple assault, minor consuming alcohol, graffiti, etc. Status offenses such as truancy or runaway may also be referred. Drug cases are not referred at this time (2011). This is an alternative to prosecution so that if a child successfully graduates from a Community Justice Board, no charges will be filed.

The Process

Upon receipt of a case, the volunteer board members hold a conference with the juvenile and parent/guardian. If the parent/guardian is a non-English speaker, an interpreter also attends the conference. (Yuma County is on the border with Mexico, and the majority of our families are of Spanish-speaking culture with some parents knowing only Spanish.)

(Continued)

(Continued)

Any family and friends, including younger siblings, are welcome to attend and participate. Conferences take place on neutral ground (not the police station or the courthouse). Our locations are churches, a school, the library, and a community center.

There will be a series of conferences on a single case because the board stays with the child and family until board members are satisfied that the child has learned enough to graduate. Sometimes the child or family encounters new problems during the term of the case. If this happens, the board continues working with them to help with the new issues.

At the first conference, the chair explains our program and establishes that the child admits the offense. Then the board members engage with the child and parent/guardian in questioning and discussion to learn about the child and family. The purpose is to discover what went wrong and to assess the child's strengths and needs. If victims are present, they are welcomed to join the discussion. The victims are encouraged to describe the impact upon them of the offense. (Careful advance preparation by staff may be necessary prior to this encounter to avoid trauma to either victim or the child offender. Often the victim is another child, and this may preclude involvement by the minor victim, depending upon the nature of the offense.)

Following this exchange, the child and parent/guardian are excused from the room and the board members deliberate on what consequences should be imposed. The child and parent, and victim if present, will have been asked what they think the consequences should be, but the child and parent do not hear the deliberations. (This is because board members must be free to discuss the circumstances without risk of inadvertently saying something harmful to the child.)

Consequences are then assigned for the juvenile to complete. These are designed to help the child learn how to make better choices and how to set and carry out goals. These consequences also lead the child to an understanding of how the child's conduct impacted others such as the victim and/or family members.

The consequences are handwritten into an agreement that is signed at the meeting by child, parent and board chair. At the follow-up meetings, further consequences may be agreed upon, depending upon what needs and issues may surface. Great care is taken to approach the child in a positive, friendly manner. We seek to inspire self-reliance, goal setting, self-confidence, and empathy toward others.

When a child satisfactorily completes all consequences, the board recognizes the child's accomplishment at a graduation meeting wherein the child is praised, presented with certificates and possibly a small gift such as a dictionary, and refreshments are shared.

Examples of Consequences

- Apology letter to parent and victim
- Report on what is bullying and how it hurts others
- Essay on what I could have done to avoid this happening
- Report on the child's dreams and goals
- Specific report on "How to become a _____ (whatever occupation or career interests the child)"

The child must stand and read aloud the letters and reports. (Depending upon the risks of further harm to the victim or the young offender, apology letters may not be forwarded to victims.) Other consequences may be to participate in counseling (referrals assisted by Juvenile Court staff). Sometimes the child is required to tour the Juvenile Detention Center (with parent). Often the child must bring in school progress reports and work to bring up grades. The child may be required to sign up for tutoring if available. The child may be sent to find out about and join activities that could occupy him or her in positive ways, such as scouting, U.S. Border Patrol explorers, sports, and life skills classes, if offered by reputable organizations.

There is no set list of consequences. The boards are free to choose whatever best fits the child's circumstances. We have a few simple parameters: Assignments should be positive learning experiences. The child should be able to bring in the results and show them to the board or bring documentation thereof. We rarely assign community service due to the lack of appropriate, safe environments for this, especially for our younger children. For example, we do not mandate our young first offenders into a highway cleanup with chronic offenders nor do we force them to work for adults who have not had background checks. The child is not mandated into any faith-based programs, although he or she may be encouraged to try these out if available.

The Boards

We began with two boards and now we have six with a seventh being planned. Each board handles no more than two cases at time and does not accept a new case until one is concluded. Hence, we usually have no more than six juveniles in the program at once. The board may work with a case for as little as one month or as long as a year, meeting every two weeks at 5:30 p.m. with the child and parent/guardian. (Occasionally, a very ambitious board may choose to handle two cases at a time but only one case is handled per meeting.)

Each board has its own chair, who is a volunteer committed to facilitate every meeting. In recognition of this commitment and by consensus of our volunteers, each board carries the name of its current chair. Our volunteers are diverse, of various ages, races, ethnicities, religions, occupations, genders, and backgrounds. Applications must be completed, and criminal history checks are done. However, we do not turn away volunteers simply because they have made mistakes in life as these people may have much to offer as a result of their experiences. As a safeguard, we do not allow volunteers to have contact with the juvenile or family except at the board meeting or in the presence of program staff.

Statistics

As of September 30, 2011, we had graduated 112 children from our program. This is a total of 66 boys and 46 girls. Our Community Justice Boards have concluded 135 cases since January 2005. This gives us a successful graduation rate of about 83%. There are currently seven open cases active before the boards.

As for recidivism, we track our graduated juveniles indefinitely. If the child is the suspect in any case that comes back through the County Attorney's Office, even as an adult, the case is included in our statistics. We count the referral as a new offense regardless of the outcome of the new case.

With the above in mind, our recidivism rate is currently about 29% (32 out of 112 graduates). We have had very few referrals of juveniles who graduated since the end of 2009. More data analysis is needed to form definitive conclusions, but we do see some trends. We notice, for example, that cases that remain with a board for a

(Continued)

(Continued)

long period of time before graduating have little or no recidivism. And cases wherein the child is involved with gangs or the parent is less cooperative with the board's efforts have a high recidivism rate.

Restorative Justice and the Community

Besides providing help for the child and family, our Community Justice Boards are an excellent model of community involvement in the criminal justice system. Community volunteers learn firsthand about the problems and issues facing young first offenders and have a chance to do something about it. The community sees how laws are being enforced in regard to their children and discovers the resources or lack thereof available to help prevent these children from re-offending.

Recognition of Pima County Attorney's Community Justice Boards

I wish to recognize Pima County Attorney Barbara Lawall, Tucson, Arizona, for implementing the first Community Justice Boards in Arizona. Her program, which has been operating successfully for many years, was the model for ours. Although our programs may diverge somewhat due to differences in our communities, we strive for the same restorative goals of repairing harm to communities and victims, helping our children make better choices, and involving our communities in restorative justice.

Conclusion

These examples show how responsive involvement with the family and professionals can open up room for different kinds of conversations that usually occur in courts and clinical offices, but they require people to work in quite different ways than they may be used to working. Vermont remains at an early stage of rolling out the use of family engagement in situations involving youth justice and/or child welfare, and the state faces all the usual systemic pressures to make family engagement fit with institutionalized, forensic, and risk-averse ways of working. Few families and young people get family meetings, as they are offered on a wholly discretionary basis. Despite the existence of enabling legislation, change comes slow. Like in other systems, it is through the sheer determination of leadership and local practice champions that practice shifts. The adage that the best teacher is experience certainly seems to apply to family meetings. The state has undertaken a major effort to align its policies and legislation with what is known about good practice and to create organizational and team climates that are hospitable to the practice of respect at all levels. Collaboration among professional systems remains the most challenging aspect of systems change.

Bringing the extended family together for case conferences in child welfare and youth justice is still treated as a luxury in many settings in the United States, a "Cadillac" approach to the delivery of services, meaning that it seems to defy "efficiency" in the use of time, energy, and money. Like other efforts to "empower" persons affected by a problem and involve them meaningfully, the institutional pressure is toward reducing their roles to those of token involvement; add-ons to the work of the professionals. It is a long-range venture, the outcome of which will be determined at local, state, and national levels and, as has been said many times, seriously puts to the test our beliefs about family and youth empowerment and democratic decision-making.

Critical Thinking Questions

1. What are some advantages and disadvantages of involving extended family members in decision making for teens who have gotten into trouble?

2. Discuss two of the case examples provided in this chapter with reference to turning points. What were the events leading up to the turning points, and how did the Family Group Conferencing elicit them?

References

American Humane Association. (2009). FGC in Restorative Justice Restorative group conferencing for dual-jurisdiction youth. Retrieved from http://www.americanhumane.org/assets/pdfs/children/restorative-group-conferencing-dual-jurisdiction.pdf

American Humane Association. (2010). Restorative Conferencing for Youth Justice Practice Manual. Unpublished.

Ashby, C. M. (2003, July). Child welfare and juvenile justice: Several factors influence the placement of children solely to obtain mental health services. Washington, DC: United States General Accounting Office, GAO-03-865T.

Bazemore, G., & Umbreit, M. S. (1998). Guide for implementing the balanced and restorative justice model. Washington, DC: U.S. Department of Justice, Office of Justice Programs, Office of Juvenile Justice and Delinquency Prevention.

Burford, G. (2005). Family group conferences in the youth justice and the child welfare systems. In J. Pennell & G. Anderson (Eds.), Widening the circle: The practice and evaluation of family group conferencing with children, young persons and their families (pp. 203–220). Washington, DC: NASW Press.

Burford, G., Connolly, M., Morris, K., & Pennell, J. (2010). Annotated bibliography on engaging the family group in child welfare decision making, Vol. 15. Englewood, CO: American Humane Association. Retrieved from http://www.americanhumane.org/children/programs/family-group-decision-making/bibliographies/research-and-evaluation/

Burford, G., & Hudson, J. (2000). (Eds.). Family group conferencing: New directions in community-centered child and family practice. New York, NY: Aldine de Gruyter.

Day, S. E., & Bazemore, G. (2011). Two generations at risk: Child welfare, institutional boundaries, and family violence in grandparent homes. Child Welfare, 90(4), 97–116.

Goodmark, L. (2009). Autonomy feminism: An anti-essentialist critique of mandatory interventions in domestic violence cases. Florida State University Law Review, 37(1), 1–48. Retrieved from http://www.law.fsu.edu/journals/lawreview/downloads/371/goodmark.pdf

Keeling, J., & van Wormer, K. (in press). Social worker interventions in situations of domestic violence: What can we learn from survivor's personal narratives? *British Journal of Social Work.* doi: 10.1093/bjsw/bcr137

Marsh, P., & Piper, K. (2009, Spring). The practical implications of the newly enacted Vermont Juvenile Judicial Proceedings Act (JJPA). *The Vermont Bar Journal,* pp. 1–6. Retrieved from http://www.vtbar.org/images/journal/journalarticles/spring2009/JJPA.pdf

Maxwell, G., Kingi, V., Robertson, J., & Morris, G. (2004). *Achieving effective outcomes in youth justice: Final report to the Ministry of Social Development.* Wellington, NZ: Ministry of Social Development.

Morris, K., & Burford, G. (2009). Family decision making: New spaces for participation and resistance. In M. Barnes & D. Prior (Eds.), *Subversive citizens: Power, agency and resistance in public services* (pp. 119–135). Bristol, UK: The Policy Press.

Pennell, J., Burford, G., Connolly, M., & Morris, K. (2011). Introduction—Taking child and family rights seriously: Family engagement and its evidence in child welfare. Child Welfare Special Issue: Taking Child and Family Rights Seriously: Family Engagement and its Evidence. *Child Welfare, 90*(4), 9–16.

Pennell, J., Shapiro, C., & Spigner, W. (2011). *Safety, fairness, stability: Repositioning juvenile justice and child welfare to engage families and communities.* Washington, DC: Georgetown University Center for Juvenile Justice Reform. Retrieved from http://cjjr.georgetown.edu/pdfs/famengagement/Family EngagementPaper.pdf

Tuell, J. (2003). *Understanding child maltreatment and juvenile delinquency: From research to effective program, practice, and systemic solutions.* Washington, DC: Child Welfare League of America.

Walker, L. (2005) E Makua Ana youth circles: A transition planning process for youth exiting foster care. *VOMA Connections, 21*(4), 5–12.

11

Creating Healthy Residential Communities in Higher Education Through the Use of Restorative Practices

Ted Wachtel and Stacey Miller

This chapter was originally published as the introductory chapter in Building Campus Community: Restorative Practices in Residential Life *(2011) by Joshua Wachtel and Ted Wachtel published by International Institute for Restorative Practices of which Ted Wachtel is the president. A former public school teacher, Ted Wachtel was one of the first educators to recognize the positive impact of restorative practices in school, family, and workplace settings. Today, he gives keynote speeches around the world.*

Stacey Miller, the director of residential life at the University of Vermont, has brought the use of circles and other restorative practices to campus life with excellent results.

Every year during the summer orientation program this chapter's coauthor, Stacey Miller, director of residential life at the University of Vermont (UVM), tells parents the unvarnished truth—that even under the best of circumstances, living in a campus

Source: From *"Restorative Circles in Schools: Building Community and Enhancing Learning",* by Bob Costello, Joshua Wachtel, and Ted Wachtel. International Institute for Restorative Practices, © 2011.

residence hall is a difficult undertaking. Many parents, some being former college students, nod in agreement. She goes on to describe the residence hall as a unique environment where almost everyone is in young adulthood (except for a few student-affairs professionals). It is devoid of children, middle-aged adults, the elderly, and with the exception of fish, any animals. Yet new students enthusiastically embrace this artificial reality because their goal is simple. They want to escape parents, family members, and any kind of adult supervision in their quest for independence and adulthood.

Those of us who have already experienced college life are painfully aware that, without the right support systems, residence hall living can be a recipe for disaster. Why? Because people who are in youthful stages of their emotional, mental, and social development often behave in ways that are not socially responsible, civil, or respectful—of themselves or others. To envision how easily civilization can turn to chaos when the young are left to their own devices, one only has to remember the boys who devolved into savagery in William Golding's classic novel *Lord of the Flies*.

Every year, college and university residence halls open their doors to hundreds of thousands of first-year students who will occupy shared living settings with a population density more concentrated than most urban residential buildings. With the exception of a few encounters at orientation or Facebook exchanges, most of these students do not know each other. Nor have most of them ever lived away from their families, except for a customary summer camp excursion. More and more students entering college have never shared a bedroom with a sibling and in some instances have never even shared a bathroom. Outside of directed social group activities or participation on a sports team, most have not had to live or work cooperatively with members of their peer group.

Some students have problems with alcohol and drug use. Others are boisterous, noisy, messy, and rude. Some struggle with personal relationships, mental health issues, or hold racial and religious biases that interfere with their ability to connect with others. Others come with even more serious problems, a history of stealing or violence that is not disclosed, that eventually manifest itself in the close quarters of residential living.

In some ways, residential hall living and the students who occupy these spaces are just a microcosm of the larger world, but with the inherent behaviors and characteristics of youth. Soon after their arrival on campus they will face the demands and stresses of their academic programs—classes, assignments, exams, and papers—and tensions and conflicts with roommates and friends. These are the circumstances that, every year, frame the fundamental challenge faced by the residential life staff at colleges and universities—how to build healthy communities quickly and effectively so that students can live together productively and harmoniously.

As a student affairs practitioner for more than 17 years, Stacey Miller spent much of her career in residential life looking for a formula, for a "magic potion," that when dispensed would enable students in residential settings, at a minimum, to get along with each other. Many years ago she found half of that formula for healthy residential communities in the theoretical model known as "community standards." Developed at the University of Nevada, the community standards process allows students to create mutually agreed upon expectations that define how their "community will engage and function on an interpersonal level." The model relies on dialogue to create and maintain standards because peer-to-peer interaction has been found to be the "single most potent source of influence on growth and development during the undergraduate years" (Astin 1993), and the simple act of sharing feelings can influence and change peer perspectives and behaviors.

Through the community standards process, community members meet to discuss their needs and wants as they relate to residential hall living, make agreements based on these needs and wants, and resolve difficulties that arise when agreements are not honored. Use of the community standards model is supposed to change the role of staff from authorities to facilitators and the role of students from recipients to creators of their own experiences. Theoretically, staff members are no longer expected to control, but rather guide the community toward individual and group responsibility and accountability (Piper 1996).

But what sounded great in theory was difficult to implement in practice. Residential life professional staff members must train young resident advisers (RAs), who are in the inherently ambiguous position of simultaneously being both peer support and authorities in their relationships with the other students in their living area, to implement the community standards process. Often relying on an *implicit* understanding of how to develop community, residential life professional staff members would often *tell* RAs to build community, but struggle to *explicitly show* them how. RAs were then left to figure out their own strategies and techniques to bring students together.

While some RAs are naturally communicative or charismatic, few are prepared to herd 50 or more diverse 18- to 22-year-olds together and run a meeting for any sustained period of time. How do RAs create an environment where boisterous, bored, distracted, impatient, posturing, nervous, and occasionally "too cool for school" young adults will engage in meaningful dialogue about issues like roommate relationships, cleanliness, and vandalism? Stacey Miller found the answer to that question—the second half of the formula for her long-sought magic potion—in "restorative practices."

Although her colleague Gail Shampnois had for more than a year advocated restorative practices (RP) as a means for helping students engage and connect with each other, it was not until Stacey Miller actually participated in a restorative conversation facilitated by Charles Johnson, the safe schools consultant for the Vermont Department of Education, that she fundamentally "got it." In only a 15-minute RP circle, she learned more about some of her colleagues than she had in the eight years she had worked with them. The circle was simple, structured, and provided equal status for all the participants. While the facilitator took part in the conversation, he did not dominate or artificially control it. Rather, the "talking piece," as it was passed around the circle from person to person, ensured that respect was paid to each individual who was talking while they held the object. Although the circle is but one aspect of the RP framework, it is a very symbolic and powerful mechanism to help those students get to know each other and begin the process of openly discussing their needs and wants, consistent with the community standards process.

The IIRP Graduate School (International Institute for Restorative Practices) in Bethlehem, Pennsylvania, is a leading provider of restorative practices training that fosters both proactive community building and reactive restorative justice, which responds to wrongdoing. To date, restorative strategies implemented at colleges and universities largely have been limited to restorative justice, which is the area of restorative practices that responds to crime and wrongdoing, in contrast with the proactive elements of restorative practices that build community and create social bonding. Although IIRP's Real Justice program was among the first to use restorative conferences to respond to wrongdoing in college settings (Wachtel, 1997), Ted Wachtel, coauthor of this chapter and IIRP president, at a 1999 restorative justice conference in Australia called for "Restorative Justice in Everyday Life: Beyond the Formal Process." He suggested the systematic use of restorative strategies not just as a response to wrongdoing but "to guide the way people act in all of their dealings" (Wachtel & McCold 2001).

In 2010, in collaboration with the IIRP, UVM's residence life staff began using restorative practices both proactively and reactively. Pleased with the first year's results, UVM is now institutionalizing restorative practices so that each August RAs will participate in three days of IIRP-designed restorative practices training. (IIRP has a training of trainers program that will transfer the training responsibility to UVM's own residence life staff.) The training and related books teach RAs how to begin the school year with proactive circles that foster community standards and then how to use a range of informal and formal restorative practices to respond to problems, conflicts, and wrongdoing as they arise.

The initial circle of the school year is held with first-year students when they arrive. Passing a talking piece around the circle, RAs ask them to respond to questions such as, "What are you hoping for in your first year here?" "What are your concerns?" "What are some of your long-term hopes and dreams?" These simple questions allow students to share as much or as little of themselves as they choose—but provide opportunities for students to become acquainted with each other and with the restorative circles that will be held periodically in their residence halls during the school year.

A few days later, when returning students join first-year students in the residence halls, RAs hold circles with questions designed to establish and support community standards: "What do you think the ideal residential community looks like?" "What kind of behaviors might interfere with achieving that ideal community?" "What can we as individuals and as a group do to overcome those obstacles to achieving an ideal community?" Those unfamiliar with circles are often surprised by how engaged college students become in addressing and solving behavioral issues and conflicts that are usually considered the domain of those in positions of authority. Yet IIRP's experiences, even with students in the most challenging urban public schools and in its own model programs for delinquent and at-risk youth, have repeatedly demonstrated the validity of its fundamental premise regarding restorative practices—that "people are happier, more cooperative and productive, and more likely to make positive changes when those in authority do things *with* them, rather than *to* them or *for* them."

UVM residence life staff use circles throughout the school year for a variety of purposes: to foster positive relationships, to raise consciousness about bias issues, and to respond to conflicts and problems. The key to a successful circle is for facilitators to be clear in their own minds what the goal of each circle is going to be and then structure questions that promote that goal.

The most dramatic circles in UVM's first year of restorative practices dealt with a tragedy. A student who lived in the residence halls committed suicide. RAs immediately recognized the healing power of circles for resident students who were shocked, saddened, and deeply troubled by the incident. Convening restorative circles within 24 hours of the tragedy allowed young people to express their feelings and support one another.

In response to substantial incidents of wrongdoing, UVM staff members have decided on two strategies. They use responsive circles when they do not know the identity of the wrongdoer and use formal restorative conferences when they do. When there is anonymous vandalism or bias graffiti, RAs convene a circle that allows students to express their feelings about the situation and to brainstorm ideas to prevent a reoccurrence. The culprit is often in the circle, hearing others' reactions to their actions and gaining an understanding of how they have adversely affected their peers. That understanding and perhaps the fear of being discovered often discourage further problems.

When the wrongdoer is known, the formal restorative conference has greater impact and is more complete. The conference facilitator asks a series of open-ended "restorative questions" that provide everyone with an opportunity to express themselves: first the offender, then those directly harmed, their supporters, and then those who are there to support the offender. Lastly everyone has an opportunity to discuss what actions might help to restore the harm. After the formal conference refreshments are served, providing an opportunity for informal conversation and social reintegration.

The most significant conference of the first year of restorative practices at UVM was held after a student, who was skateboarding in a hallway in violation of residential rules, inadvertently hit a sprinkler head. Water surged through the hallway into bedrooms. Firefighters arrived and the building was evacuated. Students could not return to their rooms until 4 a.m., with 10 rooms suffering such serious water damage that those residents had to sleep in other quarters. Books, clothing, laptop computers, and beds were damaged or destroyed.

Although the student came forward to admit what he had done and his family's homeowners insurance reimbursed the losses, the young man was ashamed to face his peers. Students were angry and upset, as rumors further exacerbated feelings by creating distorted accounts of what actually happened. While the authorities did not plan to impose punitive sanctions, in the past such an incident would result in the young man moving to another residence hall in an effort to avoid the stigma. But since the advent of restorative practices at UVM, the residence life staff now had a healthier and more effective way to deal with the emotional aftermath, by inviting the young man to participate in a restorative conference.

The conference was scheduled for a Sunday evening with 30 participants, including all the students whose rooms and property had been damaged. The young man's roommate and RA sat with him at the conference as his supporters. The staff that organized and facilitated the conference appropriately prepared everyone beforehand by letting them know what to expect.

The "offender" had the first opportunity to speak to his "victims" (these terms are never used to address or refer to anyone but are just used here to describe the conference process). When the other students realized that the incident was truly an accident, their anger subsided. Contrary to the rumors, the young man had done nothing deliberately. While he was not supposed to be skateboarding in the hallway, the consequence was obviously unintentional. He had no way of anticipating the damage that his inappropriate actions would cause. As the other students spoke, he had an opportunity to truly understand how he had adversely affected so many people in his residential community.

The conference facilitator reported that the conference went better than she had expected. The next day the student sent her an email saying, "I was skeptical going into the conference. However, I'm really glad that I was able to participate in this and I really understand how my actions affected my neighbors and fellow students." Satisfaction over the resolution of the incident was high because the conference resolved angry feelings, allowed the offender to be reintegrated into his community of peers, and put the whole incident to rest.

Lesser problems in the residence halls are handled more informally. RAs might simply respond to loud music or late-night commotion or other violations with simple affective statements, telling students how their behavior makes them feel. Or they might be slightly more formal by asking a "restorative question" derived from the formal conference script, such as, "How do you think you are affecting others?" or after exploring feelings, "How can you make things right?" Or they might move to a small, impromptu conference, bringing a few people together for an exchange, using the restorative questions to frame the discussion.

"For many, being restorative is not a comfortable way of confronting behavior," states coauthor Stacey Miller. For decades housing professionals have taught RAs to "lay down the law" and simply stop negative behavior. The RA is the "boss," the person who is in charge of the community, and is supposed to use that authority accordingly. Restorative practices is a huge paradigm shift in which staff confront behavior, but also share their own feelings as part of that process. We now are telling RAs to make themselves vulnerable, express how the inappropriate behavior is impacting them and ask questions of residents to help them understand how their behavior is affecting others. Restorative practices puts the emphasis on sustaining good relationships because ultimately that is more effective in achieving behavior change. While RAs may, at times, still have an obligation to "document" students, writing up and reporting their violations of residence hall regulations, they have moved beyond a strictly legalistic and punitive approach by allowing people to have a voice, to explain what happened, and to share how they have been affected, which creates a more cordial and cooperative atmosphere in the residence halls.

Conclusion and Follow-Up

While both UVM and IIRP are committed to refining the training and restorative protocols for residential life in their second year, they are delighted with the outcomes so far. One statistic dramatically highlights the success of the first year of restorative practices at the University of Vermont. Typically each year, by the time the winter break arrives, a dozen or more RAs have resigned from their positions, having found the job of being both peer and authority figure too frustrating and stressful to continue. However, since the implementation of restorative practices, having learned a set of strategies that allow them to be facilitators of community standards, rather than dictators, only one of UVM's 129 RAs resigned. Miller seems to have found her magic potion.

Critical Thinking Questions

1. What is the evidence of success of this university residential program?

2. How could this approach be modeled at your college? What would be some of the challenges to its implementation?

References

Astin, Alexander W. (1993). *What matters in college? Four critical years revisited*, San Francisco: Jossey-Bass.

Piper, T. (1996). The community standards model: A method to enhance student learning and development. *ACUHO-I Talking Stick* November, 14–15.

Wachtel, T. and McCold, P. (2001). Restorative justice in everyday life. In H. Strang and J. Braithwaite (Eds.), *Restorative justice and civil society.* Cambridge, UK: Cambridge University Press.

Wachtel, T. (1997). *Real justice.* Pipersville, PA: The Piper's Press.

PART III

Pretrial: Before or After Arrest—Diversion Programs

RJ is used successfully after wrongdoing has occurred but before involvement of the courts. It can be used before arrest or after arrest but before court involvement. In this section we learn how social workers, community board members, or the courts can use RJ for youth and adults alike to divert them to RJ interventions instead of sending them to court.

The topics covered in this section are diverse; the uniting theme is diversion from the traditional court and/or criminal justice system. We have a lot to learn from New Zealand, probably the country that has done the most in terms of the institutionalization of restorative justice strategies originally borrowed from the culture of the indigenous population—the Maori people. Chapter 12 by Gabrielle Maxwell chronicles this unique history. We editors have added Box 5 on a parallel example of the use of circles to confront and curb violence among minority youth in Oakland, California.

Moving into adult situations in Colorado, Mona Schatz describes in Chapter 13 the diversion of cases from the police to the community. Chapters 14 and 15 concern diversion in cases of serious violence. Anne Hayden and Katherine van Wormer review the literature on the use of restorative strategies in cases of domestic violence and rape and present original data from research in New Zealand. Chapter 15, a major contribution to this book, reveals the appropriateness of restorative processes to cases of clergy sexual abuse. The author is Theo Gavrielides, who is working to promote a wider use of restorative justice principles in member nations of the European Union.

12

Restorative and Diversionary Responses to Youth Offending in New Zealand[1]

Gabrielle Maxwell

A criminologist and senior associate at the Institute of Policy Studies, University of Victoria, New Zealand, Gabrielle Maxwell is widely published in the field of restorative justice as a leading expert on Family Group Conferencing, a process with its roots in New Zealand. Her chapter describes New Zealand's historic and pioneering experience applying RJ to divert youth from court processes and her numerous research studies of the outcomes. The boxed reading, Circles of Change: Bringing a More Compassionate Justice System to Troubled Youth in Oakland, describes a U.S. innovation that was inspired by work with indigenous populations in New Zealand.

The New Zealand approach to youth offending came into being with passage of the Children, Young Persons, and Their Families Act 1989. The legislation sets out a number of principles for the future, including that practice in child welfare and juvenile justice must involve parents, extended family, and *whanau, hapu,* and *iwi* (family groups, clans, and tribes) in developing solutions to problem situations and provide support to them in caring for their children. These principles emphasized diverting children and young people from court and keeping them within their family and community groups. They require that responses should respect cultural values, adopt culturally appropriate procedures, and cease using intrusive and disempowering interventions.

---

[1]This contribution is based on an extract of a published paper by Pennell, Maxwell, and Nash, 2011.

This act was a revision of an earlier bill affecting children and young people that had evoked widespread outrage among Maori, the indigenous people of New Zealand. The government set up a working party of Maori (Ministerial Advisory Committee, 1986) who reported on the widespread dissatisfaction among Maori with the treatment of their families and children within a social welfare system that they saw as having led to the systematic removal of Maori children from their homes, families, and culture. The results of adopting the working party's recommendations can be seen in the act's inclusion of Maori terms and concepts; its principles of diversion, empowerment and family support; and the involvement of families and the wider community in decisions. These are the ideas that were the direct antecedents of the family group conference (FGC).

The Youth Justice System in New Zealand

The 1989 act heralded the introduction of a radically new approach to respond more effectively and appropriately to young people (those under the age of 17 years) and their families when there were issues around the care or control of children and young people. The act acknowledged the responsibility of the state for providing services and support to children and families in need; encouraged a new sense of the obligation of the state to respect cultural differences, involve family and *whanau* at all times and the rights of children to remain with their families and in their communities wherever possible; emphasized the rights of children and young people to be fully informed about what was happening and to be involved in the processes even when there had been serious offending; and placed a strong emphasis on the recognition of Maori culture.

The most radical aspects of the act were provisions that placed an obligation on the state to involve families and young people and, in the case of youth justice, the victims of any offending in the decision-making processes. Consistent with the new philosophy, police have increasingly consulted with young people and families to make diversionary arrangements that could include apologies and making amends for offending as well as referrals to programs and arrangements about school attendance (Maxwell & Paulin, 2004). When cases were referred to the youth court, it too became more concerned about ensuring that young people made amends for their offending and were provided with the support that they needed to build a new life.

The FGC is at the heart of the new system for more serious offenders. When a young person is referred to an FGC (either directly by the police or the Youth Court), a meeting is arranged by a Youth Justice coordinator to discuss possible responses to the offending. The coordinator will contact family, the young person, any victims, and other relevant people to inform them about the conference and arrange a time and place for it. Meetings can occur anywhere but most commonly are held on neutral ground, such as in a community center.

All those invited are welcomed and the purposes are explained: to discuss what has happened and to decide what should be done. A police officer normally describes the events, and then the discussion of what happened will be opened up to include the young person, the victim, and others present. This is usually the point at which the young person acknowledges his or her responsibility and the group discusses what can be done to make amends. Following this discussion, the family and the young person meet privately to decide what they would like to do and prepare a plan.

In the final stage of the conference, the proposals made by the family and the young person are discussed with all participants (including any victims of the offending) until a consensus agreement is reached. The agreed plan is written up for action or, if applicable, reporting back to the Youth Court. If all the requirements of the plan are satisfactorily completed, this will normally be an end to the matter, although there are provisions for reconvening the conference if unforeseen problems arise. This conference is almost always able to reach an agreement about what is needed for the young person to be accountable for their offending, about provisions for making amends and the support that will be needed for the young person in starting a new life. Victims who attend for the most part report feeling better for having taken part and satisfied with the decisions that have been taken although inevitably complete repair of the harm that has been done often is not possible. On the other hand, some leave feeling that the conference has not met their needs and, indeed, this is a limitation. The needs of victims who have been traumatized or suffered major losses are rarely able to be met by relatively impoverished young people and their families. Their needs for support and help require the help of other agencies, and the state is gradually moving to strengthen services for victims that are independent of criminal justice processes.

The Defining Characteristics of Successful Conferences

There have been two major studies in New Zealand that have identified factors relating to effective conferencing (Maxwell & Morris, 1993; Maxwell, Kingi, Robertson, Morris, & Cunningham, 2004) and several other studies have focused on additional aspects of the youth justice system.[2] These studies identify factors that predict satisfaction with the process for the key participants and successful life outcomes for the young people after the conference.

Participation. Conferences work best when families, victims, and young people are well informed about what is likely to take place and what their roles will be; when they are actively involved both in deciding the arrangements for the conference and who will be present; and when they are fully involved in presenting their views and in reaching the decisions that are made.

The presence of all these people in the conference is important, but victims can choose whether or not they would like to attend. If they choose not to be present, finding ways their views can be reported to the group is important. Those responsible for coordinating the conference need to make sure that all those most affected are enabled to have their views heard. At the same time, it is important to ensure that the professionals

---

[2]These include studies that focus on understanding re-offending (Maxwell & Morris, 1999), the role of the youth advocate (Morris, Maxwell, & Shepherd, 1997), and police youth diversion (Maxwell & Paulin, 2004).

(such as police and social workers) all see their role as supplying information as needed and do not dominate the decision making. The conference is intended to be a process where those most affected by the offending—the victims, young people, and their families—are expected to be responsible for deciding on responses. The role of professionals is intended to be to facilitate the process and provide information about relevant options. They are not expected to be responsible for decision making except to ensure that this is consistent with legal requirements.

Empowerment. Full participation in the process is likely to lead to feelings of empowerment in the key players. A sense of control over one's own life can be restored not only to the young people but also to the victims and the family members who take part. However, participation is not enough—real empowerment will only happen when everyone leaves the conference feeling that their views have been listened to, their feelings have been understood, and their concerns have been reflected in the resulting plan.

Repairing the harm. Repair does not usually involve deciding on a punishment. Crucial factors for victims are feeling that they have been listened to and treated with respect. It is often impossible for the young person to right the wrong that has been done, but the key for both victims and the young people themselves is that something has been done to make amends that they have both agreed on: this may include apologies, reparation, and work for the victim or in the community or anything else that is important to the victim. For many victims, simply knowing that this young person recognizes what he or she has done and the harm caused, is truly sorry, and is not likely to repeat that behavior is sufficient. Outcomes that have positive results for both the young person and for others are frequently valued more highly than curfews, detention, and actions designed to cause pain.

Addressing the causes of offending. The conference often needs not only to repair the harm that the young person has caused to the victims, families, and others who have trusted them but also to repair some of the damage that he or she has suffered. Some of the most common issues are a history of abuse and neglect, a dependence on alcohol or other drugs, mental health problems, having effectively dropped out of the education system, and lacking both the life skills and the vocational skills and qualifications that are needed to find a place in the adult world. To succeed, young people need support in rebuilding their own lives. Effective programs are often the key to rebuilding lives, and they are the first step towards reintegration into community and society.

Reintegration. Building a new life requires not only support and help with needs and the opportunity to gain skills and qualifications, but also requires the ongoing support and help of people who care about the young person. For most young people, the commitment and support of family is an ongoing part of their development; this is enriched by the support and friendship of peers and mentors as they move into the adult world. Where families cannot or do not provide that support, new close relationships need to be developed with others who can play a constructive and continuing role in the life of the young person. The successful conference will locate those people who will continue to play a part in the young person's life for a long time after this particular episode has been closed (a community of care). The effective support of these people is crucial to any plan for reintegration and the building of a new life.

Conclusion

Assessing effectiveness of justice outcomes is a complex matter. There are many different perspectives on how to measure effectiveness. Reducing re-offending is a common criterion. In New Zealand, research has been carried out that compares young people with similar backgrounds, life skills, and experiences who have committed similar offenses. The overall conclusion is that the way they are treated in the justice system can make a difference to whether or not they will re-offend.[3]

The first and most important factor is to divert young people from the formal criminal justice system wherever possible and for as long as possible. If young people are kept out of courts and prisons, then re-offending is less likely. In the last 30 years, the percentage of young people who offend and appear in court has dropped to a third of the earlier level. Most of the decrease in the use of the Youth Court for young offenders has occurred since the introduction of the 1989 act that allowed for diversionary responses and introduced FGCs.

The New Zealand system is radical in its design, is restorative in its processes, and is successful in responding effectively to young people. It has served as a model for many other countries that have chosen to develop inclusive diversionary processes for resolving youth offending. It makes young people accountable, includes victims and the families in the processes, and enables young people to put the past behind them and receive support in building a new life.

Box 5

Circles of Change: Bringing a More Compassionate Justice System to Troubled Youth in Oakland

Micky Duxbury

Almost 50 years ago, a notorious church bombing in Birmingham, Alabama, killed two of Fania Davis's closest friends—and launched Davis, then a teenager, into a lifetime of social justice work. Today, the well-known Oakland, California, resident directs Restorative Justice for Oakland Youth (RJOY), an innovative organization that aims to turn teenagers accused of crimes or troublemaking into responsible citizens.

(Continued)

---

[3]The New Zealand system does not collect data on re-offending, but research shows that youths who are diverted are less likely to re-offend even when controlling for the seriousness of the offense (Maxwell & Paulin, 2004).

(Continued)

"The murder of my friends was sort of an initiation," Davis recalls from the program's light-filled office in Oakland's Preservation Park. When her sister, Angela Davis, was accused of murder and conspiracy in 1970, Davis worked for her sister's defense, following a stint as a supporter of the Black Panthers and other militant groups. After her sister was acquitted, Davis went to law school and embarked on a career as an impassioned, hard-driving—and, by her own admission, enraged—civil rights attorney. Over the years, Davis has lost none of her passion, but today it's tempered by a softer, more compassionate sensibility—one that's 100% in keeping with the Restorative Justice program's nonpunitive approach to school discipline and juvenile justice.

"Rather than suspending a kid who gets in a fight or steals, a [Restorative Justice] facilitator organizes a 'circle' that might include allies of the youth, the parents, the youth that was harmed, and the youth causing the harm," Davis says, explaining the program's it-takes-a-village method of addressing rule-breaking. Following a system adapted partly from Native American traditions, the assembled members of the circle try to answer deep questions that can lead to healing: "What happened and how did it make you feel? What does the victim need to repair the harm? What does the person causing the harm need to do to make amends? And what do the youth, family, and community need to do to prevent its recurrence?"

The approach has been so successful that the program recently received a three-year, $850,000 grant from The California Endowment, a private health foundation. The money will be used not only to extend programs into Oakland's Castlemont Community of Small Schools (a group of three public high schools), but will also give young people in trouble with the law an alternative to incarceration.

Davis, a tall, lean woman with an engaging smile, says that learning about restorative justice—an ancient approach for victims and criminals that has enjoyed a worldwide revival in the last 30 years—resulted in a life-changing epiphany, one that "integrated the warrior and the healer in me." In 2005, with the support of Oakland City Councilwoman Nancy Nadel, she convened key members of Alameda County's juvenile justice system—judges, the district attorney, the director of health and human services, and representatives of organizations that serve youth—and founded Restorative Justice for Oakland Youth. In 2006, the program at Cole Middle School in Oakland was launched. Within two years, violent fights at the school stopped, and suspension rates dropped by more than 80%, Davis says.

Eric Butler, the site coordinator for the program at Oakland's McClymonds High School, says he relies on the circle approach daily, for everything from theft to fighting. For example, he says, "Jason," a 16-year-old boy, recently stole a classmate's cell phone. The program staff explained that he could opt for a restorative justice circle instead of punishment. Jason initially worried that the circle would be too embarrassing. But after staff explained more about the approach, he chose to accept responsibility—not simply consequences—for his actions. Personally returning the stolen phone, which contained photos of the classmate's grandmother, and seeing the classmate's reaction, he realized the pain he had caused.

"He said it felt good to make it right," says Butler, adding that when young people are given a chance to repair harm instead of being punished, they begin to understand that what they do matters.

The approach is especially effective for students who have suffered years of trauma, says Hattie Tate, principal of Dewey Academy, an alternative continuation high school in the Oakland Unified School District (OUSD). "Some of our OUSD students have been either the shooter, a victim, or witnessed a shooting," she says. The restorative justice circle helps "create an environment of safety and acceptance"—a rare phenomenon for some of the academy's students, and one that requires some explanation.

"When students enter our school from the juvenile justice system," Tate says, "we start off with circles to help them understand the difference between the schoolyard, the prison yard, and the graveyard, and we talk about how to stop making choices that lead to incarceration or death."

For one traumatized 17-year-old student—known in the community, Tate says, as one of the toughest girls in Oakland—the restorative justice circle has been a tool for transformation. "She knew about every shooting incident in her neighborhood and said that she felt that death was following her," says Tate. "Whenever she was triggered, she would get hostile and start yelling at teachers." Rather than punishing the girl, the school has taken a more compassionate—and, seemingly, effective—course. "We started to allow her to leave the classroom whenever she became upset," Tate says. "After that, we have a circle that asks, 'What happened? What did you want? What can you do differently?' Sometimes we call in the [person] she is angry with, so we can work it out together."

These small, compassionate steps are crucial in breaking the "school-to-prison pipeline," Tate says. "Once our youth of color get into the criminal justice system, it is hard to get them out."

Davis was 16 years old in September 1963 when she received a call from her mother, Sallye Davis—a participant in the early Civil Rights movement—about the Birmingham church bombing. Members of the Ku Klux Klan had dynamited the building, known as a center for protesters working to end segregation. Four girls between the ages of 11 and 14 died, and 22 people were seriously injured. "The news was devastating," Davis says. "My mother described walking through the rubble of the church to be with our close family friend when she went to identify her daughter's body."

Ironically, Davis had just returned from the historic March on Washington. "I was giddy with the hope of the Civil Rights movement, but the bombing was a turning point," she recalls. "I was very angry for a long time, and that is why I was attracted to the Black Panthers and the Black Nationalist movement. Then I became involved with the women's movement, the anti-apartheid movement, the socialist movement—you name it, and that was my path."

Davis has practiced civil rights law since the late 1970s, specializing in employment discrimination litigation. But in the mid-'90s, for her own peace of mind, she says, she began to feel "that I had to change. I had too much fire and too much anger." Following in the footsteps of her mother, a spiritual woman who "embodied nonviolence," Davis started meditating, becoming "interested in more than just yoga postures, but in the whole Eastern philosophy." She adds with a grin, "I had to hide this from my friends in the movement as I thought the Marxist police would come and get me!"

At this point, she says, "I could no longer pursue a vision of social transformation that didn't include spiritual transformation." Entering a PhD program in indigenous knowledge, Davis shut down her law office in 1988; learned about restorative justice

(Continued)

(Continued)

at a conference in 2003; and "started going to conferences all over the world and talking with the leaders of restorative justice movements from South Africa to New Zealand."

To bring restorative justice to Oakland, Davis enlisted the support of Gail Bereola, then the presiding judge of the Alameda County juvenile court. Like Davis, Bereola was impressed with the effectiveness of programs around the country, and in 2008, she launched an Alameda County Restorative Justice Task Force.

While there have been many success stories since then, Bereola acknowledges that restorative justice is not a panacea. "Some offenders are so hardened that they are not willing to take responsibility for their actions, and this program is not for them," she cautions. "But in our current system, we put almost all our resources into punishing offenders, while victims play a minimal role. Restorative justice allows the victim to come face to face with the perpetrator and tell him, 'This is how you harmed me; this was the impact you had on my children, on my spouse, on my coworkers.'"

Typically, a juvenile offender might be required not only to meet face to face with his victim—say, a woman whose house he has vandalized—but to cut her lawn or bring home her groceries as a way of compensating for the damage he caused. In certain cases, those who successfully complete the Alameda County program have the charges against them dropped and wiped from their records.

Results of current studies about similar programs' effectiveness are promising: A recent study in Sonoma County found that only 10 percent of program participants returned to committing crimes, and 90 percent of the victims were satisfied with the process. In 1989, New Zealand's juvenile justice system—restorative justice comes partly from Maori traditions—adopted a nationwide, family-focused, restorative justice approach. Today, juvenile incarceration in New Zealand for crimes other than homicide is almost obsolete, according to a New Zealand government study.

And, for some, a brush with restorative justice inspires a new, more law-abiding way of life. "Many of these youth might have a parent who is strung out on drugs or incarcerated," says Bereola. "When they feel that no one cares about them, they do not care about others." That's no excuse, she says—acknowledging a lawbreaker's challenging home life "does not mean that we condone the acts they perpetrate—but restorative practices allow us to get to the root causes of crime by bringing in people who care about the victim and the perpetrator."

Over almost half a century, Davis's response to violence has evolved from one that fights fire with fire to one that meets fire with reconciliation and restoration. "Our greatest security is not in more arrests and suspensions, but in creating healthier families, schools, and communities," she says. "Harmed people harm people. Healed people heal people. If we are to interrupt the cycle of violence in Oakland and throughout Alameda County, we need a justice that heals."

Micky Duxbury, a Berkeley, California, freelancer, is the author of *Making Room in Our Hearts: Keeping Family Ties Through Open Adoption* (Routledge 2007). She is currently writing about restorative justice and the effects of mass incarceration in the East Bay. This article first appeared in the *East Bay Monthly* March, 2011 issue. Available online at http://www.themonthly.com/upfront1103.html. Reprinted with permission of the *East Bay Monthly.*

Source: From "Circles of Change: Bringing a More Compassionate Justice System to Troubled Youth in Oakland," Micky Duxbury. East Bay Monthly, March 2011, Vol. 41, No. 6. This article first appeared in the East Bay Monthly.

Critical Thinking Questions

1. Review the therapeutic qualities that go into making FGC a success in New Zealand.

2. What does the Oakland, California, experience show about the potential for using this model in the United States as shown in Box 5? What do the results show?

References

Children, Young Persons, and Their Families Act. (1989). Retrieved from www.legislation.govt.nz/pdf Link.aspx?id=DLM147087

Maxwell, G. M., Kingi, V., Robertson, J. R., Morris, A., & Cunningham, C. (2004). *Achieving effective outcomes in youth justice: Full report.* Wellington, New Zealand: Ministry of Social Development. Retrieved from http://www.msd.govt.nz/documents/about-msd-and-our-work/publications -resources/research/youth-justice/achieving-effective-outcomes-youth-justice-full-report.pdf

Maxwell, G. M., & Morris, A. (1993). Families, victims and culture: Youth justice in New Zealand. Wellington, New Zealand: Social Policy Agency and Institute of Criminology, Victoria University of Wellington. Retrieved from http://www.msd.govt.nz/about-msd-and-our-work/publications-resources/ publications-index-1988-1999.html#1

Maxwell, G. M., & Morris, A. (1999). *Understanding reoffending.* Wellington, New Zealand: Institute of Criminology, Victoria University of Wellington.

Maxwell, G. M., & Paulin, J. (2004). *The impact of police responses to young offenders with a particular focus on diversion. Report to NZ Police.* Wellington, New Zealand: Crime and Justice Research Centre, Victoria University of Wellington.

Ministerial Advisory Committee on a Maori Perspective for the Department of Social Welfare. (1986). *Puao-te-atu-tu (Daybreak): The report of the Ministerial Advisory Committee on a Maori perspective for the Department of Social Welfare.* Retrieved from http://www.msd.govt.nz/documents/about -msd-and-our-work/publications-resources/archive/1988-puaoteatatu.pdf

Morris, A., Maxwell, G. M., & Shepherd, P. (1997). *Being a youth advocate: An analysis of their roles and responsibilities.* Wellington, New Zealand: Institute of Criminology, Victoria University of Wellington.

13

Community Members: Vital Voices to the Restorative Justice Process

Mona Schatz

The Longmont Community Justice Partnership (LCJP), a Colorado restorative justice program connected to the Catholic Church, has been conducting community restorative justice group conferencing for over a decade, resolving cases referred by the police. Mona Schatz is director of the Division of Social Work at the University of Wyoming.

Can the restorative justice process impact the community more positively than more traditional corrections approaches? Is restorative justice able to heal the damage arising from harm, both harm to victims and harms that is perpetrated upon the community as a whole? Do communities regain their much-needed community safety when criminal or civil concerns are brought to resolution through restorative justice? This chapter introduces some of the ideas and perceptions of community members who participate in a restorative justice conferencing process in a Colorado community. Some of the information presented emerged from a case study done by the author and graduate social work student (Jaeckel, 2005)

Community as Central to Restorative Justice

Communities exist when groups of people form a social unit based on common location, related interests, shared identification, prescribed civic culture, and common activities (Erlich, Rothman, & Tropman, 2001). Building partnerships within any localized community serves as "glue" for that community (Evans, 1997; Erlich, Rothman, & Tropman, 2001). Social deviant behavior threatens community safety, and communities need to identify strategies to respond to acts of deviance. Restorative justice programs may serve as a specialized partnership process that contributes to and sustains community structures.

When community members join a community restorative justice conference, they are identifying themselves as members of the same community that the offender has harmed. Such involvement by representatives of the community is a central premise of restorative justice. It is the absence of this central tenet that some believe has contributed to the poor outcomes of today's highly structured, formal justice system.

Restorative justice brings victims and offenders into a process that has the potential to resolve issues not only among themselves but also on behalf of the community. For example, in a shoplifting offense, the business owner is invited to a conference meeting with the perpetrator of the offense, the arresting officer(s), the county attorney, and friends or family members who may provide support for the victims and/or the offenders. In the conferencing meeting, the trained facilitator initiates a process of fact finding and reflections about the illegal experience that occurred. How the criminal action affected all parties is examined. Listening to the stories of all parties helps identify both direct and indirect impacts of this wrongful action.

Through the restorative justice process, the harms are identified, repairs to those harms are explored, and a contract that provides clear remediation to the victim and community is agreed upon and written into a formal agreement. Including the community voice by requiring community members to be participants in the process promotes and strengthens communities. The community component of a community justice restorative group conference offers a unique perspective, a perspective that offers the offender a deeper sense of the commonalities that exist in communities. An equally unique goal of restorative justice and group conference process is to let the offender know that the community members are there to provide support for the offender and to show that the community cares about the actions of all the members of their community.

To better examine the restorative justice community group conferencing process for community members we will focus on a single case and an evaluation of community members who participated in the process.

APPLICATION OF RESTORATIVE JUSTICE: THE LONGMONT COMMUNITY JUSTICE PARTNERSHIP

The Longmont Community Justice Partnership (LCJP), a Colorado restorative justice program, has been conducting community restorative justice group conferencing since 1996. Longmont is nestled among six or seven other urban communities that make up a sprawl tied to Denver, a large metropolitan city. Once an agricultural community, the community has almost doubled in population in the past 20 years and is a suburb of the Denver metropolis. Over 75,000 people make up this community, with some varied ethnic groups, e.g. Hispanic, African American, and Anglo.

The community is both protestant and Catholic. County government is well-organized and includes city police and fire services. One hospital provides secondary medical services. There is a significant population in this community with historical ties to the area. Crime, both felony and misdemeanor offenses, has risen dramatically.

The LCJP facilitates a restorative justice process to address the complex problems of crime in this fast-growing suburban community. The founding principles of the LCJP (Siedler & Title, 1996) include viewing the nature of crime as a harm committed against human relationships and community safety and secondarily against the law or the state. They seek to hold offenders accountable for their actions. An independent evaluation of LCJP (Bernstein, 1998) noted that of the 250 offenders who have come through LCJP in the program's first two years, there was a 90% completion rate for agreements. Bernstein also found that among those who completed their agreements, 92% had no further contact with police in the following year. This demonstrates an extremely high victim success/satisfaction rate.

The Specific Situation

One of the areas that the LCJP addresses is the legal infractions of young people who attend schools in the local school district, a subgovernmental unit of the community. The case situation described in the remainder of this chapter arose because of the wrongful acts of two junior high school teens. The case involved a junior high school setting, youths aged 13 to 16. The specific situation involved two 16-year-old female youth offenders. They were charged with a felony offense because they set off the school's fire alarm and sprinkler system. The sprinklers flooded the rooms and hallways, causing significant material, physical, and emotional damage to the school. During the alarm, faculty and students were pushed into chaos; most had never experienced sprinklers pouring water all over everything. Cleanup of the school took several days and a large effort from staff and volunteers to remove the water from the building to restore the school to working order.

When the police responded to the alarm and arrived at the junior high school, the two female offenders were pointed out to the police rather quickly. The two young women were apprehended immediately and taken to police headquarters. The girls confessed to setting off the alarms and were charged as juveniles. The police and the school superintendent agreed to remediate this criminal offense through the restorative justice process, referring this case to LCJP.

The Restorative Justice Group Conference

Three school officials attended the restorative justice group conference. These three were: the school administrator, the nurse (who had suffered an asthma attack during clean up), and the special education director. These three represented the "victims" of this illegal act. The two teenage young women attended this conference process with their parents. Three community members were selected from the pool of trained community members. The restorative justice conference facilitators were both trained and experienced volunteers. Both facilitators (one male and one female) have been involved in facilitating LCJP community restorative justice conferences for over three years.

Community Members Reflect on Their Restorative Justice Involvement

Three community members were involved in the community justice restorative conference. After the conference, they were invited to share their experiences and perspectives with LCJP staff as a way to gain more depth of understanding about their unique role in the conferencing process. Some of their perspectives and views are contained in the following summary. The following statements were all provided in follow-up interviews conducted by Mona Schatz; the names have been changed to protect the respondents' anonymity.

Each of the three community members interviewed provided a unique perspective. All three were middle-aged and professionals. Ron is a local attorney who has been involved with LCJP for about six months. Prior to this conference process, he has attended three community restorative justice group conferences serving as a community member. Maggie has lived and worked in the community for several years. Maggie's previous experience with restorative justice was as a parent when her son was an offender at an earlier period of time. Leila, the third community member, is in her mid-50s. She is a small business owner in the community. At the outset of this interview, Leila said, "I didn't actually know the techniques that would be involved or the exact process, but I knew it was a way to minimize the black and white judgmental thinking about criminal behavior and instead look at more the gray area and allow community members to be involved and explore new ways to dissolve problems."

Ron believed that in this group conference he represented the "average citizen." He said that in this particular conference session, he attempted to convey this perspective and respond to the group discussion from this position. He commented that the process provided each participant with the opportunity to speak without interruption or disturbance from other people. Ron was emphatic when he stated, "That is an important aspect, allowing people who may not have been intimately involved in the specifics to be able to speak what is in their hearts and on their minds."

When he was asked if the restorative justice conferencing process was adequate, Ron responded, "I thought it was excellent, actually a very moving experience for a participant and community member. . . . You feel changed as a person having gone through that, and I felt that the offenders were dealt with [with] great respect by the facilitators and equally so the parents and all the other people involved. . . . You come away with a sense of a process that respected the dignity of everyone there." The emotion in his voice was evident. He felt deeply about this aspect of restorative justice.

Since previously Ron had been involved in three other community group conferences he had experienced outcomes that were not as positive as in this current group conference situation. Ron was able to express what he perceived as potential limitations in a restorative justice approach. He said, "One instance was where there were two offenders and one did not want to participate and did not accept responsibility for what he had done. In that case, the conference ended without a contract, without an agreement, and there was a sense of disappointment that we all felt, but that was the right outcome. He went on to clarify: "In the end, this group conference was a positive experience, helping the youth to recognize the importance of community involvement along with the prerequisites of attending a restorative justice conference.

These prerequisites include full acceptance of responsibility in both an emotional and verbal sense by all those involved in the conference, particularly the offender[s]."

Regarding the sense of community, Ron remarked,

> There was a sense of community among the members who were seated there, coming from different places: parents, teachers, victims, offenders, community members and facilitators. We were all coming from different perspectives, and we were there spending time together because of the common goal, which was to participate in this community endeavor. That's a way that community cohesiveness is built, and I felt it powerfully.

> The community is not even considered in other forms of reaching justice. There is a sense in the criminal justice system of a procedure: to follow laws, to examine facts … very rarely, that community interest, which may differ in important ways, forms a sense of crime punishment. It does not get a place at the table in other formal systems and in this one it does and that's important. (Interview conducted by Schatz.)

Since Maggie had only been involved in one other conference, in a very different position (as a parent of a son who had violated the law), she offered a unique view of serving in the "community" seat. Maggie also held a dual role in this community justice conference. She was a teacher at the school where this action took place and was present during the event. Now, she was representing the community as well. She began by saying, "At first, I felt like I was there representing a 'punisher role.' But later, I felt like I also had had an opportunity to talk to the girls about my role as a teacher." (Interview conducted by Schatz.)

She reflected that even in the first moments of the community restorative justice process she experienced a change in her stance. She said, "I think it was pretty clear up front that when the facilitator explained the process to all of us that everybody's input would be valued including the offenders and their families. We were going to take everybody's ideas and listen, learn, clarify, and eventually come up with a final contract."

Maggie identified the value of the process for the youth involved. She said, "The kids [who got into trouble] have the opportunity to listen to how they made other people feel, to address the damage that they had done. We were all heard; I think every individual was heard. The families had a chance to talk to their kids about how they felt, that what they [the youths] had done reflected upon them." She went on to say, "Any time a person sits in a conference like that, in regard to what they have done to negatively impact others, it is going to be threatening, but it is less threatening than going to court."

Maggie went on to explain that the offenders had an opportunity to tell the participants what they had done, what they felt when they pulled the alarm, and afterward what happened. "I remember one of them [the young women in the room] telling how scared she was when the police came, and she had to call her home. Each of the girls had an opportunity to open up and share feelings. It was a safe place to do that. Every one of us had an opportunity to talk about how we felt. That's part of the healing process, and that was important to all of us."

When asked about the adequacy of the group conference, Maggie stated, "It is an experience that a lot of young people do not have the opportunity to go through. In my role as a parent, in the conference that I was involved in prior to this one, not one of those kids offended again, it was a very . . . tense, moving, an impacting experience for those kids involved in that." Because Maggie shares the "school community" with the young women in this restorative justice conference, she was able to reflect on how these young women changed over the next several months because of this experience. She described the young women as being more receptive to interacting with other students and adults. One of the girls even changed the way that she dressed and the makeup that she wore. Maggie says, "Her whole persona softened."

Maggie described the restorative justice process as an opportunity to obtain "closure to an event that impacted the school community." Her reflections are in this statement: "There was an opportunity for the girls to repair the harm and make retribution in a lot of different ways, and they have not done anything like this since." Building on that thought, she stated, "I think it can be a life-changing experience."

Maggie was "glad, as a member of the community, that there is a program like this helping kids to not only see the harm but to repair it and to feel like they're being heard; that the kids are not just 'bad kids.' This is one of those programs that tries to make sure that kids walk away with their self-esteem intact, and that's really important. I don't think that the court system is concerned with that." She ended the discussion saying, "I think the [restorative justice conference] is a really important place for us as a community to put our resources rather than just the court system. I really think or wish that all first time offenders would have the opportunity rather than just going through the court system."

Leila understood her role was "to witness the process and reflect back to the girls [offenders] my feelings as if I was representing the community." When asked if the community members were presented as important to the group conference process, she replied, "Yes, yes (pause), that's the strength of how I thought it would work, that everyone would come in being equal in capacity, sharing exactly what their emotions were. I felt like I was an equal player." She related how the facilitation process, even in the early moments of introductions, served to provide information and bring about healing.

In contrast to the other two community members, Leila left the conference feeling frustrated because she saw a piece of the puzzle that others gave little attention to. Leila said, "I thought that the emphasis was put in the wrong place in a lot of ways. I felt like the girls were really the victims of a much larger problem endemic in the school systems. Maybe the perpetrator was the hierarchical system, the school that used the girls' 'boredom in the classroom' as the reason that they ended up getting into trouble. Why were they bored? The school officials also said the girls were kind of pushed by their classmates. So I question who the real offender was in this situation."

Leila viewed her role as a community member as important to the process. She says, "To have someone there as a microcosm of the macrocosm, saying, 'I as a community member feel this way.' Then you represent to the girls, 'think about the whole community, how this has effects beyond your parents, beyond your family, beyond your school, and into the whole community.' So I think it's real important to be there."

When asked how she felt regarding the facilitation that brings in the community's concerns and interests, Leila saw the value of the remediation process. She said, "I was impressed by how the remedy seemed so far reaching but it went right into it at a large level. It was not perfect, but I can see, despite the endemic problems in the school, it was still apparent to the girls what was happening. I think they were taken along into something that was cosmic to the process."

Looking for the Community Through the Narratives of Community Members

The original question that spurred the process of interviewing community members focused on how restorative justice helps in repairing harms to a community, strengthening the culture of the community and bringing justice for the offenses committed. The narratives provided by these community members appear to support the concepts of repairing harms, strengthening the culture of the community, and providing justice for offenses committed. These narratives support the ideas and theories of proponents such as Johnstone (2002) and Kurki (2000).

The varying perspectives of each community member are beneficial to this process. Though the interviews with these members could provide only a glimpse into the perspectives and views of these people, their ideas are valuable. Each participant brings a different perspective to the conference, to their roles, and to the community at large. This is the beauty of a restorative justice conference.

Critical Thinking Questions

1. Do you think your community could handle some instances of minor crime through a community board such as is described in this chapter. Why or why not?

2. Discuss why the process described in this case history was successful as compared with an earlier case that did not go so well.

References

Bernstein, D. (1998). *Longmont restorative justice project report.* Longmont, CO: Longmont Restorative Justice Project.

Erlich, J. Rothman, J., & Tropman, J. (2001). *Strategies of community intervention.* Itasca, IL: Peacock.

Evans, D. (1997). *Using partnerships to build communities.* Cleveland, TN: Penman.

Jaeckel, M. (2005). Finding the "community" in restorative justice: A case study (Master's thesis). Fort Collins, CO: Colorado State University, School of Social Work.

Johnstone, G. (2002). *Restorative justice: Ideas, and values,* Willan: Devon, UK.

Kurki, L. (2000). Restorative and community justice in the United States. In M. Tonry (Ed.), *Crime and justice: A review of research,* (pp. 235–303). Chicago, IL: University of Chicago Press.

Siedler, M., & Title, B. (1996). *Longmont community justice partnership: Building a better community one circle at a time.* Longmont, CO: Teaching Peace.

14

Restorative Justice and Gendered Violence

Anne Hayden and Katherine van Wormer

Because both Anne Hayden and coeditor Katherine van Wormer have written extensively on the application of restorative justice to situations involving serious crimes against women, the two of them coauthored this chapter on the controversial use of a restorative approach to situations of intimate partner violence and sexual assault.

What is the relevance of restorative justice strategies to violence with special meaning to women, to such situations as rape with an emphasis on university date rape and, more controversially, domestic violence? These questions are dealt with in this chapter, which draws on results from innovative programming in the United States and New Zealand.

The authors acknowledge that both genders can be victims and perpetrators of intimate violence. However, in consideration of the fact, as shown in the literature on domestic violence as well as in the official statistics, that women usually are more seriously affected by such violence than are men, this chapter refers to women as the victims and men as offenders.

How does restorative justice compare to standard forms of criminal justice and how does it meet the needs of female victims and offenders? Unlike the Anglo-Saxon-derived system, which harks back to primitive practices related to combat, restorative justice can be considered to be on the feminine end of the masculinity-femininity continuum of sex role behavior. Unlike conventional processes, restorative justice is more about making amends and providing restitution than about punishment. Representing a paradigm shift in judicial philosophy, this new vision focuses attention on the harm to victims and communities and less on the act of lawbreaking (Van Ness, 2004; Zehr, 2002). At the macro level, restorative justice is about peacemaking, at the micro level about relationship. In both instances, people come together from various sides of the law and from various backgrounds and lifestyles. From the point of view of the offender, restorative justice is about change and redemption; from the view of the victim it is about healing. Above all, this form of justice is about empowerment.

A major argument of this chapter is that restorative principles are consistent with those of feminist criminology, both in terms of core values and areas of interest. The core values of restorative justice, as succinctly summarized by Adams (2002) are healing rather than hurting, moral learning, community participation and caring, respectful dialogue, apology, and making amends to the victim. Consistent with feminist values, restorative philosophy is holistic in its concern with the whole person; the emphasis is on nondichotomous communication (as opposed to adversarial litigation); and the process is responsive to the voices of people whose voices are rarely heard.

RJ in Situations of Intimate Partner Violence

Intimate family violence (IPV) can be likened to chronic disease blighting the private lives of many in our communities. Although we know they are there, we don't talk about them. This chapter looks at IPV and sexual violence, and their impact on families. The potential of restorative justice processes offers hope to the many afflicted by these forms of violence. But its use in these areas is not without controversy and is inappropriate in many situations. Power and safety issues come to the forefront of concerns expressed.

No discussion about IPV is complete without the inclusion of power. A major theme of empowerment theory is a concern with the need for personal power or choice. Choice is the hallmark of social work's strengths model, its aim is to help clients find their own way, to carve out their own paths to wholeness. The focus of empowerment theory, similarly, is on the process rather than simply on outcomes (Gutiérrez & Lewis, 1999) and on means rather than ends. Frederick and Lizdas (2010) found in their study of victims of domestic violence that many of the women affected by family violence had little faith in the criminal justice system. The women expressed a desire to retain choice and be treated as mature adults in any decisions that were made about how to stop the abuse.

The dilemma facing abuse victims' advocates is whether the process—giving the victim the power of choice of how to proceed—or whether the outcome—pursuing IPV cases to the full extent of the law regardless of the victim's wishes—is more important. The criminalization of IPV following the creation of the Duluth model of power and control in domestic violence (Minnesota) represented the most progressive thinking of the 1970s through the 1990s. Pro-arrest policies made arrest of abusive partners mandatory, and in some jurisdictions jail terms were also mandatory. Victims who filed charges were not allowed to drop them and sometimes forced to testify against their partners. All this was done for the victim's protection and it seemed to make a lot of sense at the time. However, it took away from victims their decision-making power regarding how they dealt with the violence. They might not have wanted their partner arrested and perhaps had just wanted the violence to stop (Morris & Gelsthorpe, 2000; van Wormer, 2009.)

It is important for us to remember that the coercion of victims/survivors is inconsistent with the feminist movement's and social work's goal of self-determination (Presser & Gaarder, 2004). Research from the 1990s to the present (Morris & Gelsthorpe, 2000; Hayden 2011) has shown that IPV victims who have a say in legal or less formal proceedings may feel more empowered to get help if not to terminate the abusive relationship. Thus, their rights to determine their own needs and the means of attaining them are more likely to be protected than in a criminal justice jurisdiction on its own. Hayden's 2011 research findings, which supported this perspective, will be discussed more fully later.

Complicating these policies has been the increasing use of dual arrests or the arrest of both partners—of the aggressor and the one who fought back (van Wormer, 2010), especially likely if both parties were injured (Hayden, 2011). If a case comes to trial and the victim is forced to testify, what she says against her partner could compromise her safety later. Moreover, child protection services could investigate a mother for failing to protect the children from witnessing the violence.

Few conventional programs address the psychological needs of victims in any meaningful way nor do they address the context of the offending. Women of color often see both the courts and social services as adversaries rather than allies, so an emphasis on judicial intervention may turn them away. The women, moreover, often are dependent on men for financial support or may have undocumented immigration status or drug problems that deter them from pursuing criminal prosecution. These are among the reasons only one quarter of all physical assaults, as indicated in the Violence Against Women Survey, were found to be reported to the police (Tjaden & Thoennes, 2000).

In as much as practices in the realm of IPV have always started at the grassroots level, it is time, as Grauwiler and Mills (2004) argue, to expand our efforts to focus the needs of victims who avoid the criminal justice system. Community-based interventions that do not rely on criminal prosecution may be applied. Alternatively, such practices could become an additional process for justice available under the umbrella of the criminal justice system (Jülich, 2010).

Relevance of RJ

The least controversial form of RJ for use with offenders who have engaged in domestic and sexual violence is the use of victim-survivor panels. This is a prevention approach commonly used in batterer intervention programs. The process is basically this: Victim-survivors, not victims of the particular men in attendance, form a panel in which each participant shares her personal story. Listening to the narratives can be very painful to the listeners; the hope is that on hearing of and feeling the pain of which the speakers talk, feelings of empathy will be evoked. This can be a significant turning point for some men who previously have lacked empathy for the women they have victimized and even blamed for their own violence. In listening to these accounts, more sensitive offenders may not only feel for the victims but might also get in touch with their own past victimization and earlier feelings upon being so assaulted. In short, the process involves two themes: offender accountability and the empowerment of crime victim-survivors. Just as offenders in these encounters see the human face of survivors of violent crime, so the victims may come to see the human face of offenders and be further confirmed that what happened to them was in no way their own fault.

Restorative justice processes as a way of effecting justice for victims of interpersonal violence have been practiced in New Zealand under the criminal justice jurisdiction with favorable results (Braithwaite and Daly, 1998; Kingi, Paulin, & Porima, 2008). Presentence conferences attended by the victim-survivors and offenders and their support people have been conducted by community restorative justice service providers. Power imbalances have been addressed in various ways, such as order of speaking (starting with the victims), equal speaking rights, appropriate support people, and seating arrangements. The inclusion of community members whose roles are to monitor and support the offender's compliance and give victims ongoing support has been especially important in IPV cases.

Similar reports involving successful community conferencing in cases of severe family violence have come from traditional native community ceremonies in Canada, where community involvement changes the balance of power. Griffiths (1999), for example, presented the case of a Canadian aboriginal sentencing circle that took up the case of a man who, when drunk, beat his wife. Seated in a circle, the victim and her family spoke about their distress and a young man told them about contributions the offender had made to the community. The judge suspended sentencing until the offender entered alcoholism treatment and fulfilled the expectations of the victim and of her support group. The ceremony concluded with a prayer and a shared meal. Sometime later, the victimized woman expressed satisfaction with the process. While this case was within the conventional system, others have been handled more discreetly by tribal members. Griffiths emphasized the need for victims to play a key role throughout the process to ensure that their needs were met and that they were not re-victimized. This way, the emphasis was on restoration rather than retribution and could empower all parties.

Prevention of IPV is a very important public health objective. This is even more crucial in ongoing relationships or when shared parenting continues. Restorative justice processes have greater potential to help these couples than conventional criminal justice systems. Rather than pursuing retributive processes concerning the offender primarily, the goals of restorative processes in IPV are multiple. Offenders are encouraged to take responsibility for their actions, develop empathy for their victims, and become reintegrated into their communities. Victims are empowered, heard, supported, and assisted in their recovery. Violence prevention programs coupled with close supervision of men who have engaged in IPV are important elements in curbing further family violence. Attending such programs can be voluntary or court-ordered.

Participation in a restorative justice process by all parties is strictly voluntary, and intensive preparation precedes all such conferencing. Issues of power and control for the victim must be addressed (Umbreit & Armour, 2010). Hearing directly from the offender of his guilt and remorse while receiving support from family members can help the woman heal while reducing any feelings she may have of self-blame. In situations of violent crime, a restorative justice process can help victims by bringing the gravity of the violence that they have experienced out into the open. The message to all concerned is that any form of family violence is unacceptable.

From a feminist standpoint, restorative justice is a process consistent with women's "ways of knowing" and communication through storytelling (van Wormer, 2010). Feminist criminologists generally are welcoming of this new vision as a relatively informal, community-oriented form of justice that is focused on victims and allows offenders to "come clean" about what they have done and why (Failinger, 2006). The lack of legalism and chance to get away from a winner-take-all mentality are appealing qualities to feminists who seek a caring, interactive process. By the same token, feminist criminologists are correct to be skeptical of any process that involves dialoguing in cases of domestic violence.

Conferencing can attend to the psychological as well as physical abuse and counter victims' sense of helplessness by their involvement in the process (Koss, 2000). It can also consider other contextual and emotional factors relating to the offending that would be disregarded by the courts (Hayden, 2011). This restorative process can help both parties to understand what happened and why. Furthermore, measures can be taken to reduce the victim's vulnerability in practical ways such as making a safety plan, the provision of access to a personal bank account, safe accommodation, or transportation.

A process built on a close collaboration between victimized women, the authorities, and facilitators of RJ dialogue may be counter-indicated in working with certain cultural groups, especially those in which women have carefully defined domestic roles. Cultural factors, accordingly, need always to be taken into account. Goel (2005) cautions that restorative justice processes are ill-suited to immigrant South Asian communities for IPV. Her reasoning is that women from South Asian culture might be placated by the familiar values of community, cooperation, and forgiveness into seeking restorative justice solutions and ultimately into staying in an abusive situation. Restorative justice is based on the premise that participants are equal and can speak freely in a consensus-based proceeding. But in the South Asian (Indian) cultural tradition, such an assumption cannot be made. Tradition portrays the husband as the sole source of status and support, and Indian women are apt to feel responsible for pain inflicted by the husband.

The exact opposite argument is made by Grauwiler and Mills (2004). Their recommendation is for what they call Intimate Abuse Circles as a culturally sensitive alternative to the criminal justice system's response to domestic violence. Such Circles are especially helpful, they suggest, to immigrant, minority, and religious families where it is more likely that the family will remain intact. This model acknowledges that many people seek to end the violence but not the relationship. Such restorative processes also help partners who would like to separate in a more amicable fashion than through standard avenues. Hayden (2011) similarly argues that Chinese women might welcome the opportunity to resolve conflict in a community setting in which respect is shown to all parties and which thus avoids loss of face for their partners (Hayden, 2011).

While more conventional interventions such as imprisonment may still be used for offenders who do not change their behavior, Braithwaite and Daly (1998) see community involvement in decision-making as more beneficial for offenders than terms of imprisonment. When the victim and other members of the community are heard and are able to bring social pressures to bear on the offender in a supportive but safe setting,

Kingi et al. (2008) suggest that such restorative processes can lead to positive change. This process can help couples gain some resolution, especially when there are children involved.

Restorative processes are clearly inappropriate in situations involving a high level of violence and danger for the victim. An important research question that has not been adequately explored is this: For whom, for which type of batterers, would a restorative justice approach be effective? More precise knowledge of batterer typologies may ultimately be used to discriminate between offenders who might reasonably be expected to benefit from such an approach and those who are unlikely to benefit or who pose too great a safety threat. While batterer typology systems currently have limited clinical utility (Langhinrichsen-Rohling, Huss, & Ramsey, 2000), mental health practitioners are able through psychological testing to screen out those who show antisocial tendencies, severe depression, or who have a history of violence directed toward others outside the family.

One use for restorative justice, not considered in the literature, would be to have a gathering years later following the abuse that took place, perhaps once the former partners have gone on to lead other lives. This might be healing in situations where some form of resolution is desired, where the former batterer has turned his life around and wishes to make amends to his former victim, while his ex-partner wishes to describe the pain she has lived with in the years since the violence took place, to receive support and understanding from her family members, and finally to accept the apology and even to forgive. Consider that other restorative practices, for example, truth and reconciliation commissions and victim-offender dialogue, take place years after the crimes have taken place, and, in many ways, that is their strength.

RJ in Situations of Rape

Rozee & Koss (2001) have criticized the handling and outcomes of acquaintance rape at every level of the criminal justice system, from the police callout to the courtroom where the credibility of the victim-survivor as chief witness is challenged if not demolished. They found that racial-ethnic differences between state officials and the victim-survivor compounded the lack of consideration and respect. In fact, the clash between the Anglo-Saxon handling of criminal matters and indigenous values can sometimes be palpable. In Canada, Aboriginal justice is about restoring balance to the community (Green, 1998). Again, this is in stark contrast with Euro-American forms of justice, which, as Rozee and Koss suggested, has been experienced as "White imposed" (p. 306). Women of color have had to contend with tension between their needs for justice and their experiences of racism in the criminal justice system. Some Black and Latina women have avoided seeking help from the criminal justice system or women's shelters to protect the image held of a minority group in a racist society (Presser & Gaarder, 2004). Women of color, well aware of the brutal and prejudicial treatment inflicted upon their menfolk by the criminal justice system, have been reluctant to turn to that system for justice.

If criminal justice treatment of victims of crime in general leaves much to be desired, treatment of rape victims is unconscionable. Three main failings of the conventional system were discussed by Braithwaite and Daly (1998). The first of these was the low rate of accountability in the criminal justice system due to lack of reporting, the low prosecution rate, and the low conviction rate. Secondly, rapists sentenced to prison were often guilty of numerous undetected offenses with greater likelihood of re-offending upon release. Thirdly, women have been re-victimized under cross-examination, especially if, at the time of the offense, they were drinking, in an unsafe place at night, or their past histories could be used to support the defendant.

Because of the high level of dissatisfaction with the treatment rendered to rape victims through the criminal justice system, and because rapist and victim do not have an ongoing relationship apart from spousal and partner rape, some feminists are looking into alternative forms of justice, especially in situations of date or acquaintance rape. Restorative justice responses are consistent with the community focus of women's grassroots movements. At the community level, such strategies have been found to create positive social change in communities with chronic sexual abuse problems, for example, Hollow Water (Manitoba) which used circle conferencing (van Wormer, 2010).

Landmark research by Rozee and Koss (2001), which was in a university setting, found that a restorative justice format resulted in a number of advantages for the victim-survivor. These were increased community trust, empowered victims, reduced workload for legal authorities, advocacy of antirape messages, and increased offender accountability with possibly less stigmatization. Thus, restorative justice processes allow victims to experience justice because truth-telling rather than denial of the truth is encouraged in the process (van Wormer, 2009).

Case histories of restorative justice dialogue following rape are very rare. One story that comes from Britain narrated by Jo Nodding and available on DVD is "Jo's Story." Four years after a young man she knew pleaded guilty of raping her and was serving time in prison, Jo, who had been told by a victim liaison officer of the possibility of restorative justice—of having a meeting with Darren, her rapist. After another four years, the idea appealed to her and Darren, who was contacted, agreed to the meeting. Over the next nine months, RJ workers provided counseling to prepare both parties for the encounter. At the RJ meeting, Jo told of the impact of the offense while Darren listened; the impact on both was enormous. Then, in Jo's words,

As the meeting was finishing I was asked if there was anything else I wanted to say, and I gave him what I've later come to think of as "a gift." I said to him, "What I am about to say to you a lot of people would find hard to understand, but I forgive you for what you did to me. Hatred just eats you up, and I want you to go on and have a successful life. If you haven't already forgiven yourself, then I hope in the future you will."

This had a massive impact on Darren—I could see he was shaken by the parting "gift" I had given him. As I was leaving, I wished him good luck for the future. His step-mum, who was there with him, looked at me and just said, "Thank you."

As I left that room I felt on top of the world. Meeting him gave me closure, because I had said everything I had wanted to say and I had taken back some kind of control over my life. I know it had an impact on him. I'm not a victim any more, I'm a survivor. I've been able to make sure something good has come out of something bad. (http://www .restorativejustice.org.uk/resource/the_meeting_jos_story__surviving_rape)

Recent New Zealand Research

Research into non-reporting of IPV was conducted by Hayden (2011) to establish whether the use of restorative justice would increase reporting. The work was motivated by Hayden's awareness that couples experiencing IPV had few options open to them besides remaining in the situation or reporting it to the police and facing uncertain consequences. Although an opportunity had arisen to do a small qualitative study in the New Zealand Court-Referred Restorative Justice Pilot (Ministry of Justice, 2005), family and sexual violence were specifically excluded. Victim advocates and police had continued to withhold information about restorative justice from many victims, and the restorative justice process has, for a long time, been much more accessible to offenders through their defense counsel.

The predominantly qualitative study used a triangulated methodology with a small sample of nonrandomized victims of IPV (n=8), perpetrators (n=6), and key informants (n=15) who worked in the field of IPV. The key informants included victim advocates, judges, men's group leaders, restorative justice practitioners, and cultural advisers. None of the victims or perpetrators had been participants in a restorative justice conference, and few had any knowledge of it. Of the eight victims, four had reported the IPV to the police. Only two of them were satisfied with the police response, and one of these had experienced the IPV and reported it in the UK. Thus, only one of the eight victims was satisfied with the New Zealand criminal justice response.

Despite the fact that only half of them had reported the violence to the police, all victims had reasons for not reporting. These included fear of their partner; fear of retribution; "it wasn't real violence"; children; shame; nonrecognition of IPV; self-blame; verbal abuse and threats; it was "only an isolated incident"; poor police response the first time reported; "it's not important"; imagined it would stop; abuse led to self-doubt; and fear of family disapproval.

Participants were given a scenario of a cofacilitated model where the victim and offender each had support people, were participating voluntarily, and the conference was held in a safe place. Over the total sample of 29 participants, 79% considered that the use of restorative justice would increase the reporting of IPV. No one totally excluded the possibility of using restorative justice for IPV.

Because most objections in the literature to using restorative justice for IPV concerned safety, this theme was explored in depth. The respondents considered that restorative justice would be safer than the conventional criminal justice process in that it was speedier; could improve relationships earlier; could help couples relearn how to relate to each other; support people would be present; children could attend a separate conference after adult issues had been dealt with; and follow-up conferences could monitor undertakings made at the initial conference.

Qualities that the respondents believed would make restorative justice less safe were the potential for violence at a conference; the risk that the facilitator would have his or her own agenda, inadequate skill or knowledge about IPV or lack of cultural sensitivity; manipulation of the process by the offender; insufficient focus on the needs of victims; imbalance of power; unrepentant offender; and retribution by the offender. It was believed that the process could be made safer by both the victim and offender having realistic expectations of the process; appropriate timing; participants under-standing the need to be honest; voluntary attendance; and choice of facilitators spe-cialized and well-versed in IPV.

Conclusion

This chapter has highlighted dissatisfaction about conventional justice systems' response to intimate violence and rape and discussed the potential of restorative jus-tice to offer victims of such violence an alternative. Hayden's New Zealand research demonstrates the importance placed by victim-survivors and perpetrators on their relationships, including those of their families, as well as the complexity of how power is used in IPV by both victims and offenders. It also showed that informal reporting of IPV was a preferred option with potentially more benefits than formal reporting alone.

Restorative justice is a form of justice that we believe to be highly compatible with feminist values. The ethics of caring and sharing are common to both. We agree with Burford and Adams (2004), that the adoption of restorative principles can help bridge the gaps between formal and informal helping, between care and control, and between empowerment and coercion. The victim-survivor of crime has much to gain in receiv-ing an honest admission of guilt from the offender and some form of compensation for the harm that was done.

Critical Thinking Questions

1. Name some of the advantages of restorative justice over conventional forms of jus-tice for handling situations of partner violence. Why do you think its use is more controversial for situations of IPV than for rape?

2. What is the difference between the sentencing circle and other restorative justice processes described in this chapter?

References

Adams, P. (2002, February 24–27). Learning from indigenous practices: A radical tradition. Paper pre-sented at the Council on Social Work Education Conference, Nashville, TN.

Braithwaite, J., & Daly, K. (1998). Masculinity, violence and communitarian control. In S. Miller (Ed.), *Crime control and women* (pp. 151–180). Thousand Oaks, CA: Sage.

Burford, G., & Adams, P. (2004). Restorative justice, responsive regulation and social work. *Journal of Sociology and Social Work, 31*(1). 20–27.

Failinger, M. A. (2006). Lessons unlearned: Women offenders, the ethics of care, and the promise of restorative justice. *Fordham Urban Law Journal, 33*(2), 487–527.

Frederick, L., & Lizdas, K. (2010). The role of restorative justice in the battered women's movement. In J. Ptacek (Ed.), *Restorative justice and violence against women* (pp. 39–59). New York, NY: Oxford University Press.

Goel, R. (2005, May). Sita's trousseau: Restorative justice, domestic violence, and South Asian culture. *Violence Against Women, (11)*5, 639–665.

Grauwiler, P., & Mills, L. (2004). Moving beyond the criminal justice paradigm: A radical restorative justice approach to intimate abuse. *Journal of Sociology and Social Welfare, 31*(1), 49–62.

Green, R.G. (1998). *Justice in aboriginal communities: Sentencing alternatives.* Saskatoon, Saskatchewan, Canada: Purich Publishing.

Griffiths, C. T. (1999). The victims of crime and restorative justice: The Canadian experience. *International Review of Victimology, 6,* 279–294.

Gutiérrez, L., & Suarez, Z. (1999). Empowerment with Latinas. In L. A. Gutierrez and E. A. Lewis (Eds.), *Empowerment of women of color* (pp. 167–186). New York, NY: Columbia University Press.

Hayden, A. (2011). Why rock the boat? Non-reporting of intimate partner violence (PhD dissertation). Auckland, NZ: Auckland University of Technology.

Jülich, S. (2010, December). Beyond conflict resolution: Towards a restorative process for sexual violence. *Te Awatea Review: The Journal of Te Awatea Violence Research Centre,* Christchurch: University of Canterbury, 8(1 & 2), 21–25.

Kingi, V., Paulin, J., & Porima, L. (2008). *Review of the delivery of restorative justice in family violence cases by providers funded by the Ministry of Justice: Final report.* Wellington, NZ: Victoria University of Wellington.

Koss, M. (2000). Blame, shame, and community: Justice responses to violence against women. *American Psychologist 55*(11), 1332–1343.

Langhinrichsen-Rohling, J., Huss, M. T., & Ramsey, S. (2000). The clinical utility of batterer typologies. *Journal of Family Violence, 15*(1), 37–53.

Ministry of Justice. (2005). *New Zealand court-referred restorative justice pilot: Evaluation.* Wellington, NZ: Crime and Justice Research Centre, Victoria University of Wellington.

Morris, A., & Gelsthorpe, L. (2000). Re-visioning men's violence against female partners. *The Howard Journal, 39*(4), 412–428.

Norton, Jo (2011). Jo's story. Restorative justice council. Retrieved from http://www.restorativejustice.org .uk/resource/the_meeting_jos_story__surviving_rape_

Presser, L., & Gaarder, E. (2004). *Can restorative justice reduce battering?* In B. Price and N. Sokoloff (Eds.), The criminal justice system and women: Offenders, prisoners, victims, and workers (3rd ed.) (pp. 403–418). New York, NY: McGraw Hill.

Rozee, P., & Koss, M. (2001). Rape: A century of resistance. *Psychology of Women Quarterly, 25,* 295–311.

Tjaden, P., & Thoennes, N. (2000). *Full report of the prevalence, incidence, and consequences of violence against women: Findings from the National Violence Against Women Survey.* Research report. Washington, DC: National Institute of Justice and the Centers for Disease Control and Prevention.

Umbreit, M. & Armour, M.P. (2010). *Restorative justice dialogue: An essential guide for research and practice.* New York: Springer Publishing Company.

Umbreit, M., Vos, B., Coates, R., & Brown, K. (2003). *Facing violence: The path of restorative justice and dialogue.* Monsey, NY: Criminal Justice Press.

Van Ness, D. (2004). Justice that restores: From impersonal to personal justice. In E.H. Judah & M. Bryant (Eds.), *Criminal justice: Retribution vs. restoration* (pp. 93–109). Binghamton, NY: Haworth.

van Wormer, K. (2009). Restorative justice as social justice for victims: A standpoint feminist perspective. *Social Work, 54*(2), 107–117.

van Wormer, K. (2010). *Working with female offenders: A gender-based approach.* Hoboken, NJ: Wiley.

Zehr, H. (2002). *The little book of restorative justice.* Intercourse, PA: Good Books.

15

Clergy Child Sexual Abuse: The Restorative Justice Option

Theo Gavrielides

Dr. Gavrielides is the founder and director of Independent Academic Research Studies (IARS). He is also a visiting professor at Buckinghamshire New University, a visiting professorial research fellow at Panteion University of Social & Political Science (Greece), a visiting senior research fellow at the International Centre for Comparative Criminological Research (ICCCR) at Open University (UK) and a visiting scholar at the Centre for Criminology and Justice Research Department of Justice Mount Royal University (Canada). Recently, Theo Gavrielides was appointed to be the project leader of the 3E Model for a Restorative Justice Strategy in Europe. The focus of this project is the development of restorative justice as a response to crime in 11 European countries. This project is under the auspices of the European Union.

Recognized for his pioneer research on restorative justice, Gavrielides in this chapter directs his attention to cases of clergy child sexual abuse in a contribution with significant implications for the resolution of such tragic and destructive situations—for the individuals, the religious institution, and the community.

Child sexual abuse is real. By definition it involves the person entrusted with protecting the child violating their position of power. School teachers, parents and family members, doctors, scout leaders, and coaches have all been included in the perpetrators' list. This chapter is exclusively focused on clergy child sexual abuse, particularly in the context of the Catholic Church. This is not to suggest that abuse by members of other religions or denominations is not also a reality.

The sex abuse crisis within the Roman Catholic Church has surfaced first and has been attracting researchers, policymakers, politicians, and public attention since 1985. This refers to the Louisiana case of Gilbert Gauthe, a parish priest had molested young boys and was transferred from parish to parish since the 1960s. As Gavrielides and Coker argue (2005), the Catholic Church seems to have moved through two identifiable phases and may be entering a third. The first stage included a series of hidden crimes and its cover-up by the hierarchy. The second began with the entrée of traditional justice investigations in specific cases. Other alternatives are now being sought. More importantly, "having been forced to accept responsibility publicly, the Catholic Church may be entering a phase of open dialogue and constructive shaming" (p. 347).

The possibility of entering into a dialogue and sharing power with victim-survivors opens the door for alternative solutions other than those available within the dominant punitive paradigm of criminal justice. One of these forms of dialogue may be restorative justice (hereafter RJ). It is not the intention of the paper to speak for or against RJ. Gavrielides argues that the focus of RJ researchers should not be on the superiority of the RJ paradigm, but on the development of its processes and principles (Gavrielides, 2008). Gavrielides also warns that "RJ might not be a 'bed-time story' any more, but it is not a panacea for all the deficiencies of the current criminal justice system either" (2007, p. 9).

The scale of clergy sexual abuse within the Catholic Church is frightening. In the United States alone, according to the 2004 U.S. National Catholic Conference of Bishops report (John Jay College of Criminal Justice, 2004) for the period 1950–2002, there were 4,392 priests who were the subjects of allegations of sexual abuse that were not known to be false (4% of all clergy in the 50-year period). These allegations involved 10,667 victims; 226 of these cases were criminally charged and 138 resulted in convictions. Lawsuits were far more common, reaching $573 million for compensation. This figure does not include 14% of the dioceses involved as they refused to give financial data. It does not include settlements made after 2002 either. For instance, the Diocese of Orange, California, was asked to pay $100 million for the settlement of 90 abuse claims in 2004, while the Diocese of Los Angeles, California, was asked to pay $660 million for the settlement of 550 claims in 2007.

Clergy sexual abuse within the Catholic Church is by no means exclusively a U.S. phenomenon. The 2009 Ryan and Murphy reports revealed "a chronic problem" in Ireland involving priests, Brothers, and social workers in schools and churches (Hogan, 2011). Abuse cases also came to light in Belgium, France, Germany, and the Netherlands.

The truth is that we will never know the full extent of the abuse to which children have been subjected by clergy. Many victim-survivors have taken their secret with them while it is assumed that thousands still remain silent (Frawley, 2004). The limited scope of this chapter does not allow us to look into the reasons that kept these survivors silent. We cannot investigate the factors that could help survivors to come forth, either. Our research is concerned only with cases and victim-survivors who have come forth (or who wish to come forth) and the accused dioceses that are willing to enter into a voluntary and constructive dialogue of healing, restoration, and forgiveness.

From the outset, we have to accept that genuine dialogue requires voluntary and honest participation. This also includes RJ, which is defined as "an *ethos* with practical goals, among which is to restore harm by including affected parties in a (direct or indirect) encounter and a process of understanding through voluntary and honest dialogue" (Gavrielides, 2007, p. 139). According to Gavrielides, "RJ adopts a fresh approach to conflicts and their control, retaining at the same time certain rehabilitative goals" (p. 139).

We define sexual abuse as "any conduct between a child and an adult when the child is used as an object of sexual gratification for the adult. A child is abused whether or not this activity involved explicit force, whether or not it involves genital or physical contact, whether or not the child initiates it, and whether or not there is discernible harmful outcome" (John Jay College of Criminal Justice, 2004, p. 22).

This paper makes three arguments. First, it looked at extant scientific studies and faith-based papers to assess the extent to which clergy sexual abuse cases constitute a different phenomenon that stretches beyond criminology and the rules governing the breach of law (civil or criminal). The paper concludes that these cases have an additional dimension not identifiable within other child sexual abuse cases. This dimension is of a dual nature. It relates to the violation first of an individual's basic human right to faith and to the sacramental culture of Catholicism.

Secondly, the paper argues that because of the unique nature of these cases, it is only through a user-led process that long-lasting and genuine solutions can be sought for both parties. The argument is based on research studies conducted with victim-survivors and accused dioceses. The paper also provides a summary of what the parties involved in these cases really want. Finally, the paper argues that these user-led processes can be delivered by various forms of dialogue, one of them being RJ.

Beyond Law and Order

There is a large body of scientific research on the impact of sexual abuse on victims (Sgroi, Blick, & Porter, 1982; Finkelhor, 1984; Fleming, Mullen, Sibthorpe,& Bammer; 1990; Ferguson, 1997; Whiffen, Thompson, & Aube, 2000). For the sake of brevity, these are grouped into 11 categories: (1) depression, (2) fear, (3) anxiety, (4) feeling of isolation, (5) poor self-esteem, (6) anger and hostility, (7) self-destructive behavior, (8) substance abuse, (9) sexual maladjustment, (10) propensity towards revictimization, and (11) difficulty in trusting others (Shea, 2008). The two most common psychological effects are post-traumatic stress disorder and depression (Gover, 2004).

The extent to which these effects will manifest themselves depends on the survivor's story, personal circumstances, support systems, and other variables that have occupied scientists' attention for some time (Briere & Elliott, 1993). Kendall (2002) and other neurologists (King et al., 2003) went as far as proving that traumatic experience such as physical and sexual abuse can affect the chemistry and structure of a child's brain.

This paper argues that in addition to these detrimental effects on the victim, clergy child sexual abuse has a further dimension. This is of a dual nature. The first nature involves the violation of an individual's basic human right to faith and identity. This raises two additional questions: first, of public law and human rights and, secondly, of neglect and revictimization; this time not by the accused dioceses, but by the state. Here, we will deal only with the latter.

According to Guido, "The sexual abuse of children and adolescents by Roman Catholic priests entails a violation of meaning as well as persons" (2008, p. 255). He quotes Danny, a victim-survivor of clergy sexual abuse: "Tell them what he took away from me . . . not just my innocence but my faith. I am like a spiritual orphan, betrayed by what I loved, and feel lost and alone" (Guido, 2008, p. 257). Table 15.1 illustrates specific aspects of clergy sexual abuse cases as recorded by Farrell (2009).

McLaughlin's (1994) and Rosetti's (1995) studies with victims of clergy sexual abuse indicated the manifestation of a strong emotional impact and various spiritual effects. Sipe (2001) suggested that effects such as withdrawal, depression and acting out may be observed, but the abuse might not always be evidenced. He also pointed out that this kind of abuse makes the children feel helpless and unable to disclose; the children lose their sense of identity and feel confused and lost.

Furthermore, according to Farrell, Keenan, and Spierings, clergy child sexual abuse is "a distinct form of sexual trauma" that "generates unique post-traumatic symptoms not accounted for within the existing post-traumatic stress disorder conceptual frameworks" (2010, p.124). These include significant anxiety and distress in areas such as theological belief, crisis of faith, and fears surrounding the participant's own mortality.

Moreover, Lothstein (1999) argued that abuse by a Catholic priest is akin to murdering a person's soul. Many are the documented cases of victim-survivors who took their own lives. For instance, Thorpe & Barry (2004) indicated that persons who were sexually abused by a priest experienced thoughts of suicide. They cited the evidence submitted by a widow of a male who had been abused as a child by a Catholic priest. Her

Table 15.1 Specific/additional aspects of survivors trauma experience (Farell, 2009)

Existential	Spiritual
Dissonance in accepting inner freedom and direction within life	Difficulty praying
Fearful of death and/or dying	Discomfort with religion assuming ownership of the spirit
Being robbed of an important philosophy of life	Generalized sense of inner emptiness
Generalized uncertainty surrounding the purpose of life itself	Locked into continual conflict with God
Omnipotence = collusion = powerlessness = insignificance	Inability to engage in any of the sacraments Political anger

Source: From "Sexual Abuse Perpetrated by Roman Catholic Priests and Religious," D. Farrell (2009). Mental Health, Religion & Culture, 12(1), 39–53.

husband kept the abuse secret and did not disclose it until the Boston cases came to light. Just hours after he revealed his secret to his wife, he committed suicide. The accounts of victim-survivors are particularly helpful in grasping this additional dimension (e.g., see Sullivan, 2004). For instance, Smith, writing under a pseudonym, said, "my separation from God almost killed me, emotionally and psychically" (2004, p. 10).

The second nature of this additional dimension relates to what Guido (2008, p. 257) calls "the sacramental culture of Catholicism," which "maintains that the created order of people and things manifests an otherwise invisible divine order." Guido explains that for Catholics "this is more than a matter of symbols," and he is right in saying that unlike other Christian denominations, the priest-perpetrator is "not only a trusted and honored figure but is by virtue of ordination an *alter Christ*, another Christ" (p. 257). Much is thus at stake for the church. As Hussey (1991) explains, the Catholic Church understands that the sacrament of holy orders changes a man fundamentally and permanently and leaves him uniquely able to act in the name and in the person of Christ (see also Osborne, 1988). Therefore, priest-perpetrators' betrayal of that trust and dishonoring of their role cannot be separated from their sacramental character and Christ.

To conclude, clergy sexual abuse has additional implications for victim-survivors and the involved dioceses. For the former it *also* entails a violation of their faith, sense of identity, and place in the world. For the latter it *also* entails a violation of the Church's sacramental culture and, indeed, Christ. These implications sit on top of the undeniable fact that these cases also constitute a breach of law (civil or criminal), and may also bear any of the 11 aforementioned effects that are associated with child sexual abuse cases.

Due to the public exposure of clergy abuse cases but also the severity and extent of their impact, the response was swift and can be grouped into four categories: (1) institutional and policy changes (e.g., the U.S. church's 2002 Charter for the Protection of Children and Young People, the creation of the National Review Board, a new church Office of Child and Youth Protection, and the Committee on Sexual Abuse); (2) research and audits of dioceses (Noll & Harvey 2008); (3) mobilization of civil society (e.g., the Restorative Justice Council on Sexual Misconduct in Faith Communities); (4) legislative reforms (Hamilton, 2005). By nature, none of these responses are user-led.

The cases that did come to light and for which justice was pursued were dealt with either as matters of criminal or civil law (see above). Independently of whether one is an advocate, adversary, or a skeptic of the current justice system, it has to be accepted that the focus of the available (criminal and civil) processes is not the pursuit of what parties (victims and dioceses) want. Any first-year law textbook will indicate that the focus of criminal law is on *the harmful act* and the punishment of *the perpetrator*, while for civil law is on *the harmful act* and *the damage or loss* caused by it.

According to the Trauma Transmission Model (Figley, 1998), the restoration of survivors' faith, sense of identity, and place in the world as well as the amelioration of the psychological, neurological, and other damages they endured, empowerment, and participation must be secured. The same applies for reaching the remaining outcomes listed by victims and accused dioceses. According to Figley's Empowerment Model (1998), there are five phases to facilitating a healing process: (1) building commitment to therapeutic objectives, (2) framing the problem, (3) reframing the problem, (4) developing a healing theory, and (5) closure and preparedness. Figley's model of intervention emphasizes a communication process aimed at developing a healing theory. This process gives opportunities for storytelling, a reinterpretation of symptoms, a clarification of insights and correction of distortions, and answers to questions central to healing.

For truly reaching what parties want, first there must be a willingness to enter into honest, safe, and constructive dialogue. One form of such dialogue is restorative justice (Rea, 2009) as revealed in the following situations involving resolution of priest abuse cases.

Milwaukee Archdiocese Restorative Circle

Geske (2007) reports on the outcomes of a pilot restorative circle that was carried out in Milwaukee Archdiocese between four survivors of clergy sexual abuse, one priest who had admitted abusing a minor, non-accused priests, and the Milwaukee Archbishop. The circle, which was carried out under the auspices of Marquette University Law School, provided a safe space for a dialogue, which according to Geske (2007) helped restore faith and harmony in the church. The circle was filmed and was used by Geske in parishes nationwide to promote the use of RJ with clergy sexual abuse. In the film, victims of clergy abuse share and dialogue with members of the community and clergy as a means of healing past and present wounds. The initiative has become a resource for other restorative justice organizations in the state, has formed partnerships with local community groups that work with criminal justice issues, and has been providing victim/offender dialogues for crimes of severe violence through the Wisconsin Department of Corrections (DOC), Office of Victim Services and Programs.

In 2005, a pilot program was established in New Zealand under which sexual assault cases could be referred for conferencing to a provider with special expertise in this area (see Jülich et al., 2010). Project Restore New Zealand is based on the U.S. Restore program (see Koss, Bachar, & Hopkins, 2003), which facilitates conferencing both for court-referred cases and for self-referred cases.

Project Restore places emphasis on preconference preparation and risk assessment while its practice model is a modified version of the conferencing model used by the New Zealand Court-Referred Pilot Programme for Restorative Justice (Jülich et al., 2010).

According to Professor Shirley Jülich, who led the initiative, the project "aims to provide victim-survivors with an experience of a sense of justice, support offenders to understand the impacts of their behavior, and facilitate the development of an action plan that might include reparation to the victim and therapeutic programs for the offender (Jülich et al., 2010, p. 1).

Anecdotal information reported for the U.S. Restore Program by Koss, et al. (2003), indicated that after two years of operation, participation rates are 71% for victim-survivors and 84% of those offenders where victims agreed to enter the program. Further, they noted that in some instances conferences have been convened without the victim-survivor's attendance, but in all such cases, victim-survivors have given their permission for the conference to go ahead.

THE CASE OF THE MOUNT CASHEL ORPHANAGE, ST. JOSEPH'S TRAINING SCHOOL FOR BOYS, AND ST. JOHN'S TRAINING SCHOOL FOR BOYS

Between 1962 and 1990, 10 members of the Catholic Christian Brothers Order sexually abused 30 or more boys in their care at the Mount Cashel Orphanage in Newfoundland, Canada. Additionally, members of the same order who were running St. Joseph's Training School for Boys in Alfred, Ontario, and St. John's Training School for Boys in Uxbridge, Ontario, also faced criminal charges of child sexual and physical abuse that occurred starting in the 1930s. The remarkable nature of mass abuse, especially of orphans, provoked the direct intervention of Canadian courts and the legislatures of Ontario and Newfoundland.

Only in August of 2002 did two Christian Brothers educational institutions legally connected to the Mount Cashel Orphanage—Vancouver College and St. Thomas Moore Collegiate—reach an out-of-court settlement with victims in order to avert the Vancouver schools' liquidation. Christian Brothers Order members managed to garner $19 million Canadian in bank loans to compensate Mount Cashel victims (Dawes, 2002).

Over 700 former St. Joseph's and St. John's training schools students came forward to allege abuse. Four hundred of them formed a union to pursue their legal options. However, instead of opting for traditional criminal justice procedures, they chose to enter a restorative justice process. According to Robinson, the former students perceived this form of resolution could offer a number of advantages, which they considered crucial in reaching true justice.

In 1992, the students reached an agreement with the Brothers of the Christian Schools of Ottawa, the government of Ontario, the Roman Catholic Archdiocese of Ottawa, and the Roman Catholic Archdiocese of Toronto. *Inter alia,* successful outcomes included "(a) facilitation of apologies by those responsible for physical and sexual abuse; (b) reasonable financial compensation for pain and suffering; (c) financial advances for medical/dental services, vocational rehabilitation, educational upgrading, and literacy training; (d) provision of counseling services; (e) payment to ex-students who had not been paid for farm work and menial work while they were at the schools; and (f) a commitment by the participants to work towards the eradication of child abuse" (Robinson, 2002, para.16).

According to Robinson, restorative justice was thought to be the right procedure because it (a) avoided the adversarial process of conventional litigation with its financial costs; (b) allowed for a broader, more creative range of solutions than are possible in a legal settlement; (c) empowered the victims; (d) was more cost effective" (Robinson, 2002, para. 14). Through conferencing, past relationships had a chance of being preserved—particularly those between the student victims and their church, Robinson claims. Although research on the long- and short-term impact of the restorative process on the specific victims and offenders of this case has not been carried out, the outcome and the process itself were more aligned with what parties wanted.

THE FRASER REGION COMMUNITY JUSTICE INITIATIVES ASSOCIATION (FRCJIA)

This is a community-based, nonprofit organization in British Columbia, Canada, that uses restorative processes with severe forms of violence including sexual offending. This is believed to be the first government-authorized and -funded victim-offender conferencing program designed for use in severe crimes. It has been running for almost two decades. Various evaluations have been carried out measuring its impact over the past 15 years.

Their findings are encouraging as they report a significant positive impact on all participants. "Victims frequently report that this approach has contributed to their trauma recovery in profound ways, including a diminishing of severe symptoms of post-traumatic stress disorder. Offender participants also describe the process as deeply "'healing.'" Therapists and prison program facilitators have reported seeing significant increases in victim empathy and a commitment to relapse prevention in those who have participated" (Gustafson, 2005, p. 225).

SCHOOL OF CRIMINOLOGY AND CRIMINAL JUSTICE, GRIFFITH UNIVERSITY

Based on 387 sexual offending cases (227 court, 119 restorative conferences and 41 formal cautions) during a 6.5-year period (January 1, 1995–July, 1, 2001), the program, which is run for both victims and perpetrators of sexual abuse, reported

- Victims believe that they are better off if their case is handled restoratively.
- If a sexual offending case goes to court, the chances of being proved is half (51%). This has severe consequences on the victim, including deep psychological and emotional stress, depression and personality disorders.
- It appears that the potential problems of a restorative process may be less victimizing than the formal legal process.
- The traditional criminal justice process has proved to do very little for victims as long as offenders can deny they have done anything wrong.
- Restorative processes can open a window for those who have offended to admit to what they have done.

THE RESTORATIVE JUSTICE COUNCIL ON SEXUAL MISCONDUCT IN FAITH COMMUNITIES (RJC)

RJC is a national body of restorative justice practitioners, theologians, ministers, victim-survivors, and lawyers that facilitates restorative services and solutions for those affected by sexual misconduct in faith communities. RJC has argued strongly that RJ offers a viable form of dialogue that they have used to help victim-survivors heal and dioceses to amend and restore. Details of the cases it has dealt with and the teachings they have developed can be found on its website.

Concluding Thoughts

Sexual abuse and its impact vary from case to case. It involves the dignity we all carry by virtue of our human nature. Clergy sexual abuse may cause additional layers of psychological and other consequences for victim-survivors. It also constitutes a violation of Christ and the sacramental culture of Catholicism. Identifying what is appropriate for each case is not easy and advocates of various practices claiming ability to provide solutions need to be vigilant and responsible.

One such alternative has been offered by RJ proponents. This paper made the argument that due to their unique nature and additional implications, clergy child sexual abuse cases are best addressed through user-led solutions; one form of such a process is indeed RJ. The paper looked at the extant limited literature on the matter to identify actual cases and research projects that can shed light to those claims. Although it is safe to argue that when RJ values are respected and the process is offered under its voluntary and complementary nature, outcomes are indeed user-focused and significant for reaching parties' wishes. However, further and more detailed research and testing are warranted.

Critical Thinking Questions

1. How is trauma in situations of clergy sexual abuse unique as compared to other situations of sexual assault? What is the unique nature of the loss?

2. What does restorative justice offer to clergy abuse situations that could help heal the harm that has been done?

References

Briere, J., & Elliott, D. M. (1993). Sexual abuse, family environment, and psychological symptoms: On the validity of statistical control. *Journal of Consulting and Clinical Psychology, 61*, 284–288. Retrieved from PsycARTICLES database.

Dawes, D. (2002). *Catholic schools granted reprieve.* Retrieved from http://www.canadianchristianity .com/cgi-bin/bc.cgi?bc/bccn/0802/catholic

Farrell, D. (2009). Sexual abuse perpetrated by Roman Catholic priests and religious. *Mental Health, Religion & Culture, 12*(1) 39–53.

Farrell, D., Keenan, P. and J. Spierings. (2010). Using EMDR with survivors of sexual abuse perpetrated by Roman Catholic priests. *Journal of EMDR Practice and Research, 3*(3), 124–133.

Ferguson, A. G. (1997). How good is the evidence relating to the frequency of childhood sexual abuse and the impact such abuse has on the lives of adult survivors? *Public Health, 111*, 387–391.

Figley, C. R. (1998). *Burnout in families: The systemic costs of caring.* New York, NY: CRC Press.

Finkelhor, D. (1984). *Child sexual abuse: New theory and research.* New York, NY: The Free Press.

Fleming, J., Mullen, P. E., Sibthorpe, B., & Bammer, G. (1999). The long-term impact of childhood sexual abuse in Australian women. *Child Abuse & Neglect, 23*, 145–159.

Frawley O'Dea, M. G. (2004). The history and consequences of the sexual abuse crisis in the Catholic Church. *Studies in Gender and Sexuality 5*(1), pp. 11–30.

Gavrielides, T. (2007). *Restorative justice theory and practice: Addressing the discrepancy*. Helsinki, Finland: HEUNI.

Gavrielides, T., (2008). Restorative justice: The perplexing concept. Conceptual fault lines and power battles within the restorative justice movement. *Criminology and Criminal Justice Journal, 8*(2), 165–183.

Gavrielides, T., & Coker, D. (2005). Restoring faith: Resolving the Catholic Church's sexual scandals through restorative justice: Working paper I. *Contemporary Justice Review, 8*(4), 345–365.

Geske, J. (2007). Restorative justice and the sexual abuse scandal in the Catholic Church, *Gardozo Journal of Conflict Resolution's 2006 Symposium, 8*, p. 651.

Gover, A. R. (2004). Childhood sexual abuse, gender, and depression among incarcerated youth. *International Journal of Offender Therapy and Comparative Criminology, 48*, 683–696.

Guido, J. J. (2008). A unique betrayal: Clergy sexual abuse in the context of the Catholic religious tradition. *Journal of Child Sexual Abuse, 17*(3–3), 255–268.

Gustafson, D. (2005). Exploring treatment and trauma recovery implications of facilitating victim offender encounters in crimes of severe violence: Lessons from the Canadian experience. In E. Elliott & R. Gordon, (Eds.), *New directions in restorative justice: Issues, practice, evaluation* (pp. 193–228). Devon, UK: Willan Publishing.

Hamilton, M. (2005). *The laws we need to pass to properly punish child abuse*. Retrieved from http://writ.news.findlaw.com/hamilton/20050616.html

Hogan, L. (2011). Clerical and religious child abuse: Ireland and beyond. *Theological Studies, 72*, pp. 170–186.

Hussey, M. (1991). The priesthood after the council: Theological reflections. In K. Smith (Ed.), *Priesthood in the modern world* (pp. 19–28). Franklin, WI: Sheed & Ward.

John Jay College of Criminal Justice. (2004). *The nature and scope of the problem of sexual abuse of minors by Catholic priests and deacons in the US*. Retrieved from http://www.usccb.org./nrb/johnjaystudy

Jülich, S., Buttle, J., Cummins, C., & Freeborn, E. (2010). *Project Restore: An exploratory study of restorative justice and sexual violence*, Auckland, NZ: Auckland University of Technology.

Kendall, J. (2002, September 24). How child abuse and neglect damage the brain. *The Boston Globe*. Retrieved from http://www.ssurvivorsnetwork.org

King, N. J., Heyne, D., Tonge, B., Mullen, P., Myerson, N., Rollings, S. (2003). Sexually abused children suffering from post-traumatic stress disorder: Assessment and treatment strategies. *Cognitive Behavior Therapy, 32*, 2–12. Retrieved from Academic Search Premier database.

Koss, P., Bachar, J., & Hopkins, C. (2003). Restorative justice for sexual violence: Repairing victims, building community, and holding offenders accountable. *Annals New York Academy of Science, 989*, 384–396.

Lothstein, L. (1999). Neuropsychological findings in clergy who sexually abuse. In T. Plante (Ed.), *Bless me father for I have sinned: Perspectives on sexual abuse committed by Roman Catholic priests* (pp. 59–85). Westport, CT: Praeger.

Marshall, T. (1996). The evolution of restorative justice in Britain. *European Journal on Criminal Policy and Research 4*, 21.

McLaughlin, B. (1994). Devastated spirituality: The impact of clergy sexual abuse on the survivor's relationship with God and the Church. *Sexual Addiction & Compulsivity, 1*, 145–158.

Noll, D., & Harvey, L. (2008). Restorative mediation: The application of restorative justice practice and philosophy to clergy sexual abuse cases. *Journal of Child Sexual Abuse, 17*(3 & 4), 377–396.

Osborne, K. (1988). *A history of the ordained ministry in the Roman Catholic Church*. New York, NY: Paulist Press.

Rea, L. (2009). *The legacy of clergy sexual abuse: A cry for restorative justice*. Retrieved from http://www.restorativejustice.org/RJOB/the-legacy-of-clergy-sexual-abuse-a-cry-for-restorative-justice

Robinson, B.A. (2002). *Sexual abuse by Catholic clergy: the Canadian situation*. Retrieved from http://www.religioustolerance.org/clergy_sex3.htm

Rosetti, S. (1995). The impact of child sexual abuse on attitudes toward God and the Catholic Church. *Child Abuse & Neglect, 19*, 1469–1481.

Sgroi, S. M., Blick, L. C., & Porter, F. S. (1982). A conceptual framework for child sexual abuse. In S. Sgroi (Ed.), *Handbook of clinical intervention in child sexual abuse* (pp. 9–38). Lexington, MA: Heath & Company.

Shea, D. J. (2008). Effects of sexual abuse by Catholic priests on adults victimized as children. *Sexual Addiction & Compulsivity*, 15, pp. 250–268.

Sipe, R. (2001). *Sipe Report: Preliminary expert report*. Retrieved from http://www.thelinkup.org/sipe.html

Smith, M. (2004, Spring). A survivor's story. *Human Development, 25*, 5–10.

Sullivan, J. (2004, Spring). Into the fire of hope. *Human Development, 25*, 11–20.

Thorpe, B., & Barry, W. (2004, Spring). Boys' tears in men's eyes: How can we help? *Human Development, 25*, 40–44.

Whiffen, V. E., Thompson, J. M., & Aube, J. A. (2000). Mediators of the link between childhood sexual abuse and adult depressive symptoms. *Journal of Interpersonal Violence, 15*, 1100–1120. Retrieved from Professional Development Collection data.

PART IV

In Correctional and Reentry Programs

W e come now into the heart of the criminal justice system. The starting point in Chapter 16 is a case study of a victim-offender dialogue that took place after the offender served his time in prison for manslaughter. This true story is told to us by Amy Holloway and Gale Burford, who provide much insight into the feeling-side of victim-offender interaction. The remaining four chapters are authored or coauthored by Lorenn Walker and take us into a variety of situations, all of which are offender-focused. Chapter 17, by Walker, Andrew Johnson, and Katherine van Wormer, describes the absolutely unique situation of a prison designed and run along lines consistent with the principles of restorative justice. The prison is in Brazil, operated by volunteers from the Catholic Church rather than by the state.

In Chapter 18, Walker and Ted Sakai describe an interesting experiment in which the teaching of restorative skills is provided to prison inmates to help in their communication and assertiveness. The final two chapters of the section focus on helping people who have served time in the criminal justice system make a successful reentry or return to society. Walker and Rebecca Greening introduce us to a process that is relationship-focused to help about-to-be-released inmates work on issues related to the people in their lives, some of whom they have harmed. Restorative rituals of celebration are an innovation practiced experimentally in Hawai'i and described by Walker in Chapter 20.

Viewed as a whole, the common ground in the variety of the topics covered in this section is that all of them take us beyond theory into the applied area. We can therefore consider this as the "how-to" section of the text. Chapter 16 provides details of how the victim-offender dialogue springs into action; Chapter 18 teaches about skills building from a cognitive perspective. Highlighting the chapter is the inclusion of Box 6, in which Walker recalls her experience as facilitator of a powerful restorative session at Walla Walla Prison. This case example is real, recent, and was featured on the Oprah Winfrey Network. The final chapter in this section describes a restorative ceremony that could be modeled for programming in other correctional facilities or programs.

16

"Hate Left Me That Day": Victim Offender Dialogue in Vermont

Amy Holloway and Gale Burford

Amy Holloway, who has an MSW from the University of Pennsylvania, is director of victim services at the Vermont Department of Corrections and Gale Burford, MSW, PhD is one of the foremost pioneers in the promotion of restorative strategies in the Canadian justice system and today, professor of social work, University of Vermont. In this essay, they provide one of the most moving accounts of a victim-offender dialogue in this book. This is a story of healing, forgiveness of the self and others, and of resilience.

Restorative justice has a long history in Vermont with a variety of practices having been used. The Victim Offender Dialogue (VOD) is a restorative justice program available to victims of severe and violent crimes through the Vermont Department of Correction's Victim Services Program. The process is victim-initiated and victim-centered and designed to give victims the chance to meet and ask questions of the individual who caused them harm. The dialogue is facilitated by a trained facilitator after a significant period of individual preparation when the facilitator engages both the victim and the offender in conversations about the enduring impact of the crime and helps each party identify issues of concern and inquiry. The process is voluntary for offenders, who do not get any special consideration in their sentence or release status for participating.

One of the first Victim Offender Dialogues to take place in Vermont was between two people we refer to as Sarah and Peter. The following was prepared from case file materials with the assistance of Sarah and Peter with the understanding that they did not want their real names used in the publication. We are grateful to them for letting us offer their story to you, the reader, and for their comments and recollections in the final draft.

Sarah's husband, Dan, and her 20-year-old son, Ben, were killed in a car accident. The accident also left two younger boys in the home without a father and their oldest brother.

Thinking about the day her husband and son died, it stuck in Sarah's mind that Dan had phoned to say he was picking Ben up at his work and that they would be home shortly. She did not think further about it until it seemed late and they still were not home.

What happened and the meaning for her would be pieced together over time, first through emergency responders and police, then through a criminal justice process and victim support services, and finally through a Victim-Offender Dialogue.

While her husband and son were driving in the northbound lane of their familiar drive home, Peter was behind the wheel of his car traveling in the opposite direction on the same road, headed toward his own home. Peter had just left a party where he always acknowledged that he consumed excessive amounts of alcohol and marijuana. Peter was driving well in excess of 30 miles above the speed limit for that stretch of the road, and his judgment was diminished. He crossed the center line into the lane of oncoming traffic, and collided head-on with the car driven by Dan, killing both Dan and Ben instantly. The bodies of the father and son were so badly burned that members of the emergency team who responded to the crash site failed to recognize in the moment that victims were a colleague from the rescue squad and his son. Only when they went to the house after midnight to tell of the accident, when Sarah answered the door, did they realize whose bodies they had seen. And only then did Sarah learn that her husband and son were dead. The moment was telling of the nature of the emotional ripple effect that would overtake the family and the community.

Sarah and Dan had lived most of their married life in this community. The family was well known and beloved in the area. Dan was involved in many community activities and Ben was recognized for his abilities as an artist and his work with developmentally challenged and emotionally disturbed children. The aftermath of the deaths was felt throughout the community as a devastating blow, and community support was enormous, but it was Sarah who was most personally affected. Throughout the court proceedings, she looked into the face of the person who had taken away her husband and child and struggled helping her surviving children absorb the loss.

Sarah's initial reaction of "total shock" shifted as time wore on through the court proceedings to what she says was "anger turning to hatred." She was clear from the beginning that the only thing she wanted was "as much jail time they could get" for the driver. She wanted the court to treat the deaths of Ben and Dan as two separate charges to maximize the possible length of imprisonment. She worried that if the defense was able to get a combined charge it would result in less jail time. She wanted to see a sentence of 30 years with no possibility of parole and she wanted a "full trial" in the hope that by bringing out every detail it would cause the judge to show no mercy in sentencing. At that stage, Sarah rejected the idea of seeking restitution or an apology stating to the presentence investigator, "How do you apologize for the loss of a son and a husband?" It was not a question.

Sarah attended every hearing and described herself as "very vocal." Sarah says that she and the driver never addressed each other directly during any part of the court proceedings. She said, "Each time I saw him he didn't look like he cared at all about what he had done to me or my family."

Peter was a recent college graduate and was headed toward graduate school at the time of the crash. He received injuries including a head injury, five broken ribs, a broken ankle and an eye laceration, in the collision. While the bodies of Dan and Ben were being taken from the scene, Peter was being rushed by ambulance to the hospital where after a period of hospitalization he made a full recovery. During his time in the hospital and afterward, Peter said that because of his head injury he "didn't remember what had happened right before the crash." He said that he was "crushed" by what he did and that he was afraid of going to prison. From the start he said that he planned to take full advantage of any programs prison had that would help him stop drinking. During the presentence investigation he told the investigator, "Not a day goes by that I don't think about the two people I killed."

The court proceedings lasted for a year, during which time Peter was allowed to leave the state for visits with his mother. Peter was eventually convicted and sentenced to 5–20 years. He served three and a half years in jail and was released on furlough in 2003. Records confirm while Peter was in jail he took full advantage of every program he could, including treatment for substance abuse, and that his remorse for his actions was demonstrably genuine from the beginning.

Thanks to the connection with the Victim Services program, Sarah actively kept track of Peter's progress while he was incarcerated through his caseworker and she too believed, even during the period of incarceration, that he was "taking his sentence seriously."

Despite justice seeming to have been served through the criminal justice system, Sarah says that she was not healing. Instead, she says she was nurturing "active hate." Eventually, she began to realize that this "active hate was playing too prominent a role in my healing process." She "had become someone I didn't recognize and didn't like very much." The hate was "getting to me," and she was "trying to figure out how to get rid of it." Around this time one of the Victim Service specialists who had been working with Sarah mentioned to her that the DOC was starting a Victim Offender Dialogue Program and said if she was interested in meeting with Peter, it could be arranged. Initially Sarah said she was not ready, but after giving it some thought she decided to "try it as a way to give up my anger and hate and to heal differently." She contacted the Victim Services Program, and the process began.

When Peter was approached about doing the Victim Offender Dialogue with Sarah, he was surprised that she wanted to meet with him. He was apprehensive and afraid. It was not the process itself he feared. He had already participated in a Victim Offender Dialogue with one of Dan's relatives. What concerned him was his memory of Sarah's anger during the court process and his uncertainty about "what she needs from me." Peter stated later of the criminal court process: "I knew she was angry, and I didn't know how to deal with it."

By the time they met, however, Peter says that he had surrendered to his fear. He credits the careful preparation he received over several months. Sarah also acknowledged the importance of the preparation and said the facilitator "asked hard but good questions." Peter had been released and was living in the community by the time Sarah and Peter met for their dialogue.

Reflecting on the meeting itself, Peter confirmed that as expected there were no surprises as to the content of the dialogue, but he was surprised at his experience of feeling ashamed, embarrassed, and sad as he listened to Sarah tell her story of how she was impacted by his crime. Peter demonstrated mindfulness in fully listening to what Sarah had to say and knowing that "this was the one thing I could do to help her" and the only way he might "make a positive difference." He acknowledged that there was little else he could or any offender can do to make things better and he could not "undo" his crime.

In helping the authors prepare this description, Peter acknowledged that he "might have felt more afraid to be out in the community" if I hadn't done the dialogue with Sarah. He said it was Sarah's anger that made him so uneasy and fearful about "what she or other members of her family would do if they saw me out in the community."

Peter acknowledges there were things he wanted from the dialogue. He wanted to be able to tell Sarah about the changes he had made in his life and that he had taken full advantage of the opportunities given to him while he was incarcerated. He wanted her to know that he accepted the consequences of his actions, and the way they have and will always impact her life. He wanted her to know that he has grown up emotionally, mentally, and spiritually.

Sarah felt surprised that Peter initially had been afraid of her because of her anger. During the preparation stage, Sarah said that even though she felt prepared, she really did not know what to expect when she walked into the room on the day of the dialogue. She cannot now remember who spoke first, but she does remember Peter asking her to tell him about who it was that he had killed. She says that opened the space to talk about both Dan and Ben. She remembers making a point of telling him that Ben had been a young man who had not been involved with alcohol at all.

Sarah now believes that what she interpreted during the court process as evidence of Peter lacking remorse for what he did was really his confusion about how to respond to her or how to tell her how terribly he felt about what he had done to her and her family. She is not surprised that during the dialogue "my maternal instincts took over." She gave him a hug, which she thinks helped him relax, and in the end her feelings signified that her hate and anger were gone.

Sarah does not think that she will ever be friends with Peter, but she feels certain that she could not have lived much longer with her hate. She says she is comfortable knowing that Peter is back in the community. She believes that without the dialogue there is a good chance she would have continued feeling she must leave the state out of fear. "Hate left me that day," and Sarah says that was her goal.

As of this writing, both Sarah and Peter are regular speakers for DUI Victim Impact Program sessions. Peter speaks every three months on the first night of the program, which is devoted to the direct impact on the offender, and Sarah speaks the second night, which deals with the impact on others. Sarah says she has never "built up the nerve" to go listen to Peter speak about the impact on him. In her speech, she talks about their Victim Offender Dialogue, although she adds that in her presentations she never uses his real name out of respect for his new life and the efforts he has put into making changes. For his part, Peter speaks about turning the negative into something good and the obligation that offenders have to their victims to do better in the future in honor of those who have been harmed. He says he knows that "not everyone is ready to undergo change" but reasons that "if only a few in the group are inspired, it is worth it."

Critical Thinking Questions

1. Draw a "map" of the emotional ripple that you imagine might widen out from Sarah and Peter into their relationships from the start. How do you imagine that impact changes during the court process and after the dialogue?

2. What, if any, questions would you ask Peter if you could and why? How about Sarah?

17

Brazil's Restorative Prisons

Lorenn Walker, Andrew Johnson,
and Katherine van Wormer

Brazil imprisons thousands, but a small percentage of fortunate people are imprisoned in APAC (Association for the Protection of the Condemned) prisons, where they are treated with respect and trust. This chapter describes the work of volunteers from a Catholic Church community association that helps administer the prisons in collaboration with the recuperandos ("people in the process of recuperating," aka inmates). Select recuperandos have the keys to the cells and prison. No governmental or other correctional officers work at the APAC prisons. Walker, who spent two days, including a night at a men's APAC prison, and Andrew Johnson, a PhD student who spent several weeks at an APAC prison, and Katherine van Wormer describe this remarkable restorative prison that has significantly low recidivism rates. Andrew Johnson is a doctoral candidate in the Sociology Department at the University of Minnesota. As part of his dissertation research, he spent two weeks living inside the cells as a recuperando in two APAC institutions. He is a graduate of Bethel University in St. Paul, Minnesota, and received his master's degree in geography and urban studies from Temple University in Philadelphia, Pennsylvania.

APAC Prison's Restorative Approach to Rehabilitate Incarcerated People

The teachings of restorative justice are consistent with those of the world's great religions (Zehr, 1990). There is the Jewish concept *tikkun*, to heal, repair, and transform the world, and the Christian notion of forgiveness and belief in the duty to overcome evil with good. Zehr describes the three dimensions of the Jewish *shalom* as including material or physical well-being, right relationships with other people and God, and moral or ethical "straightforwardness," referring to both honesty in dealing with others and having integrity without guilt or fault (Zehr, 1990). In this chapter you will see how one person's journey to put his religious values into practice led to an awakening concerning the treatment of prisoners in his country of Brazil. The brutality of the prisons struck him as a sharp contradiction to the teachings of the Christian church.

The Brazilian prison system is infamous for the brutal and often inhumane conditions of its facilities. Overcrowding and corruption are rampant, violent prison gangs control entire wings of many prisons, and the recidivism rate hovers around 70% (International Bar Association, 2009). But in Minas Gerais, an interior state of Brazil, an innovative prison system is being implemented that has the potential to change the trajectory of incarceration in Brazil and possibly beyond. APAC (*Associacao de Protecao e Assistencia aos Condenados*), translated from Portuguese as the Association for Protection and Assistance of Convicts, is a prison system that has fully integrated restorative justice principles into its methodology and has achieved tremendous results.

APAC HISTORY

APAC began in San Paulo, Brazil, in 1972 when Dr. Mario Ottoboni, a lawyer and passionate Catholic, faced a crisis in his personal faith. "I was questioning my life's purpose. I felt I could no longer be absent from any human and social problems" (e-mail correspondence from M. Ottoboni to Lorenn Walker, August 1, 2010).

Ottoboni found Catholicism's tenets hollow if only experienced in the abstract intellectually. During this time, he heard what he believed to be God's voice telling him to visit the men and women in the local prison (Creighton, 1999). Ottoboni began visiting the prison with lay members of his local Catholic parish. He was appalled by the conditions of the prison and treatment of the incarcerated people, and in the midst of this misery, he found his life's work.

Ottoboni and a handful of volunteers from his community set out to revolutionize the way people administer prisons. They started with a unique application of the golden rule: *Treat imprisoned people the way you would want them to treat others* (Ottoboni, 2003, p. 24). Ottoboni understood that this idea was a radical approach. He knew that he would face opposition, but he strongly believed that "a person who wants to change the society cannot have timid ideas" (p. 23).

The APAC system began with a prison in Sao Joao dos Campos, and now its methodology has spread to over 30 facilities in three Brazilian states and about a dozen other countries (Minas Gerais Department of Justice, 2011). In the United States, Prison Fellowship International (PFI), a Christian organization doing restorative justice work with prisons, has adopted APAC methodology and affiliated with APAC. APAC is recognized as the "first contemporary prison" to apply a completely faith-based approach to all parts of prison administration (Sullivan, 2009, p. 247).

APAC prisons promote a restorative response to crime by encouraging the community and incarcerated people to be accountable for their lives and for society. One of APAC's foremost goals is that incarcerated people "see that it is not enough to avoid wrongdoing; it is necessary for them to do good" (Ottoboni, 2003, p. 52). Service, community, care, and compassion, along with emphasizing repairing and maintaining relationships, are driving values in APAC prisons.

APAC'S RESTORATIVE APPROACH

APAC's restorative approach to incarceration begins from the moment an incarcerated person enters the prison. Instead of labeling people as *inmates* or *prisoners*, APAC calls them *recuperandos,* which translates into English, as "people who are undergoing a process of rehabilitation" (Creighton, 1998, p. 2). When a recuperando passes through the heavy iron door into the prison, they pass under a painted phrase that is one of APAC most enduring maxims: *A person is always more than the mistakes he or she makes* (Ottoboni, 2003, p. 24).

There is a symbolic removal of the recuperando's handcuffs and shackles when they initially enter APAC, and are told, "You are free now to become the man [woman] who you truly are." Treating incarcerated people with dignity and believing that they can change their lives is at the core of the APAC approach and is best understood through the eyes of a recuperando.

"I like it here because the food is good, there are no drugs, there is sunshine, and I can work. I can see my family," says Fernando with a wide grin. He is about 6 feet tall and slender, with warm green eyes, blond hair, and tan skin. He is sitting in an outdoor courtyard on a sunny morning at the APAC men's prison in Itauna, Minas Gerais. Bright pink and orange bougainvillea and banana trees line the trimmed courtyard that abuts a paved basketball court. Two men are busy tending to the plants and flowers; the smell of freshly baked bread is coming from the kitchen. It looks like a school campus. There are no prison guards. It is surprising that Fernando is being interviewed in a medium security prison that houses about 150 men convicted of the crimes ranging from the most serious, including murder, to simple theft and drug offenses.

Fernando explains how APAC has helped him:

I am 35 years old and have been in and out of prison since I was 20. This time for drug trafficking. I was busted selling 50 grams of pot and the judge gave me three years and 8 months. I was in prison in Rio de Janeiro and was so lucky to come here. This place has given me hope. I have been a drug addict since I was 14. I never believed I could live without drugs and alcohol, but since I came here, now I can believe I can live without drugs. I have been clean for 12 months, the longest ever in my life. I now see I wasn't enjoying life on drugs like I am now. I love working, and I love helping other people. APAC has changed my life.

APAC in Itauna, Minas Gerias, Brazil

The men's APAC prison in Itauna is one of nearly two dozen in Minas Gerias. This prison has two guest rooms in its administrative wing where visitors, including authors of this article, may be allowed to sleep overnight. Unlike other prisons, APAC actively pursues community members to enter the prison and permits interested visitors to sleep in the prison and eat meals with the incarcerated people. More incredible is that community volunteers and incarcerated people administer APAC prisons, not the government.

There are no prison guards. Selected recuperandos hold the keys to the cells, doors, and gates. The incarcerated people collaborate with the volunteers to maintain prison safety and enforce the prison rules.

APAC prisons are administered and governed by democratic principles (Ottoboni, 2003). The prisons' "bylaws, writs, and resolutions" are developed by a board of directors in collaboration with the community where the facilitiy is located. Elections are held for officers of the board whose members include legal, pastoral, police, prison, and general community at large representatives (Ottoboni, 2003, p. 156).

The atmosphere of an APAC prison is opposite to most prisons (Resende, 2009). Instead of an oppressive place where incarcerated people are constantly reminded of their failures, shame, and guilt, APAC's environment emphasizes the inherent worth of each recuperando. The atmosphere constantly reinforces the belief that all people, no matter what their circumstances and past behavior, are capable of changing and restoring their lives.

APAC METHODOLOGY

After almost 40 years since Dr. Ottoboni and a group of volunteers took a leap of faith and decided to change the prison system in their community, the APAC method has been refined through experience. Today, new APACs have been inaugurated, operating on 12 fundamental elements based on the simple premise that imprisoned people are more than the crimes that they have committed:

1. Community participation: Community volunteers regularly visit APAC prisons and teach courses. Volunteers build trust with the recuperandos and facilitate their reentry and transition back into the community.

2. Recuperandos help one another: The recuperandos are not only expected to obey the law, but are expected to "do good."

3. Work: A recuperando's security level requires different levels of work. In the "closed regime," APAC requires "labor therapy" activities "capable of fostering [the recuperandos'] creativity and making them reflect on what they are doing" (Ottoboni 2003, p. 55). The work opportunities vary at each facility and include everything from craft making and working in the kitchen to harvesting the fruits and vegetables in prison gardens.

4. Religion and the importance of the experience of God: The roots of APAC are based in the Christian faith, but it is not a "Christian" program. Recuperandos are not required to adopt a particular religion, but choosing one is encouraged. Religious participation is an important part of APAC's emphasis on personal reformation and plays an important role in reintegration into society.

5. Legal assistance: Incarcerated people need to know their legal status, including length of imprisonment, etc., and are provided with legal help.

6. Health care (physical, mental, dental, etc.): Most services are provided at the prisons by volunteers from the community or state employees. Meeting the prisoners' basic needs is viewed as the starting point for the implementation of restorative justice. (Ottoboni, 2003, p. 64).

7. Human valorization: This term describes the foundation of APAC's methodology. Treating incarcerated people with dignity, APAC seeks to "put the human being in the first place; in this sense, all the work must aim at reshaping the self-image of the man who erred. Calling them by their names, knowing their histories, expressing interest in their lives, visiting their families, satisfying their basic needs, allowing them to sit at the table during meals and using cutlery to eat, among other measures, will help them discover that not everything has been lost" (Ottoboni, 2003, p. 65).

8. The family: Some of APAC's biggest advocates are the incarcerated people's families. The families are treated with respect, are not subject to humiliating searches, and are allowed to visit their loved ones every week. Helping the families meet their basic needs also relieves some of the stress of incarceration and extends human valorization to the family.

9. Volunteers and their training: Extensive training with about 24 hours of instruction is required for volunteers.

10. Social reintegration center: The recuperandos are not simply released into society when their sentences are complete. Each person participates in a social reintegration program that starts months before their release date.

11. Merit: Merit is more than simply complying with prison rules. It is about imprisoned people realizing that what they do not only improves their individual lives but society in general. Bulletin boards with statistics of how many people have not been rearrested since leaving APAC are posted where all can see. This is a reminder of the goal to improve their lives and shows how the whole group is doing in efforts to achieve the goal.

12. Deliverance through Christ workshop: The *Jornada* is a three-day intensive religious experience. Jornada translates to English from Portuguese as "a short journey." Every six months APAC prisons conduct jornadas on varying themes with presentations, small group discussions, individual "reflection," and a closing celebration with family and food (Creighton, 1999, p. 4).

The importance of relationship development, maintenance, and repair are deeply embedded in the APAC methodology. "Relationships [are] the heart of the [APAC] system" (Burnside & Lee, 1997). Each incarcerated person has a "godparent" assigned to them "who will support him throughout his sentence and treat him as one of the family. . . . His role is to build a relationship so valued that the recuperando will not want to re-offend. Government is by men, not laws" (p. 39).

APAC SELECTION AND TREATMENT PROCESSES

In Brazil, when a person is convicted of a criminal offense, they are sent to the state's prison system where some learn about APAC, mainly through word of mouth. A judge decides if the person can be transferred to the APAC system. The judge's decision is based on input of the defendant, a review of their behavior while at the state prison, and the perspective of the APAC administration. "In general, there isn't a sentence management plan. The APAC methodology is sufficient. It's just the legal requirements of the judges that have to visit" (Parker, 2011). Brazilian law requires criminal court judges to visit prisons where they sentence defendants "once a month" (e-mail correspondence from San Paulo, Brazil, Judge Eduardo Rezende Melo to Lorenn Walker, July 7, 2011).

When an incarcerated person initially arrives at APAC, they go to the "closed" section of the prison. They are locked in this part of the facility, but not in individual cells.[1] Once a recuperando has spent the time required in the closed section, they are allowed to transfer into the "semi-open" section of the prison. Here they are allowed to leave for work weekdays at 6 a.m. and return by 6 p.m..

Recuperandos in the semi-open section are subject to drug and alcohol testing and may be returned to the closed part of the prison if they break the rules. The final step of APAC is admission into the "conditional" stage. At this minimum supervision stage, *recuperandos* may sleep outside the prison but must check in monthly with the administration to show that they are complying with the conditional release requirements.

APAC treatment includes work, job, and career training, and all forms of medical and psychological services. Restorative meetings with harmed loved ones and others are explored and provided as needed. All the services and treatment at APAC are tailored to fit the needs of individual incarcerated people.

APAC OUTCOMES

Research on people who completed their sentences in APAC prisons 1996 through 1999 were compared to people released from other prisons, and shows significantly less recidivism. The outcomes for 148 people released from APAC and 247 from another Brazilian prison were reviewed about three years after release (Johnson, 2002). The other Brazilian prison was not typical but "a more humane, clean, and self-sustaining facility" (p. 8), which was "primarily based on vocational training and the use of prison industry" (p. 7).

The study evaluated participants for re-arrest, re-incarceration, and any differences in crime severity when they were re-arrested or re-incarcerated. Recidivism was 16% for people released from APAC, and 36% for those released from the other prison. APAC's recuperandos had significantly fewer rearrests and re-imprisonments, but the sample was too small to measure severity of crime comparisons of the groups.

---

[1] One day a month, recuperandos in the closed section of the Itauna men's prison voluntarily lock themselves up for the day "to show solidarity for their brothers" who are in the other Brazilian prisons.

Results for both types of prison were extremely low compared with the Brazilian nationally estimated recidivism rate between "50% to 70%."[2] The study was labeled "exploratory" because the "Brazilian police did not provide criminal history on a large number of former inmates from both prisons" and no comparison of other Brazilian prisons was made (Johnson, 2002, p. 10). The researchers did not believe there was any "systemic bias" by the police concerning the missing data, yet "considerable caution" was suggested in interpreting the results.

APAC'S FAITH-BASED FOCUS

APAC's roots are religious. The seed was planted by Catholic Church members and has been watered by primarily religiously motivated volunteers. One of the reasons APAC has been able to expand so rapidly and successfully is because it is not overtly religious. The methodology stresses the importance of religion in the lives of the recuperandos but does not place any specific spiritual requirements beyond participation in some sort of faith. Dr. Ottoboni understood the importance of allowing freedom to choose religion:

> *Recuperandos* need to profess a religion, believe in God, love and be loved. It does not really matter whether they profess one belief or another; moreover, we should never suffocate or asphyxiate *recuperandos* [original emphasis] who feel they have to follow a certain vocation (that would generate anguish in them, instead of making them reflect) (Ottoboni, 2003, p. 61).

Recuperandos do not simply attend religious services and practice formal rituals but instead are encouraged to practice their faith in their daily lives. APAC prisons help people rehabilitate by encouraging them to practice empathy, accountability, and service for each other. Faith is used not only to reconcile the recuperando with a higher power and avoid "sinful" or high-risk behaviors but also to instill a sense of social responsibility. Fernando came to appreciate the value of service after being incarcerated at APAC. He said APAC helped him make a discovery: "I love helping other people."

While APAC's approach may marginalize an atheist, it leaves space for a variety of religious expressions in many cultural contexts. The volunteers and incarcerated leaders administering each APAC prison define its spiritual components. Specific religious mandates are not explicitly woven into the methodology. The state of Minas Gerais, where nearly all of the APACs are located, is not a religiously diverse region. Christianity is the most widely practiced faith, and most people are Catholic or Protestants.

Other cultures with different religious environments can apply APAC methodology. Muslim, Buddhist, and Hindu cultures also promote the same integrity and values that guided Dr. Ottoboni's vision. Each religion reflects the realities of where it is practiced.

Benson Iwuagwu, the executive director of a prison system near Lagos, Nigeria, that applies APAC's methodology, reports that the Christian and Muslim residents there

---

[2]There are no official recidivism records for the country, but a Brazilian newspaper reported the recidivism rate at 70% (Skalmusky, 2010).

operate under the same institutional guidelines but have separate religious services. Iwuagwu says that there are no rival and competing factions based on the different religions. He openly laments that if the rest of his country could coexist as well as the people in this prison, Nigeria would not be experiencing the religious violence that currently plagues it (B. Iwuagwu, interview with Andrew Johnson, July 1, 2011).

APAC PROMOTES PRAGMATIC FAITH-BASED PRACTICES

The pragmatic aspect of APAC's faith-based efforts, are consistent with how people have experienced religion historically. Theologian Karen Armstrong (2009) identifies *practice* as the component of major religious traditions. (She looks to the Eastern religions, a starkly different cultural reality from Brazil: "Religion as defined by the great sages of India, China, and the Middle East was not a notional activity but a practical one; it did not require belief in a set of doctrines but rather hard, disciplined work, without which any religious teaching remained opaque and incredible" (Armstrong, 2009, p. 26). Armstrong shows most religions use empathy for developing spirituality: "Every single one of the major traditions—Confucianism, Buddhism, and Hinduism, as well as the monotheisms—teaches a spirituality of empathy, by means of which you relate your own suffering to that of others" (Armstrong, 2004, p. 272). With this conceptualization of religion, APAC could be utilized in any religious environment.

In *Restorative Justice Dialogue*, Umbreit and Armour (2010), include a chapter on spirituality, which defines a reverence for life (compared to religiosity) as a set of formally structured beliefs, values, and practices. Religious components are incorporated under spirituality. All the major religions have spiritual themes consistent with restorative justice. Biblical justice, as Zehr suggests, was not "a forensic inquiry into wrongdoing to establish guilt. . . . Rather, biblical justice was an attempt to right wrongs, to find solutions that would bring about well-being" (1990, p.142). Restorative justice is not only about righting a wrong for persons harmed by crime but also for everyone involved, including communities. It is about making amends rather than punishment, restitution rather than retribution (Zehr, 2002).

Confucianism supports the Eastern theory that human nature is basically good and that we should seek the good in people (Breton & Lehman, 2001; Canda & Furman, 2010). Confucius taught his disciples the principle of *ren* or truthfulness and kindness. Confucianism, advocates a restorative approach to crime and justice and assumes that the first victim of any criminal offense is the person who has committed the wrong himself or herself (Hui & Geng, 2001).

Central to Buddhism is compassion and interconnectedness of all beings (Canda & Furman, 2010). Buddhist justice grows out of a compassion for everyone involved when one person hurts another. Loy (2001) contrasts Tibetan culture, where a citizen is seen as having a legal duty to help others, with the American legal tradition, where the truth emerges from adversarial actions. In contrast to Western justice, in Tibet there is no clear division between religion and the state, in sharp contrast with Western judicial philosophy.

Umbreit and Armour (2010) reviewed restorative justice literature and found nine basic themes compatible with spiritual teachings. Themes such as transformation head the list. Citing Zehr (1990), the authors view the restorative process as leading to personal change by many participants, which may be a transformation of the mind and the emotions. The second spiritual theme is a sense of connectedness to the community that often occurs through the interpersonal support offered to the participants. In contrast to adversarial courtroom justice, which pits people against each other with the winner taking all, restorative processes bring people together with a focus on their common goals and bonds. Far from a fight, restorative practices are cooperative and lead to understanding. Repentance and forgiveness are themes with spiritual as well as religious roots that may be experienced in the restorative process. Forgiveness is generally interpreted as letting go of the anger and resentment that the person who was wounded feels toward the wrongdoer. Another spiritual component, balance or harmony, is characteristic of peacemaking circles conducted by indigenous groups to promote healing following a hurtful event in the community. Instead of being reactive to events, this justice model uses events as opportunities for community members to feel heard, to rebuild trust, and restore harmed relationships (Breton & Lehman, 2001). The rituals are another key component shared by both restorative justice and spiritual practices. The eighth element of restorative justice singled out by Umbreit and Armour is a sense that something cannot be explained. It is an awareness of a power greater than the self. Participants sometimes describe the process as mystical and out of the ordinary. Such feelings tend to arise when the rituals include opening and closing ceremonies as well as moments of silence and meditation. Finally viewed as a whole, reverence for life is central to the philosophy of restorative justice.

Conclusion

APAC is a successful restorative prison model. Treating incarcerated people with respect and kindness can rehabilitate and prevent crime. APAC provides a profoundly humane approach to corrections.

Dr. Phil Zimbardo, who conducted the 1971 Stanford prison experiment (The Stanford Prison Experiment, 2011), says it is the lack of humanity that prevents prisons from being places of rehabilitation. Instead of prisons being places where people often learn criminal behavior, we could "use the power of the situation to produce virtue" (Zimbardo, 2007, p. 451).

Zimbardo suggests how social situations can improve behavior and points out the importance of labeling people. "Give someone an *identity label* [original emphasis] of the kind that you would like them to have as someone who will then do the action you want to elicit from them" (p. 451). *Recuperando* suggests learning to become a better person, which is what prison should be about. The labels *offender, defendant, inmate,* and *prisoner* suggest past misbehavior. Zimbardo also suggests that people be encouraged to admit mistakes and "move on. . . . Say the six magic words: 'I'm sorry'; 'I apologize'; 'forgive me.' Say to yourself that you will learn from your mistakes, grow better from them" (p. 452). This idea is consistent with having a "growth mind-set" and understanding that those who realize they continually learn achieve higher levels of success than people who believe the ability to learn is inherent or genetically endowed (Dweck, 2006). APAC gives people the opportunity to say Zimbardo's "six magic words" while promoting a growth mind-set.

The complete APAC model might not work everywhere, but aspects of its methodology could be used. Simply using positive "identity labels" and calling people by their names is a small step in treating people more humanely and improving things.

Critical Thinking Questions

1. Generally what do you believe the purpose of prison is? How successful do you believe prisons are? How might restorative justice assist prisons?

2. How would the APAC prison approach work in the United States? What aspects of APAC do you think are effective or ineffective and why? If you were to advocate for an APAC prison approach, or using aspects of it, what would you say to convince policymakers to consider it?

References

Armstrong, K. (2004). *The spiral staircase: My climb out of darkness.* New York, NY: Anchor Books.

Armstrong, K. (2009). *The case for God.* New York, NY: Knopf.

Breton, D., & Lehman, S. (2001). *The mystic heart of justice: Restoring wholeness in a broken world.* West Chester, PA: Chrysalis.

Burnside, J., & Lee, P. (1997). Where love is not a luxury. *Ethical Life.* Retrieved from http://seekjustice .co.uk/my-brothers-keeper/free-resources-for-faith-based-programmes-in-prisons/

Canda, E. R., & Furman, L. (2010). *Spiritual diversity in social work practice: The heart of helping.* New York, NY: Oxford University Press.

Creighton, A. (1999). Itauna Prison. Unpublished report. Retrieved from http://www.pfi.org/cjr/apac/ where1/reports/brazil/ituana/

Dweck, C. (2006). *Mindset: The new psychology of success.* New York, NY: Random House.

Hui, E. C., & Geng, K. (2001). The spirit and practice of restorative justice in Chinese culture. In M. Hadley (Ed.), *The spiritual roots of restorative justice.* Albany, NY: State University of New York Press.

International Bar Association. (2009). *One in five: The crisis in Brazil's prisons and criminal justice system.* International Bar Association Human Rights Institute Report. Retrieved from http://www.ibanet .org/Human_Rights_Institute/HRI_Publications/Country_reports.aspx

Johnson, B. (2002). Assessing the impact of religious programs and prison industry on recidivism: An exploratory study. *Texas Journal of Corrections.* Retrieved from http://nicic.gov/Library/018449

Loy, D. (2001). Healing justice: A Buddhist perspective. In M. Hadley (Ed.), *The spiritual roots of restorative justice* (pp. 81–97). Albany, NY: State University of New York Press.

Minas Gerais Department of Justice. (2011). Court of Justice of Minas. Retrieved from http://www.tjmg .jus.br/presidencia/programanovosrumos/apac_minas.html

Ottoboni, M. (2003). *Transforming criminals: An introduction to the APAC methodology.* Washington, DC: Prison Fellowship International.

Resende, F. (2009). Offender-friendly prisons, less costly, better results, Comunidad Segura: Networks of ideas and practices in Human Security blog. Retrieved from http://www.comunidadesegura.org.br/ en/STORY-Minas-Gerais-offender-friendly-prisons-less+costly-better+results-APAC

Skalmusky, A. (2010). The cycle of Brazilian prisons. *The Rio Times*. Retrieved from http://riotimeson line.com/brazil-news/rio-politics/the-cycle-of-brazil%E2%80%99s-prisons/#

The Stanford Prison Experiment (2011). Retrieved from http://www.prisonexp.org/

Sullivan, W. (2009). *Prison religion: Faith-based reform and the Constitution.* Princeton, NJ: Princeton University Press.

Umbreit, M., & Armour, M. P. (2010). *Restorative justice dialogue: An essential guide for research and practice.* New York, NY: Springer Publishing Company.

Zehr, H. (1990). *Changing lenses: A new focus for crime and justice.* Scottdale, PA: Herald Press.

Zehr, H. (2002). *The little book of restorative justice.* Intercourse, PA: Good Books.

Zimbardo, P. (2007). *The Lucifer effect: How good people turn evil.* New York: Random House.

18

Restorative Justice Skills Building for Incarcerated People

Lorenn Walker and Ted Sakai

Restorative justice uses behavioral, cognitive, and emotional skills that help people communicate about and cope with difficulties easier. Skills include listening, using precise language to concretely describe experiences and goals, and understanding how emotions and thinking affect situations. These skills are normally taught to restorative justice facilitators but can also be taught to incarcerated people for their benefit. Called Restorative Justice as a Solution-Focused Approach to Conflict and Wrongdoing the training program described here is provided over 12 weeks. Lorenn Walker developed and implemented the program for incarcerated people at the suggestion of Waiawa Correctional Facility (WCF) prison staff. Ted Sakai, MBA, is director of the Hawai'i Department of Public Safety, which oversees all Hawai'i prisons, and is a former warden of WCF. Almost 200 incarcerated people from the Hawai'i Women's Community Correctional Center and WCF have completed the training where they learn about restorative justice and solution building.

The major portion of this chapter is reprinted with permission from Corrections Today. *Box 6 has been added to the original article because it illustrates the concepts described in the article. Both the boxed reading and the article take place within prison walls.*

Source: From *"A Gift of Listening for Hawaii's Inmates,"* Lorenn Walker, Ted Sakai. *Corrections Today,* December 2006, pp.58–61. © 2006. Reprinted with permission of the American Correctional Association, Alexandria, Va.

"**W**e were crazy. Pushing down an old tourist lady for a purse and doing the rest of that stuff, it was all nuts. I can't believe we did it. It was the drugs." This is one inmate's assessment of his and his fellow inmates past criminal behavior. They are sitting in a classroom where 18 inmates are broken up into four groups of four or five inmates in each group. The inmates have lived together at this minimum-security prison in Hawai'i for the past year. The small groups are discussing who was affected by their criminal behavior as part of a training program in restorative justice and solution-focused facilitation skills. The inmates were chosen to participate in this pilot inmate-training program by their counselors from a drug treatment program at Waiawa Correctional Facility on the island of O'ahu. Waiawa is located about 20 miles from Honolulu at the end of an old one-lane road that winds up some low lying mountains. Bright green banana trees and other lush tropical foliage surround the prison, which provides an expansive view of Pearl Harbor and the Pacific Ocean. Waiawa is a rehabilitative facility where inmates farm the land and eat what they grow. Waiawa was a World War II military installation that the federal government leases to Hawai'i with the stipulation that education and treatment be provided to the inmates.

Program Description

Inmates participated in the facilitator training over 12 weeks, meeting once a week in the evenings for two hours a day (24 hours total). The program seeks to help them learn self-control and how to get along with others. The inmates were told, "Effective facilitators are competent, self-aware people who listen carefully and who exercise control when their emotions are triggered." The inmates were introduced to emotional intelligence skills (Goleman, 1997).

Listening was the primary communication skill taught to the inmates and was the skill they practiced most often during the training and for their homework during the week in between training sessions. The inmates reported weekly on their homework practice.

Experiential Learning

The training is conducted as a group meeting where inmates increase their expertise through experience and practice. This form of learning has been found more effective than traditional classroom lectures (Johnson & Johnson, 1994; Bandura, 1977). Inmates sit with two co-trainers in a large circle. Inmates work in smaller circles and dyads throughout the trainings, but the group begins and ends in a large circle each session.

Strengths Based

The training is strengths based. It focuses on what is positive about the inmate and his life. Research shows that focusing on strengths rather than deficits generates more positive behavior (Turnell & Edwards, 1999). In corrections it has also been shown that prisoner interventions are more effective for reducing recidivism when reinforcements are mostly positive and not negative (Petersilia, 2004).

The weekly meetings always open with each inmate sharing something that they are grateful for that happened since the last week. Sometimes it was, "My dad wrote me after four years!" Or it might be an appreciation of a simple thing, such as, "I didn't get written up or into any trouble" or "I'm still alive."

The training sessions always end with each inmate complimenting another inmate. "I want to compliment Frank for defusing a potentially hostile situation in our dorm last week. He respected both of the fighting inmates and saved everyone a lot of grief." Sometimes the inmates got up and gave each other rough bear hugs or bumped fists in more emotional displays of gratitude toward each other. Giving compliments is part of the solution-focused model that the training uses.

Solution-Focused Approach

The training follows the solution-focused approach to problem solving as developed by Insoo Kim Berg and Steve de Shazer (Berg & de Shazer, 1993). Berg was an internationally recognized author and therapist who provided her expertise and guidance on the training program's development.

The solution-focused approach uses language skills to assist people in problem solving by getting them to envision what they want and how they will behave and feel different when they experience their desired outcome. Instead of focusing on what is unwanted, thinking and talking about how terrible it is, and concentrating on why the problem exists, the solution-focused approach asks people what specifically they want and how they have succeeded in other areas. As social psychologist Albert Bandura pointed out long ago, self-efficacy transfers—as one succeeds in one area, the ability to succeed transfers to other areas (Bandura, 1977).

Solution-focused trainers and therapists are expert listeners who find out what clients care about and what they want. Throughout the training, inmates are asked to imagine in great detail how their life will be different without the problem and how exactly they will behave and feel without the problem. The trainers took great care to consistently point out the inmates' strengths. "Wow, you've been clean and sober for two years!" They also constantly ask the inmates how they managed to overcome difficulties and succeed in the past: "How have you managed to stay clean for two years now?" Focusing on how to repeat positive and successful behavior is easier than trying to change negative behavior (Berg, 1994).

Restorative Justice

Over 90% of all American inmates pleaded guilty to an offense before imprisonment (Hall, 1996). These inmates would benefit by being accountable for their offenses. Getting angry with criminal offenders, asking them "What's wrong with you?" and then punishing them, is not usually effective for getting them to take responsibility for their behavior. For most offenders to genuinely be accountable they need to consider how their behavior affected people and what might be done to repair the harm it caused. This is what restorative justice is all about.

The training introduces inmates to three basic restorative justice questions: (1) who was affected by the wrongdoing? (2) how were they affected? (3) what might be done to repair the harm? (Zehr, 1995). Asking these questions takes the focus off of the offenders and puts it where it should be, on the innocent people hurt by the bad behavior.

Everyone makes mistakes in life. Of course most people do not engage in criminal acts that lead to prison, but everyone has hurt others at times. How we respond to wrongdoing is important. Focusing only on why an offender committed a crime and how terrible he or she is without considering the harm caused victims and the community creates an unhealthy system with a lot self-absorbed inmates.

Most working in corrections and the criminal justice system know how much offenders feel sorry for themselves. This should not be surprising because the system mainly concentrates on offenders with little regard for victims. Likewise, offenders rarely consider the victims or how their behavior affects their own families. Considering victims, which restorative justice does, is the first step in developing empathy and rehabilitation for offenders, which probably explains why it is more effective at decreasing recidivism than our current system.

Forgiveness

The inmates are introduced to forgiveness as a life skill as developed by Fred Luskin. While everyone has hurt others, everyone has also been hurt in life. Hanging on to old wounds, carrying around resentment and hostility, keeps people unhappy. The energy it takes to imagine a just revenge for someone who was harmful is more wisely used for creating a positive life. No one can control anyone but himself. Inmates learn that forgiveness does not mean bad behavior is condoned or forgotten or that offenders ever have to know that they have been forgiven—it can be extended to people who are deceased. Forgiveness is simply letting go of resentment.

After the inmates learned about this concept of forgiveness, two of them shared powerful stories of how they forgave people who seriously hurt them as children. One Waiawa inmate forgave both his parents for committing suicide. His father killed himself when the inmate was 10 and his mother killed herself when the inmate was 13. He was subsequently raised in foster homes where he suffered abuse. He recognized that as a youth "many people reached out to help" but he rejected the offers. Instead, he became a heroin addict and bank robber who spent most of his adult life (the past 30 years) in prison. He functioned in life by being isolated from people and completely avoiding his painful emotions associated with the loss of his parents and suffering of his childhood. The training showed him healthy practices for dealing with his emotions that he says help make him feel confident that he will not use drugs in the future. Facing painful emotions is vital for overcoming anxiety and developing positive emotional health (Leahy, 2005).

Another Waiawa inmate forgave the man who shot and killed his father. The killing occurred when the inmate was 10 years old and his father died in his arms. His aunt was also shot and killed, and his mother was seriously wounded. The shooter is in another prison, and the inmate has struggled with his feelings for revenge for many years. Learning that forgiveness can be something extended to benefit the victim and not necessarily the offender helped the inmate deal with his pain and not remain focused on retribution against the shooter.

The Hawai'i Forgiveness Project gave each of these inmates a Student of Forgiveness Award. The Forgiveness Project also included the stories written by the inmates in a booklet that it published.

Training Outcomes

An assessment of 200 inmates' surveys on the effectiveness of the training showed that they found it helpful in teaching them new skills. Of the inmates surveyed, a majority stated that they appreciated learning listening and communication skills from the training. One inmate said, "We were given a gift, the gift of learning to listen." Learning to listen is a significant outcome as it is a precursor for empathy development.

One of the inmates in the training relapsed and used drugs several days after his release from prison. He violated his parole, but he turned himself into his parole officer. He entered a drug treatment program and became compliant again with his parole conditions. Five inmates from the training also requested Restorative Circles. Four of them had circles. A circle was scheduled for the fifth, but he was moved to a medium security prison before it was conducted.

Lots of light bulbs went off for the inmates. They went from having dull, unenthusiastic looking demeanors to being bright and excited people. They learned some skills that gave them more hope for their lives. During the training they often commented on how grateful they were for it and said things such as, "Learning all I have here makes me glad I went to prison!" "I thought this was going to be the same old thing, and I was blown away to learn and experience all I did in this circle."

Conclusion

This is an inexpensive training program that can improve a prison. The former warden said, "This program is helping to transform the culture of the prison organization from one of anger and hostility to [one of] caring and compassion. It shows people how to focus on positives and not negatives. It shows inmates a different way to resolve problems instead of through retaliation and violence, which is their typical response to disputes. This program gave meaning to some of the principles taught at the substance abuse therapeutic community."

As of 2012, over 200 incarcerated people have participated in the Restorative Justice as a Solution Focused Approach to Conflict and Wrongdoing. The program has evolved to provide a concluding evening where judges and other respected community members are invited. The incarcerated people provide a skit that they develop. The skits have all been very moving and each has addressed forgiveness to date. The group also shares some refreshments and certificates of completion are handed out.

Now we turn to a recent example that puts the concepts discussed here into practice. The situation described is an extremely compelling one that involves a homicide and takes place in a prison between a convicted murderer and the victim's family.

Box 6

Remembering Bob Shapel: A Prison Restorative Dialogue at Walla Walla

Lorenn Walker

Oprah Winfrey has shown a continuing interest in the power of restorative justice and featured several dramatic meetings between victims and offenders on The Oprah Winfrey Show. *On the Oprah Winfrey Network on October 8, 2011, on a program called* Confronting, *featured a victim-offender dialogue at the Washington State Penitentiary in Walla Walla that involved a dialogue facilitated by Lorenn Walker. In Box 6, the reader can appreciate the amount of preparation that went into this dramatic encounter between two women who lost a loved one to murder and the perpetrator of the horrific crime. After you read the following account, watch the video excerpt at the website provided in the boxed reading.*

In January 2011, I was asked to work with three people to facilitate a restorative dialogue (aka victim offender mediation) at Washington State Penitentiary in Walla Walla. The dialogue was filmed for *Confronting* on the Oprah Winfrey Network: http://www.oprah.com/own-confronting/Colleen-Meets-Her-Husbands-Killer

Colleen Shapel's husband Bob, was senselessly murdered in a February 2004 robbery. Bob had been Colleen's best friend for most of her life. Melissa, Colleen's oldest daughter, and William Schorr, a codefendant who pleaded guilty to the murder, also participated in the restorative dialogue (another defendant who was determined to be most responsible for the murder refused to participate).

After I was first contacted and before the dialogue was conducted six months later in July 2011, I spoke frequently on the phone with Colleen, Melissa, and William. I met Colleen and Melissa in person several times a few days before the dialogue and William a few hours before it.

I felt my job was to mainly listen to their pain, and simply be present with them in their suffering. All three had been struggling for seven years. Colleen was still deeply angry and resentful. No question that her feelings were absolutely justified and understandable, but her hostility was making her life miserable. "They took my best friend away," she sobbed at William Schorr's sentencing. "They took my self away. There are days I can't even function." Seven years later, Melissa described her feelings this way: "I lost my mother too and not just my father."

Since the murder, William Schorr had attempted suicide three times. He was haunted by his participation and the terrible harm he caused. He had basically given up on life and felt doomed to a life of regret and misery. His guilt and shame overwhelmed him. "I can never forgive myself for what I did. It is unforgiveable. It tears me up. I go to bed every night reliving what happened. I can't sleep and don't think I ever will be able. I deserve to die."

As my conversations continued over the months with each person, I listened and we talked about anything they wanted. Eventually the idea of forgiveness came up with Colleen.

The word *forgiveness* triggers many emotions for people. It means different things to different people. While some restorative justice practitioners and trainers reportedly advise facilitators: "Never mention the F word" to people they work with, I openly discussed forgiveness with Colleen.

Initially she explosively said, "I can never forgive for this!" I explained my understanding to her. "Forgiveness doesn't mean forgetting Bob or dishonoring him. It is never right to condone bad behavior. Forgiveness can simply be taking the energy it takes being resentful and angry and instead putting it into something positive that you want in life."

Fred Luskin's (2002) wonderful book *Forgive for Good* teaches forgiveness as a life skill and stress reducer. I sent the book to Colleen after our first discussion about forgiveness. After she read the book, she said, "It's not about people who've been through murders, Lorenn, it's about friends and stuff like that." Colleen was not ready to forgive anyone for what happened to her husband or her life.

I respected Colleen's decision to be unforgiving. I believe all adults are the experts on their own lives and everyone knows what is best for themselves. Listening to people helps them figure out what they need and what they want. I only explained my understanding of forgiveness to Colleen. Being a lawyer and trained advocate as well as a health educator and facilitator, I did not want to influence or argue with Colleen that she should adopt my view, but I admit that I silently hoped someday she might come to see forgiveness the way Fred Luskin does.

The restorative dialogue was originally scheduled for June at the prison in Walla Walla, but it was abruptly canceled. "Prison security issues" arose after William's bunkmate was allegedly found with marijuana in their cell. The prison administration canceled the meeting due to this infraction.

Colleen, Melissa, and William were upset and shaken about the prison's decision. Colleen especially felt revictimized by the system that she thought should be protecting her. "How can his bunkmate stop me from meeting with Schorr? It's all I've thought about for months. This can't be happening," she cried. A compelling and strong advocate, Colleen took her complaints to the prison administration.

William also felt defeated. While he feared meeting Colleen and Melissa, he desperately wanted them to have the opportunity to hear his answers to any of their questions about Bob's last moments and anything that might help them. He went to his counselors and asked them to help get the meeting rescheduled. I also abandoned my mainly listener and facilitator role, and actively advocated for the meeting.

Reason and compassion prevailed. After about three weeks, the prison administration reconsidered and allowed the restorative dialogue to be rescheduled. Everyone was relieved that the months spent preparing were not in vain, and there would be a chance for the three to meet and tell their stories. All were anxious about meeting. Bob's loss would forever leave a wound or at least a scar. Knowing that they would meet gave all three a slight hope that some kind of healing might be possible.

The meeting occurred on a dark cloudy day and took about four hours. They were some of the most intense hours I have ever witnessed. The dialogue and outcomes were "unbelievable" according to prison staff and other observers.

(Continued)

(Continued)

At the end of the meeting, Colleen said she wasn't "ready to forgive," but she sobbed and tightly hugged William. Earlier, she said, "You seem like a nice guy."

"I'm sorry we're meeting under these circumstances," William replied.

Many of us cried during the dialogue, including some strong-looking men with many years' experience as correctional officers. After Colleen hugged William, so did Melissa, and so did I. "It was the first time I was hugged in seven years," said William afterward.

I have kept in contact with Colleen, Melissa, and William since the restorative dialogue and plan to indefinitely. Each one of their voices sounds stronger, they are more cheerful, and they are more hopeful about the future. "My life is completely changed for the better," said Colleen. "It's like my mom's back," said Melissa. "I can sleep better," said William.

Bob Shapel and the horrible cause of his death must never be forgotten. Restorative dialogues, victim offender conferencing, and any restorative practice absolutely do not need to lead to forgiveness. Colleen and Melissa's compassion, extended after they met with William and saw he was not a "horrible monster," however, has freed them to live happier lives. Their compassion has also allowed William to find some meaning in his imprisonment, which now is about working to help other incarcerated people reenter the community and avoid the wrong choices he made. Finally, many people have been inspired by how these three people bravely faced their suffering, including me.

I will forever appreciate the Washington prison department for allowing this dialogue to occur (many prisons do not allow them at all); the Oprah Winfrey Network for its work educating people about restorative justice; and Colleen, Melissa, and William, who were courageous enough to face and share their pain so others might benefit.

Critical Thinking Questions

1. How do you want people in your community returning from prison to behave? What do you think returning inmates should know and understand that would help keep people in your community safe?

2. What difference has learning about your emotions made in your life? What have been the most effective ways for you to learn about your emotions, your behaviors, and your thinking patterns in your life?

References

Bandura, A. (1977). Self-efficacy: Toward a unifying theory of behavioral change. *Psychological Review, 84*, 191–215.

Berg, I.K. (1994). *Family based services: A solution focused approach.* New York, NY: Norton.

Berg, I. K., & de Shazer, S. (1993). Making numbers talk: Language in therapy. In S. Freidman (Ed.), *The new language of change.* New York, NY: Guilford Press.

Goleman, D. (1997). *Emotional intelligence.* New York, NY: Bantam Books.

Hall, D. (1996). *Criminal law and procedure.* Albany, NY: Delmar Publishers.

Hawai'i Forgiveness Project. (2006). Retrieved from www.hawaiiforgivenessproject.org/

Johnson, D., & Johnson, F. (1994). *Joining together: Group theory and group skills.* Boston, MA: Allyn and Bacon.

Leahy, R. (2005). *The worry cure: Seven steps to stop worry from stopping you.* New York, NY: Harmony Books.

Luskin, F. (2002). *Forgive for good: A proven prescription for health and happiness.* New York, NY: HarperCollins.

Petersilia, J. (2004). What works in prisoner reentry? Reviewing and questioning the evidence. *Federal Probation Journal, 68*(2), 4–8.

Turnell, S., & Edwards, S. (1999). *Signs of safety: A solution and safety oriented approach to child protection casework.* New York, NY: Norton.

Zehr, H. (1995). *Changing lenses.* Scottdale, PA: Herald Press.

19

Huikahi Restorative Circles: A Public Health Approach for Reentry Planning

Lorenn Walker and Rebecca Greening

Hawai'i has been experimenting with a restorative reentry group planning model where incarcerated people apply to meet in a facilitated three-hour process that addresses an individual's needs for a successful reentry into the community. The process applies current learning theory principles in a self-directed group process that repairs relationships necessary for criminal desistance. The process addressees incarcerated people's need for reconciliation with their loved ones and unrelated victims—and themselves. Research of small samples out of prison two years or more shows promise for this restorative reentry intervention. Rebecca Greening, a young lawyer who graduated from the Boston Latin School and studied social work at New York University before becoming a lawyer, saw early in her career the need for restorative justice approaches to deal with crime and social problems. Greening is currently employed as a lawyer for people involved with the child welfare department in Boston. This article is reprinted from the European Journal of Probation. (*Source: The Huikahi Restorative Circles: A Public Health Approach for Reentry Planning, Lorenn Walker and Rebecca Greening, 2010, Federal Probation, 74* (1). Available at http://www.uscourts.gov/FederalCourts/ProbationPretrialServices/FederalProbationJournal.aspx

"Oh, it was good. It brought me some closure with Ken. Gave me a different way of looking at him. It's addiction. He's choosing it over his family. I'm still cautiously optimistic about him, but I'm 100% for Rachel. I'm absolutely sure she'll make it," says Marta in March 2010.

Five years earlier, in March 2005, Marta, Ken's maternal aunt, along with Ken, Rachel, his girlfriend and mother of his three children, and his drug treatment counselor at Waiawa Correctional Facility, participated in the first Huikahi Restorative Circle. This restorative reentry planning process, developed in Hawai'i, was reported in the June 2006 *Federal Probation* journal (Walker, Sakai & Brady, 2006). This paper is a follow-up report on Marta's and other circle participants' satisfaction and includes recidivism results for incarcerated people released from prison for at least two years who had circles.

It has been four years since Ken was paroled from prison, and three since his parole was revoked after he relapsed. He is now re-incarcerated at a private prison in Arizona. Marta, who raised Ken after his mother died, reflected on her experience in the 2005 circle five years later:

> The circle addressed a lot of issues for me. I had a lot of guilt. I worried that I didn't spend enough time with him. There was a lot of self-blame. But talking in the circle helped me deal with that. Now I realize we all have trauma and we all do the best we can. Every day I think. "I did the best job I could." He had a good upbringing. I did my best. His choices now are all his own.

Besides raising Ken, Marta spent over 25 years as a police sergeant for the Honolulu Police Department. She told Ken's circle facilitator, "We're on the opposite sides. I arrest 'em and try and get 'em into prison, and you're trying to keep 'em out. But we're both in the same circle. We're working for the same thing—to keep people safe."

According to John Braithwaite, an internationally renowned expert in restorative justice, Hawai'i is a world leader in innovation for reentry planning for prisoners because of its work on restorative circles. We all look forward to the next stage in this Hawaiian leadership toward a more effective way to prevent crime by reintegrating released inmates into a supportive community (Hawai'i Legislature, 2010, p. 3).

Huikahi Restorative Circle Process and Development

The Huikahi Restorative Circle is a group process for reentry planning that involves incarcerated individuals, their families and friends, and at least one prison representative. The process was developed in 2005 in collaboration with two community-based organizations and a Hawai'i state prison: the Hawai'i Friends of Justice & Civic Education, the Community Alliance on Prisons, and the Waiawa Correctional Facility located on the island of O'ahu.

The process was originally called Restorative Circles, but was renamed Huikahi Restorative Circles to distinguish Hawai'i's reentry planning process from other restorative processes. In Hawaiian, *hui* means group, and *kahi* means individual. Together, the word *huikahi*, for purposes of this process, signifies individuals coming together to form a covenant. The addition of *Huikahi* to the name was a result of the input of a Native Hawaiian prison warden.

While the modern restorative justice movement is about 30 years old, many believe its roots trace back to "most of human history for perhaps all the world's peoples" (Braithwaite, 2002, p. 5). Circle processes are a fundamental practice of the restorative justice movement (Zehr, 2002). Peter Senge, cofounder of the MIT Organizational Learning Center says "no indigenous culture has yet been found that does not have the practice of sitting in a circle and talking" (Isaacs, 1999, p. xvi).

Today, research confirms that restorative justice is an evidence-based practice that reduces criminal recidivism (Sherman & Strang, 2007), and there is a growing movement to use restorative practices in reentry for incarcerated people returning to the community (Bazemore & Maruna, 2009).

Huikahi Circles Provide a Solution-Focused Approach

While restorative justice provides the theoretical underpinning for the Huikahi Circles, its facilitators utilize solution-focused brief therapy language during the process. Solution-focused therapy acknowledges that a therapeutic process "happens within language and language is what therapists and clients use to do therapy" (de Shazer, 1994, p. 3). In this way, language is used to help people discover their inherent strengths and establish their goals along with ways to achieve them. Insoo Kim Berg, a cofounder of solution-focused brief therapy, assisted in the design of the Huikahi Circle process.

Solution-focused brief therapy is recognized as a *promising* evidence-based intervention by the federal government (OJJDP, 2009). Solution-focused approaches have been successfully used in restorative programs by courts to reduce violence (Walker & Hayashi, 2009). The *Solution-Focused Judging Bench Book* details how a solution-focused approach can assist the courts in administering justice (King, 2009).

Huikahi Circles Apply Public Health Learning Principles

Many corrections experts have called for a "public health" approach to deal with criminal behavior (Zimbardo, 2007; Schwartz & Boodell, 2009), and specifically for dealing with prisoner reentry (Travis, 2005). In addition to a public health approach for traditional prevention uses, public health also offers a rich history for designing optimal learning programs.

Public health educators have worked to improve the health outcomes for populations for generations. "Modern public health practice extends far beyond the historic focus on infectious disease and environmental threats" (Novick & Morrow, 1987, p. 29). Health education is probably one of the oldest and most successful disciplines working to change the behavior of humans. "Both science and social factors form the basis for public health interventions" (Novick & Morrow, 1987, p. 4).

The World Health Organization (WHO) considered and established criteria that health educators should use in working to change behavior (WHO, 1954). WHO specifies that learning is more likely to occur when there is a focus on individuals' goals; uses positive motivation; is provided in group settings; and is offered through experiential activity-based processes. This is consistent with established research by Albert Bandura that *enactive learning* is the most effective learning approach (Bandura, 1997).

Huikahi Circles, and most restorative interventions, apply the criteria recommended by WHO. The circles are based on people's positive motivation to repair harm and to take responsibility for their futures. The circles are group processes, self-directed, goal-oriented, and an active learning experience for participants.

Additionally, Huikahi Restorative Circles meet the "five principles of effective reentry" that corrections reentry expert Jeremy Travis advocates in *But They All Come Back: Facing the Challenges of Prisoner Reentry* (2005). Each of the five principles requires action (p. 324):

1. Prepare for reentry

2. Build bridges between prisons and communities

3. Seize the moment of release

4. Strengthen the concentric circles of support

5. Promote successful reintegration

Huikahi Circles Provide Healing

While crime prevention and decreasing recidivism are important objectives of the Huikahi Circle reentry planning process, an equally important objective is to provide healing for people harmed. Healing for people with incarcerated loved ones is vital. "The victim's physical and emotional wounds must be healed. And the social bonds that connect individuals to one another must be reestablished" (Moore, 1995, p. 241).

Even when the loved ones of imprisoned individuals are not the direct victims of the crime, they often suffer trauma as a consequence of the incarceration. Many lose a vital economic support when their partner or family member goes to prison (Travis & Waul, 2004). Children with incarcerated parents experience serious emotional and physical consequences, such as increased drug use, sleep disturbances, stress, depression, and feelings of guilt and shame (Robertson, 2007).

In addition, recent research on the mental health consequences for victims of violent crime suggests that the traditional criminal justice system's response is often a source of secondary victimization and further trauma. Restorative justice practices are advocated to avoid the detrimental mental health consequences that victims experience as a result of their contact with the adversarial criminal justice system (Parsons & Bergin, 2010). The criminal justice system lacks mechanisms to address the damaging effects that incarceration has on the loved ones of imprisoned people. Just as restorative alternatives are suggested for the immediate victims of violent crime, so too are they appropriate for the other victims of crime—the family and loved ones of the incarcerated individual.

Huikahi Circle Results

From 2005 to 2010, a total of 52 Huikahi Circles were provided. Two incarcerated people had follow-up *re-circles*. A total of 50 incarcerated people,[1] 45 men and five women, had circles. Altogether 280 people (family, friends, prison staff/counselors, and incarcerated individuals) participated in the circles. Following each circle, participants filled out surveys about their experience: 100% of participants reported the circles to be a *very positive* or *positive* experience.[2]

Figure 19.1   Overall Satisfaction With Circle

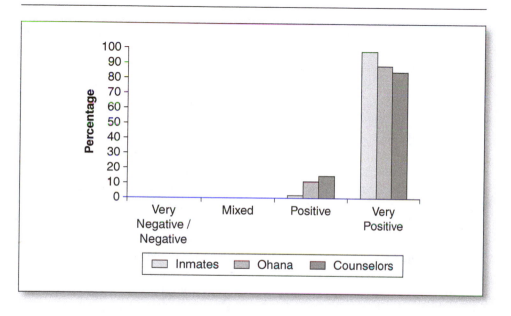

In addition to the full Huikahi circles with loved ones participating, 66 *Modified Huikahi Restorative Circles*, 36 for incarcerated women and 30 for men, were provided in Hawai'i between 2005 and 2012.[3] The modified circles developed as an alternative

---

[1] Two men who applied for circles in prison were out when they had theirs. One was held at his mother's home and one at a church. A juvenile's circle was also held in the family court with his judge participating. The judge commented afterward: "I learned a lot about the process and, most importantly, [the client]."

[2] As of April 2012, 80 circles have been held—five juveniles in Hawai'i have had them—four were in a correctional institution and one youth had his circle at court because he didn't want his family to see him in prison; three circles were held in California for people on probation; one was held in Helsinki, Finland; and one was held in New York. A total 392 people who have participated were surveyed and report 100% satisfaction with the process.

[3] An additional Modified Huikahi Restorative Circle was provided to an incarcerated woman in a California jail as part of a training program for probation officers. The woman, four of her incarcerated friends, and two support people who worked in the jail participated, and all reported the process was very positive. As of January 2012, organizations in New York, California, Virginia, and Texas were working to replicate the circle program in their communities.

for people whose loved ones were unable or unwilling to attend a full circle in a prison (Walker, 2009) and instead other incarcerated supporters participate in the circles.

Approximately 165 incarcerated people have applied for circles during the seven-year period. They mainly learned about the process from other incarcerated people who had circles or applied for one. To date, 37% of the total applicants have been able to have circles. A lack of resources and institutional support prevents delivering all the circles requested. In addition, although all of the circle participants requested a re-circle, only two were provided because of a lack of funding.

Recidivism Results

Samples to date are too small to make any judgments about whether the Circle process prevents repeat crime, but the percentages are promising. For the 2005–2012 period, a total of 23 people who had circles had been out of prison for two years or more. Ten of the 23 were out of prison for three years or more. Of the 23, 16 people (14 men and two women) remained out of prison without any new known charges against them. Seven men are back in prison either for new arrests, new charges, or parole violations. Approximately 70% have not been in contact with the criminal justice system and the remaining 30% have either been charged or convicted of new crimes, or violated the terms of their parole, and are back in prison.

Methodology for determining recidivism rates varies. A 2009 study of people out of Hawai'i prisons for three years revealed an average 54.7% recidivism rate[4] (Hawai'i Interagency Council on Intermediate Sanctions, 2009).

Although the sample size of the Huikahi project is small, and it only reviewed subjects who were out of prison for two years, the 30% recidivism rate is significantly smaller than the overall state 54.7% rate. Because of a lack of support from the former state executive office (Brady & Walker, 2008), the project was unable to provide necessary follow-up contacts and re-circles. In light of the limited services provided, the project's preliminary recidivism rate remains promising, but it is inconclusive that the circles prevent repeat crime.

Satisfaction and Healing Results

Loved ones who participated in Huikahi circles report high levels of satisfaction with the circle process and indicate that they have begun to heal. Of the 169 loved ones who participated during the 2005–2010 period, 124 felt "very positively" and 42 felt "positively" while only three felt "mixed" regarding their forgiveness toward the incarcerated person. In addition, 117 felt very positively, 50 felt positively, and five felt mixed that the Circle

---

[4]This average rate includes people on parole, on probation, and those who were released directly out of prison and "maxed out" without parole or probation. The recidivism rate for people who maxed out was markedly higher at 61.5%.

Figure 19.2 Status of 23 Circle Participants Who Had Been Out of Prison for 2 years

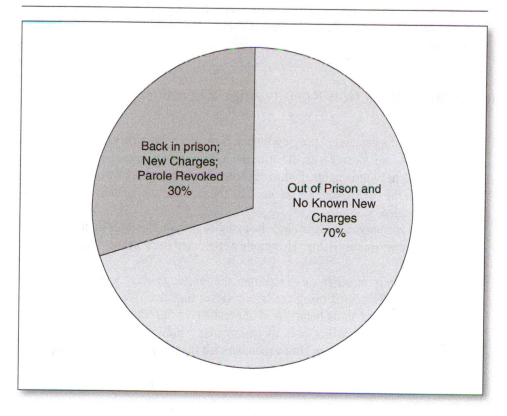

Figure 19.3 Circle Made Participants More Optimistic About Inmate Staying Out of Prison

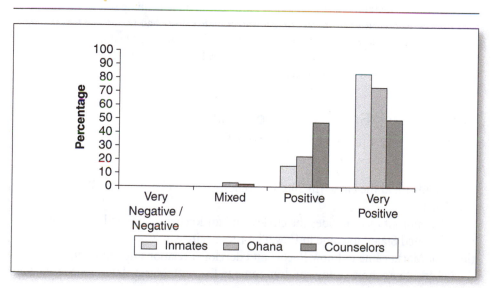

helped them reconcile with the incarcerated person. Participant optimism that the incarcerated loved ones would stay out of prison as a result of the circle was also rated highly.

A telephone survey with loved ones of the men who relapsed, were rearrested, or are back in prison shows that the circle process continues to be highly valued despite the recidivism.

Participant Satisfaction Results After Recidivism

The loved ones of incarcerated people who had Huikahi circles, who were released, and who came back into contact with the criminal justice system continue to believe that the circles had healing benefits. Follow-up with family members revealed that their experiences in the circles were not lessened by the fact that the formerly incarcerated people re-offended.

One family member said, "The circle helped give my son the tools he now has and it taught him how to apply them." This mother attributed her son's re-offending to his drug addiction.

Family members in other cases reported that although their loved one had re-offended, the circles helped bring the family closer together. "We said things in the circle we'd never talked about before," said one relative. In this way, family members see the circles as a benefit to not only the incarcerated individual, but for the family dynamic as a whole. Even when family members felt that they would not participate in a circle again, they reiterated their positive experiences with the process. Many wanted other families and incarcerated people to have the same opportunity to participate in circles.

Additionally, the girlfriend of a man who had a circle in 2005 but relapsed and has been in a private Arizona prison since September 2009, said,

> Without a doubt the circle helped him. It reinforced him maintaining sobriety. It *put the cards on the table* with his other friends who attended. They had no idea he was using, and after the circle we could all talk about how to help him. It helped him stay out of prison for four years. . . . It absolutely helped me heal. I had things I needed to say about how I was affected. The circle validated my feelings."

Huikahi Circles Build and Strengthen Healthy Family Connections and Support

"If we hadn't had the circle [in 2005] I wouldn't have gotten to know Rachel so well," says Marta.

The nonprofit that provides the circles paid for Rachel, who then lived in the continental United States, to come to Hawai'i for Ken's circle. It was through that introduction that Marta came to know Rachel and develop a relationship with her. As a result Rachel and Ken's three young children came to live with Marta. After his release, Ken, along with Rachel, lived with Marta. Since Ken was re-incarcerated, Rachel and the children have continued to live with Marta. Because of the relationship between the two women, which developed through the circle, the three children have lived in a stable home for five years.

"She pays rent and doesn't know it, but I'm saving it all up for her as a little nest egg for when they move out," says Marta.

The circles provide a conduit for building healthy family support among participants who are not incarcerated. Imprisonment harms families and children (Travis, Cincotta McBride, & Solomon, 2005). "Children of imprisoned parents are often described as the forgotten victims of imprisonment" (Robertson, 2007 p. 7). Parental incarceration often creates immediate and long-term problems for children (Travis, et al., 2005).

As Marta and Rachel's experience demonstrates, Huikahi circles offer a way to develop relationships and support that assist children hurt by incarceration. The latest research shows 52% of people incarcerated in state prisons and 63% of people in federal prison are parents of minor children (Glaze & Maruschak, 2008). How these children can be helped should be considered and made a vital feature of prison interventions. Focusing on the individual incarcerated person is insufficient to assist families and communities.

Conclusion

Huikahi circles provide a process for an incarcerated individual and their loved ones to find ways to heal from the harm created by crime and imprisonment. The circle gives all parties an opportunity to give voice to their own experience while collaborating with incarcerated individuals to create a plan that meets their needs for a successful transition back into the community. Even when the incarcerated person is re-incarcerated after a circle, the positive outcomes for families remain significant.

In addition to the need for reconciliation, incarcerated people have other basic needs, including developing and maintaining a support system, locating and keeping housing, and maintaining physical and emotional health as well as staying clean and sober. How they can meet these needs is addressed during the circle. Meeting these basic needs has been shown to shut the "revolving door" of prisons for a significant number of formerly incarcerated people (Howerton, Burnett, Byng, & Campbell, 2009).

"Correctional administrators recognize that it is probation and parole failures, not new prison admissions (due to convictions) that fuel our current prison crowding crisis" (Byrne, Taxman & Young, 2002, p. 15). We need to continue with these endeavors to reintegrate formerly imprisoned people. We must find solutions and stop giving up on people. Especially disturbing is that many people who abuse substances suffer from mental health issues, and a large number of them are in prison (Mumola, 1999). Instead of treating these people like they have health problems, and working toward helping them get well and dealing with their addictions, we have mainly punished and criminalized them. Sadly, and with moral disregard, it seems prison has become the mental health institution of the day in the United States.

The families portrayed in this chapter and who we have had the honor of meeting throughout the seven years of the Huikahi circle program, continue to inspire us with their deep insight and with their unbending love and optimism for their family members who at times seem to love drugs more than their parents and children.

"He is basically a good person. He's just lost and keeps turning to drugs. It breaks my heart. I might have to use *tough love* with him at times, but believe me it is a well of *endless love,* and no matter what, I will never give up on him," said Harold's mother two years after his circle, his relapse, and his return to prison. This hopeful sentiment is the foundation on which to build a successful reentry program.

Critical Thinking Questions

1. What difference has planning and goal setting ever made in your life?

2. What have you ever transitioned from that you think might have benefited from a circle planning process like the one described here? Explain what you transitioned from and how the circle could help. How do you think the circle process might be helpful to anyone else that you know personally or know of generally? Describe who they are, and how a circle might help them.

References

Bandura, A. (1997). *Self-efficacy: The exercise of control*. New York, NY: W.H. Freeman.

Bazemore, G., & Maruna, S. (2009). Restorative justice in the reentry context: Building new theory and expanding the evidence base. *Victims & Offenders, 4*(4), 375–384.

Brady, K., & Walker, L. (2008, summer). Restorative justice is a mandated component of Hawai'i's reentry system. *Justice Connections*, Issue 6.

Braithwaite, J. (2002). *Restorative justice and responsive regulation*. New York, NY: Oxford Press.

Byrne, J., Taxman, F., & Young, D. (2002). *Emerging roles and responsibilities in the reentry partnership initiative: New ways of doing business*. National Institute of Justice report.

De Shazer, S. (1994). *Words were originally magic*. New York, NY: W.W. Norton.

Glaze, L., & Maruschak, L. (2008). *Parents in prison and their minor children*. Bureau of Justice Statistics Special Report NCJ 222984. Retrieved from http://bjs.ojp.usdoj.gov/index.cfm?ty=pbdetail&iid=823

Hawai'i Legislature, House Concurrent Resolution 188 requesting the Department of Public Safety to facilitate the delivery of the Huikahi Restorative Circles program in Hawai'i correctional facilities. 2010. Retrieved from http://www.capitol.hawaii.gov/session2010/lists/measure_indiv.aspx?billtype =HCR&billnumber=188

Howerton, A., Burnett, R., Byng, R., & Campbell, J. (2009). The consolations of going back to prison: What "revolving door" prisoners think of their prospects,

Isaacs, W. (1999). *Dialogue the art of thinking together*. New York, NY: Doubleday.

Journal of Offender Rehabilitation, 48(5): 439–461.

King, M. (2009). *Solution-focused bench book*. Melbourne: Australasian Institute of Judicial Administration Incorporated.

Moore, M. (1995). Building a safer society: Strategic approaches to crime prevention, *Crime and Justice, 19*, 237–262.

Mumola, C. (1999). *Substance abuse and treatment, state and federal prisoners, 1997*. NCJ 172871. Washington, DC: Department of Justice, Bureau of Justice Statistics.

Novick, L., & Morrow, C. (1987). Social and behavioral determinants of health. In *Public health and human ecology*, (pp. 211–242). East Nowalk, CN: Appleton & Lange.

Office of Juvenile Justice and Delinquency Prevention [OJJDP], Model programs guide, Solution-focused brief therapy. Retrieved from http://www2.dsgonline.com/mpg/mpg_program_detail.aspx?ID =712&title=Solution-Focused%20Brief%20Therapy

Parsons, J., & Bergin, T. (2010). The impact of criminal justice involvement on victims' mental health, *Journal of Traumatic Stress, 23*(2):182–188.

Robertson, O. (2007). *The impact of parental imprisonment on children*. Geneva, Switzerland: The Quaker United Nations Office, Geneva, Switzerland. Retrieved from http://www.quno.org/geneva/pdf/humanrights/women-in prison/ImpactParentalImprisonment-200704-English.pdf

Schwartz, S., & Boodell, D. (2009). *Dreams from the monster factory*. New York, NY: Scribner.

Sherman, L., & Strang, H. (2007). *Restorative justice: The evidence*. Cambridge, UK: The Smith Institute.

Travis, J. (2005). *But they all come back: Facing the challenges of prisoner reentry*. Washington D.C.: The Urban Institute Press.

Travis, J., Cincotta McBride, E., & Solomon, A. (2005). *Families left behind: The hidden costs of incarceration and reentry*. Washington DC: The Urban Institute Press Justice Policy Center.

Travis, J., & Waul, M. (2004). *Prisoners once removed: The impact of incarceration and reentry on children, families and communities*. Washington, DC: The Urban Institute Press.

Walker, L. (2009). Modified restorative circles: a reintegration group planning process that promotes desistance, *Contemporary Justice Review*, 12:4, 419–431.

Walker, L., & Hayashi, L. (2009). Pono Kaulike: Reducing violence with restorative justice and solution-focused approaches, *Federal Probation, 73*(1), 23–27.

Walker, L., Sakai, T., & Brady, K. (2006). *Restorative circles: A reentry planning process for inmates*, *Federal Probation*, 70:1. Retrieved from http://www.uscourts.gov/fedprob/June_2006/circles.html

World Health Organization. (1954). *Expert committee on health education of the public*. Technical Report Series, No. 89. Retrieved from http://dosei.who.int/uhtbin/cgisirsi/PdnohFfGsQ/45280102/60/26/X

Zehr, H. (2002). *The little book of restorative justice*. Intercourse, PA: Herald Press.

Zimbardo, P. (2007). *The Lucifer effect: Understanding how good people turn evil*. New York: Random House.

20

Restorative Celebrations for Parolee and Probationer Completion: The Importance of Ritual for Reentry

Lorenn Walker

Under the guidance of internationally respected restorative justice expert John Braithwaite from Australia and criminal desistance expert Shadd Maruna in Ireland, Lorenn Walker, on behalf of Hawai'i Friends of Justice & Civic Education, collaborated with members of the Hawai'i justice system to develop restorative rituals for people who completed parole and probation. Over 150 people have participated in the events including judges; parole board members; parole and probation officers; state and private attorneys; drug treatment counselors; prison staff; police officers; people successfully completing parole; formerly incarcerated people no longer under government jurisdiction; people on parole and probation; and friends and family of people completing parole and other community members. This chapter describes two types of restorative rituals celebrating parole and probation completion and discusses the importance of rituals for effective reentry.

This project provided two types of reentry ritual events. One was a large group event for people completing parole held in the Hawai'i Supreme Court's chamber. Over 50 people attended each of three Parole Completion Celebrations. The other type of event was a Probation Completion Circle. It was a single individualized event for a person successfully completing probation. The man getting off probation, along with his judge and four probation officers, participated in the facilitated event.

Description of Parole Completion Celebration Ritual

"No way my friends are ever going to believe I sat in a circle with the judge who sentenced me and all the rest of you here, and it wasn't an AA meeting!" said a formerly incarcerated man during the Parole Completion Celebration held October 6, 2011. The man participated in the circle as part of a restorative ritual to celebrate the hard work and determination of people who successfully completed parole and to also honor the people working with the justice system who assisted them, especially parole officers.

There have been three Parole Completion events held in the Hawai'i Supreme Court since 2010. Hawai'i's Supreme court building, called *Ali'iolani Hale*, was built in 1874 and since then it has been used for Hawaiian governmental agencies (Fischer, 2011). The elegant two-story gray stone building has marble floors and two spiral staircases leading up to the chamber. A huge glass dome rises from the middle of the building's ceiling. The chamber is furnished with golden koa wood furniture, porcelain fixtures, and antique glass chandeliers.

A total of 150 people attended all three evening events for people who completed parole in 2010 and 2011. Participating members of the justice system including judges, parole board members, lawyers, prison staff and counselors, socialized with the other invited guests, including people being discharged from parole and others still on parole and probation. Many formerly incarcerated people and their loves ones attended. As people came up the two spiral staircases they walked into the lovely entryway to the chamber. It was decorated with huge tropical flower arrangements placed on antique tables. The people mingled in the entryway and enjoyed Mediterranean and traditional Hawaiian food, live Hawaiian music, and traditional hula dancing. Giant painted portraits of Hawai'i's past chief justices, in gold ornate frames, hung on the walls.

With the assistance of the parole office, 25 invitations designed like formal graduation announcements, with stamped RSVP cards included, were provided about a month earlier to people being discharged from parole. Each event participant received a nicely folded program outlining the evening's agenda:

6 p.m.–6:30 p.m.: Arrival, music, and refreshments

6:30 p.m.–6:35 p.m.: Circle opening

6:35 p.m.–6:45 p.m.: Chief Justice Mark E. Recktenwald, presentations

from Hawai'i Friends of Justice & Civic Education to

Judge Leslie A. Hayashi, Judicial Innovation Award

Carlo Fiore, Prison Aftercare Support Award

Jo DesMarets, The Russ Takaki Restorative Parole Officer Award

Ian Crabbe, Restorative Justice Community Award

6:45 p.m.–7:45 p.m.: Sharing in circle: People getting off parole will share whatever they want with the community, and the community will share whatever they want with them

7:45 p.m.–8 p.m.: Circle closing and completion of surveys

An inspiring quote was included on the other side of the printed program. October 2010's program stated

Our history is an integral part of ourselves. As long as we think of the past as the source of our problems, we set up, in a sense, an adversarial relationship within ourselves. The past, very humanly, responds negatively to criticism and blame but favorably to respect and stroking. The past prefers to be seen as a resource, a store of memories, good and bad, and a source of wisdom emanating from Life experience (Ben Furman & Ahola Tapani, *Solution Talk: Hosting Therapeutic Conversations*).

The program for the October 2011 event included this quote:

The promised land may be many things to people. For some it is perfect health and for others freedom from hunger or fear, or discrimination or injustice. But perhaps on the deepest level the promised land is the same for us all, the capacity to know and to live by the innate goodness in us, to serve and belong to one another and to life (Rachel Remen, MD, *My Grandfather's Blessings*).

Parole Completion Celebration Circle

After half an hour socializing and eating, the large group convened in a circle of chairs in the Supreme Court chamber. People sat in any chair they chose. A native Hawaiian opened the circle with a traditional Hawaiian chant.

Next, awards were given to formerly incarcerated people and people who work in the justice system. In 2011 two formerly imprisoned people were recognized for their efforts in helping others re-enter successfully back into the community. An innovative judge and an outstanding parole officer were also given awards.

Of particular importance is the Russ Takaki Restorative Parole Officer Award, given to an especially humane and effective parole officer. The award is named for Russell Takaki, who was the Hawai'i parole office administrator in the early 1970s. Under Takaki's leadership Hawai'i only had a 5% recidivism rate, which was the lowest in the country at that time (Bishop, 1973). Takaki was a well-known surfer and compassionate person who treated people on parole with respect and kindness. "He brought parolees home for dinner, got them jobs, and took them surfing with him" (K. Rogers, telephonic and e-mail communication, March 22, 2010).

By 2009, Hawai'i had long ago abandoned Takaki's approach, and its recidivism rate for formerly imprisoned people had grown to one of the highest in the country

(Hawai'i Legislative Blog, 2009). The Russ Takaki Award is an effort to reward parole officers for embodying practices that work to increase criminal desistance, reduce recidivism, and inspire the justice system.

After the first Parole Completion event, when Takaki's work was again discovered and appreciated, another purpose of the rituals emerged: *the encouragement and recognition of positive parole officer behavior*. After the first event, people working in the system, as well as the consumers of the system, clearly benefited from the positive emotional elements and inspiration for their beneficial and hard work. Both those who participate as recipients of the system and those who provide services benefited from seeing and appreciating the positive effects of their work.

One man who got off parole said he found the event particularly positive because "everyone's stories gave me hope." Another woman said she would remember "everything and to stay on the right path" as a result of the event. Another man said he would remember most "that there is hope in the justice system, and they really do care."

A police officer thought the event was meaningful because it "showed parolees they are not alone." The police also heard compliments for their efforts including, "I want to thank the officers here for saving my life when I was on the streets." Later a prison drug counselor said, "I never heard so much love for our boys in blue!"

Steven Alm, a Hawai'i state judge, former U.S. attorney, and creator of Hawai'i's HOPE probation program (The Pew Center, 2011), has attended all three parole completion events. After the first one he said he was "honored to participate" and what he would remember most: "Great optimism. Great sharing. A shared sense that we are all in this together." After the third event in 2011 Judge Alm said,

> People can change and make better choices in their lives. Parole completion ceremonies are important because they recognize these changes and celebrate them with the parolees and their families in an always moving and inspiring event. Everyone is a winner: the parolee, their families and friends, and society. I have always considered it a privilege to be involved, and I believe it is important for the "graduates" and their families to see judges in this happy and supportive role. Having the chief justice and the head of the Hawai'i Paroling Authority attend and participate demonstrated that compassion and support come from all quarters.

Two other state judges have attended the events since their inception and both strongly support the process. Hawai'i Chief Justice Mark Recktenwald attended the 2011 event and lauded the benefits of restorative justice, saying, "This celebration tonight is to recognize the hard work that the people getting off parole have done and the hard work Hawai'i parole officers and other members of our justice system and the community have done to help them."

The awards were framed 8-by-10-inch original color photographs of Hawai'i nature scenes. Each award was handed out in the circle by the chief justice, who also read a short paragraph of each person's achievements helping people with reentry.

After the awards were given, the circle facilitator said, "Now we will go around the circle, and the people getting off parole can say anything they want to the community here tonight. And the rest of us can say anything we want to the people getting off parole." When parolees introduced themselves, they were given a fresh flower lei, and a copy of either Viktor Frankl's *Man's Search for Meaning* or Mark Nepo's *The Book of Awakening: Having the Life You Want by Being Present to the Life You Have.* Many tears of joy were shed for the inspiring moments during the circle celebrations. Most participants agreed that there was a lot of heartfelt sharing and stories.

Probation Celebration Circle

The single Probation Celebration Circle was for a man successfully finishing probation. It was held with Judge Alm, who had supervised the man's probation, in Alm's courtroom. Four probation officers also attended. The man's two adult children, who planned to attend but could not at the last minute, provided information to the facilitator that was read during the circle. An empty chair was left in the circle signifying the missing children.

The man opened his circle and said that he was most proud of staying off drugs since relapsing 10 months earlier while being on probation. Each of the circle participants, including Judge Alm and the missing children's information, listed the man's strengths or what they liked about him. Next, the man made a plan for how he might make amends and repair harm caused by the behavior that led to his probation. The plan addressed what his children wanted, which was for the man "to stay clean." The man listened to his children's request and made a plan for how he could stay clean, including "dealing with life's adversities; working; have a sponsor, who has a sponsor; attend NA/AA meetings; reach out for help when necessary; make plans to take college classes; continue communicating with my children; practicing nonviolence when angry; and stay busy." To reconcile for harm he caused to the "community at large," the man decided to do the same things he would for his children. The circle ended with the participants complimenting the man on anything they learned about him during the circle or anything else they wanted to say. He closed the circle tearfully, saying, "Thank you for giving me this opportunity to turn my life around and for believing in me." Three probation officers, Judge Alm, and the man were surveyed and reported the process was "very positive." One probation officer rated it as "positive." All believed it could have been better if the man's children had attended.

BASIS OF RESTORATIVE RITUAL PROGRAMS FOR PAROLEES AND PROBATIONERS

The program was provided through Hawai'i Friends of Justice & Civic Education, dedicated to improving the justice system. The program is based on John Braithwaite's and Shadd Maruna's work discussing the power of rituals for rehabilitation, reentry, and restoring relationships after crime and incarceration. Both Braithwaite and Maruna have extensively studied corrections. Both also offered to assist in the development of this pilot program and were contacted for advice and guidance in designing the process and evaluation tools.

The importance of "reintegration" or "transformation" ceremonies for rehabilitation is clear (Braithwaite & Mugford, 1994). People who feel connected to and supported by communities are less likely to commit crimes. Additionally, "a symbolic element of *moral* inclusion" (Braithwaite, 1989) is necessary for effective reentry. Concepts of "atonement, forgiveness, redemption, and reconciliation" are "intangible processes of status elevation" and most likely "critical components of the reintegration process" (Maruna, 2011, p. 4).

"Successful reintegration is a two-way process, requiring both effort on the part of the former prisoner (e.g., desistance, repentance), but also on the part of some wider community (e.g., forgiveness, acceptance). As such, reintegration appears to be an ideal candidate for the implementation of rituals that, by their nature, are supposed to generate feelings of solidarity and community among participants" (Maruna, 2011, p. 13).

Maruna (2011) further reports "that successful rituals would be highly emotional occasions. Collins (2004) emphasizes that an essential outcome of a successful ritual is the generation of 'emotional energy': feelings of confidence and enthusiasm in the participants. Rituals should involve a kind of cathartic, emotional contagion, allowing one to transcend the mundane" (Maruna, 2011, p. 14).

David Wexler, law professor and cofounder of therapeutic jurisprudence (see Chapter 4), advocates judicial use of rituals for rehabilitation (Wexler, 2001). Wexler also notes the value of rituals for improving "professional satisfaction" of judges.

Rituals Must Be Engaging and Relevant for Participants

In addition to providing rituals that support positive emotions, equal care must be made to make rituals engaging and relevant for participants. To be effective, rituals need to support "social psychological dynamics" (Maruna, 2011, p. 22). Rituals should be emotionally satisfying, not boring academic affairs where "distinguished guests" stand behind podiums or tall judicial desks, giving prepared speeches and calling out long lists of names and awarding people certificates. Rituals must be something everyone attending can participate in and feel a part of.

The Parolee Completion Celebration, which included the wider community and the Probation Completion Circle for the individual and his close community of care, met the criteria for effective rituals. Participants in both processes said the events were "highly emotional" and generated "feelings of confidence and enthusiasm in the participants." Additionally, the events were engaging and participatory. Sitting in a circle is more natural and "personally meaningful" for people compared to the typical theatrical audience seating normally used for graduations, weddings, etc. The circle process gives everyone equal voice, not only the professionals or select few. This key aspect of the process is consistent with public health learning principles, restorative practices, and solution-focused approaches, which have been successfully used in reentry and court programs (Walker, 2010; Walker & Hayashi, 2009; King, 2009).

Participant Satisfaction With Parole Completion Ritual

Surveys after all four events asked people to rate and describe their experiences. Of the 81 surveys collected at the parole completion event, only one person complained it was "too long," yet this person rated the event "positive" overall.

Seventy-five of those surveyed reported that the process was "very positive." Five people found it simply "positive," and only one person found it "mixed," a formerly incarcerated man who also said the process was meaningful to him because it showed that "I am not the only one—others feel as I do."

One man getting off parole reported that it was "particularly positive" because of the "recognition of my hard work." This is important considering research that shows recognition for effort is more important for learning and success than validations based on innate personal characteristics (Dweck, 2006).

A woman supporting her son-in-law getting off parole said, "I enjoyed everyone here. I feel sorry for anyone who missed this important milestone for people on or off parole." Many people reported they were surprised by the "care" shown by people working in the justice system and felt that the event was meaningful because of the "camaraderie" and "heartfelt" stories shared. Many people mentioned the value in having the judges attend and sit in the circle. One parolee said the event "solidified my belief in myself and my fellow parolees." Another said, "It feels good inside to be acknowledged and it makes me feel stronger to be sober!" One said he would remember "the joy and love that I've seen in others." Another said, "I appreciate all the positive feedback from the people in authority." Other comments included "being able to show the judiciary system that we can do good"; "recognizing the efforts and accomplishments of people"; "there is hope"; "we are all connected"; "forgiveness for all"; "uncle sharing about forgiveness and healing"; "it was very positive and uplifting"; and "how very elegant people of all economic backgrounds communicated well with each other."

Conclusion

The Parole Completion Celebration will be continued. The judges, people discharged from parole, and all others attending overwhelmingly valued the events. More parole officers will be given the Russ Takaki Award. The parole office and the parole officer who won the previous award will be invited to help select the next awardee. More effort will also go into inviting the people being discharged from parole. The Probation Completion Circle will not be pursued. While it was a positive experience, with a scarcity of resources, we will focus on the people being discharged from parole instead of probation.

Rituals are necessary and powerful. People being discharged from parole need to be symbolically accepted back into the community. They need to be inspired, and the people who work in the justice system need to be inspired too. It is common for professionals to become cynical and jaded, which hurts the system and the people it serves. This ritual disrupts negative perceptions. From the first time the event was held to the third time, more government workers and parolees attended the events. There were stories of parole officers discounting the event, but this will not detract from providing it, rather it motivates providing the program. Our parole office and justice system are a reflection of ourselves and our community. To be a good parole officer today, one is not required to bring parolees home for dinner or take them surfing like Russ Takaki did, but if we want humane parole officers like Takaki, we need to recognize *the Russ Takaki in them*, and celebrate their successes. The same is true for the police, judges, lawyers, and others working in the justice system. Inspiration, joy, and other positive emotions can transform and strengthen our justice system and our lives. This Parole Completion Celebration is a ritual that can help everyone.

Critical Thinking Questions

1. What important rituals have you participated in your life? Which rituals were the most interesting and engaging for you and why?

2. What do you think the people working in the justice system could do to be more effective at preventing repeat crime (reducing recidivism) in working with people on parole, probation, and prison?

References

Bishop, J. (1973). Hawaii's prison reform brings low recidivism. *The Milwaukee Sentinel.* Retrieved from http://news.google.com/newspapers?nid=1368&dat=19731210&id=ds0wAAAAIBAJ&sjid=dxEE AAAAIBAJ&pg=5830,2059328

Braithwaite, J. (1989). *Crime, shame and reintegration.* Cambridge, UK: Cambridge University Press.

Braithwaite, J., & Mugford, S. (1994). Conditions of successful reintegration ceremonies: dealing with juvenile offenders. *The British Journal of Criminology, 34*(2), 139–171.

Collins R. (2004). *Interaction ritual chains.* Princeton, NJ: Princeton University Press, 2004.

Dweck, C. (2006). *Mindset: The new psychology of success.* New York, NY: Random House.

Fischer, J. (2011). Walking tour of historic Honolulu. About.com Guide. Retrieved from http://gohawaii .about.com/od/oahusights/ss/honolulu_walk_a_5.htm

Furman, B., & Ahola, T. (1992). *Solution talk: Hosting therapeutic conversations.* New York, NY: Norton.

Hawai'i Legislative Blog. (2009). *PSD briefs lawmakers on offender reentry plan,* posted by Thelma, January 23, 2009. Retrieved from http://hawaiihouseblog.blogspot.com/2009/01/psd-briefs-lawmakers-on -offender.html

King, M. (2009). *Solution-focused bench book.* Melbourne, Australia: Australasian Institute of Judicial Administration Incorporated.

Maruna, S. (2011). Reentry as a rite of passage, *Punishment & Society, 13*(1): 3–28.

The Pew Center. Hawaii's HOPE Program. Retrieved from http://www.pewcenteronthestates.org/report _detail.aspx?id=56841

Rogers, K. Telephonic and e-mail communications with Lorenn Walker March 22, 2010.

Walker, L. (2010). Huikahi Restorative Circles: Group process for self-directed reentry planning and family healing. *European Journal of Probation, 2*(2), 76–95.

Walker, L., & Hayashi, L. (2009). Pono kaulike: Reducing violence with restorative justice and solution focused approaches. *Federal Probation Journal, 73*(1), 23–27.

Wexler D. (2001). Robes and rehabilitation: how judges can help offenders "make good." *Court Review, 38*(4), 18–23.

PART V

Community Restoration and Reparation

This section of the book takes us to macro-level resolution of conflict in which whole nations are involved in peacemaking, often following the overthrow of governments with a legacy of mass cruelty and oppression. In some cases even more catastrophic events, such as the mass slaughter of whole populations following war, have left a nation in ruins and the people overwhelmed with despair. In order to help heal the nation's wounds, national commissions may be set up to conduct public hearings and take testimony from injured citizens while members of the former regime are held publicly accountable. This form of restorative justice is known as reparative justice when compensation is given to tribes and minority groups whose rights were violated and truth and reconciliation commissions when the process involves lengthy, highly publicized investigations into the wrongs that were committed.

Chapters 21 and 22 both describe truth and reconciliation commissions that were of historic proportions. The most famous of all these commissions, the one that has been emulated by many others, is the peacemaking that took place in South Africa following the end of apartheid. Carl Stauffer and David K. Androff discuss this historic event from different angles. From these historic accounts, the reader will learn of major efforts to restore the peace following horrendous events, such as the genocide of indigenous populations that took place in East Timor (now Timor Leste). And on a much smaller scale, readers will learn of a little-known truth and reconciliation commission that was set up in Greensboro, North Carolina, to resolve hard feelings following racial attacks that were directed against African Americans in that town.

Marta Vides Saade, drawing on international social work organizations, reveals in Chapter 23 how closely the values of the profession of social work coincide with those of restorative justice. This chapter also provides some of the history of how social work moved away from the field of criminal justice and corrections in the United States in the conservative era of the 1980s, but now is showing a renewed interest in this field in light of promising developments, including the proliferation of restorative practices.

The subject of Chapter 24 similarly concerns national attempts to right a wrong that was committed against minority groups, in this case Japanese Americans who were treated as war criminals during World War II on the basis of their ethnicity. Rita Takahashi informs us of the facts surrounding that sad event in American history.

Unique to this book and to the restorative justice literature is Chapter 25 by Fred H. Besthorn. This chapter applies the principles of restorative justice to our natural environment. The focus is on our need to repair the damage that has been done and continues to be done to Mother Earth. Such reparation must be done not through advanced technology, he argues, but through listening to the earth's voice. Traditionally, North American Native populations looked to the earth as teacher. Box 8 by Laura Mirsky describes Native forms of justice geared toward the restoration of balance and harmony as are found in nature.

21

Restorative Interventions for Postwar Nations

Carl Stauffer

Carl Stauffer teaches restorative justice at Eastern Mennonite University and is a colleague of Howard Zehr. His international experience is extensive; Stauffer lived for many years in different parts of the world, including South Africa and Sierra Leone. His expertise is on restorative justice approaches at the post-conflict stage, involving truth and reconciliation commissions.

Introduction: Justice in Transition?

The heavy heat of the tropical afternoon sun was almost as oppressive as the news of blanket amnesty being granted to the rebels who had fought the vicious 12-year civil war in Sierra Leone, a country in West Africa. I was with the Sierra Leone refugee community in 1999, listening with shock to the BBC announcement of total impunity as it crackled and sputtered out of portable transistor radios clutched to the refugees' ears. In silence, I searched for understanding in the haunted and tearing eyes of my refugee friends—people who had seen their families killed, who had their villages pillaged and burned, and many whose limbs were amputated in horrific terror campaigns perpetrated by the rebels. These were broken, heavy-hearted, traumatized people, tired of war.

As they struggled responding to the news, some of their eyes sparked with flashes of rage and vengeance, "If these rebels enter my village, I will kill them!" While many others, with eyes glazed in a hollow stare, shrugged their shoulders saying, "What can we do, this is the only way to have peace—we must figure out how to live together somehow." The injustice of blanket amnesty brought with it another blanket of heavy apathy about the future. The polarizing and paralyzing emotions of revenge on the one hand and apathy on the other were thick in the air. Unable to bridge this emotive chasm, I left the refugee gathering wrestling with my own anger, despair, and despondency. In the darkness of the night, I cried out to God, "There must be a better way—this is not justice—where is real justice in this all?" The foundations of Sierra Leone, struggling to rebuild itself, will crumble if its future generations are resigned to scripts of justified revenge or resigned apathy. We needed another way—a path between violence and hopelessness.

The Sierra Leonean refugees were crying out for justice. But what does justice require? How is justice satisfied? What does justice feel like? Many say justice meets violence with violence—a revenge justice characterized by a visceral form of honoring the memory of the dead who have been immortalized in a premature death (Eisler, 1987; Erenrich, 1997; Girard, 1972; Ignatieff, 1998). The civilized expression of punitive justice comes in the form of state-sanctioned legal retribution in response to illegal violence. This form of retributive justice is the dominant model of the Western legal system. It is based on the notion that punishment results in individual rehabilitation and collective deterrence. Others believe justice comes from a divine command, a universal power beyond humans. Today, Mosaic law and Sharia law are political applications of ancient legal codes and believed to be a direct revelation from God. Others see justice as a human construct, a natural law. This concept emphasizes the rational law of cause and effect. Every action results in a ripple of consequences. "You reap what you sow" illustrates this idea. Social contract theorists including Hobbs (1651), Locke (1689), and Rousseau (1762) are some of the best-known proponents of this form of justice. Still others understand justice as social equity (freedom of choice), rights-based egalitarianism (fairness), and the search for the maximization of the "common good." This is utilitarian or distributive justice (Rawls, 1971; Sen, 2009). Elements of these justice concepts permeate the guiding principles of transitional justice, which aims to reconstruct societies that have experienced mass atrocities.

Transitional justice, which relies on the concepts of restorative justice, involves a range of approaches that nations employ to address past human rights violations. These approaches include trials and prosecution, truth commissions, lustration or vetting, reparations, reintegration of ex-combatants and war-affected populations, and institutional reform. Transitional justice objectives are truth-telling at all levels; giving voice to victims (public platforms that "bear witness" to atrocities); ensuring accountability (perpetrator acknowledgement and responsibility); providing victim and survivor restitution and reparations; and advocating for institutional reforms for the prevention of future violence.

Below, the restorative values and practices of three African nations are examined to evaluate the restorative influence of transitional justice.

South African Truth and Reconciliation Commission

While the South African Truth and Reconciliation Commission (TRC) moved away from blanket amnesty (the primary experience of Latin/South America) and embraced impunity only on the condition of full disclosure of the truth, it overlooked several critical measures. First, it was perceived to be perpetrator-centered as opposed to victim-centered, partly because of the amount of time and attention given to the legal rights and procedures of the amnesty applicants. For example, victim-offender interactions were seriously hampered by the legal constraint confining perpetrators to only discuss the past within the parameters of the amnesty hearings. Perpetrators were liable for any confessions, admissions of guilt, or apologies expressed outside the amnesty hearings in a court of law. The law resulted in a barrier to relationship-building and reconciliation. Secondly, the South African TRC functioned from a top-down approach, which was successful in opening up a robust debate on reconciliation at a national level, but it failed to translate that reconciliation experience in practical application at the local community level. In South Africa, there was no formal interface between the TRC and other traditional indigenous practices of justice, healing, and reconciliation. Thirdly, the South African TRC made a one-time payment of money to victims, which failed to engage perpetrators and communities in creative, meaningful efforts to compensate and make reparations (Van der Merwe, 1999).

The South African TRC teaches three main lessons. First, the legal framework giving the TRC's an inherent perpetrator focus resulted in victims and survivors seeing it as offender-biased. Secondly, it cannot be assumed that a national TRC process can be automatically or easily translated from the state level to the local community. To implement the measures of a "top-down and bottom-up" approach takes intentional and strategic planning, time, and energy. Thirdly, a meaningful transitional justice effort must go beyond confessions, testimony, and apology and must enact tangible (material or structural) compensation and reparation for the general public's satisfaction.

Gacaca Courts in Rwanda

Building on the South African TRC experience, Rwanda took its transitional process a step further and engaged in a local, community-based approach to justice. Gacaca runs parallel, both complementary and supplementary, to the formal legal process of an international tribunal launched previously in Arusha, Tanzania. The Gacaca process involves the community electing nine community leaders who function as third-party judges in each case. These nine community arbitrators are tasked with gathering as much information as possible about the genocide activity in their local village. Then they bring together the survivors, accused offenders, family support networks, and the community at large. Truth telling is core to the process with witnesses corroborating the findings. Opportunities for guilt admissions, confessions, and apologies, as well as survivor-offender mediation and reconciliation, are emphasized throughout the process. The community judges then decide if forgiveness, reduced prison sentences, compensation, or punishment is appropriate. The benefits of Gacaca are myriad, and the world is watching with bated breath to see the potential long-term success of this effort for reconciliation and healing in Rwanda (Wolters, 2005).

Interestingly, some of the most stinging critiques of the Rwandan experience of transitional justice have not been about Gacaca's internal structure or effectiveness but instead the political interference of governmental ideology and policy concerning its definition of "genocide." Vigilant against any language or action that smacks of "genocidal ideology," the Rwandan government has outlawed the use of the ethnic designations of "Hutu" and "Tutsi." It keeps tight surveillance on any organizations that appear to favor one ethnic group over the other. While this is quite understandable, given the ethnic genocide horrors that have transpired in Rwanda, it has had the unintended consequence of silencing a rigorous and honest national debate about ethnicity and genocide (Tiemessen, 2004).

Additionally, in an eagerness to exonerate the government from the horrific 1994 violence and suppress genocide ideology in the country, the ruling party has instituted a rigorous campaign to carefully distinguish the language of genocide (organized violence intent on eliminating an entire ethnic group) from all other forms of violence (mass killings or massacres). On the surface, this linguistic difference seems straightforward, but it has dangerous implications for healing processes. First, it has allowed the ruling Rwandese Patriotic Front (RPF) to excuse itself for past violence, claiming that massacres or mass killings that transpired under its watch were strictly a consequence of war and an effort to stop genocide. Secondly, this definition infers that only Hutus could have had genocidal intentions. Thirdly, as the Gacaca process was set up to deal with the aftermath of genocide specifically and not the past Rwandan violence generally, the Gacaca process implies a bias in favor of Tutsi against Hutu (Mamdani, 2001).

Any process of truth and reconciliation (whether amnesty or prosecution) must maintain an impartial standard for all people and organizations involved in perpetrating gross human rights violations. There must be impartiality regardless of which side one favors or whether or not one claims a moral high ground in violent struggles. Without a demarcation against violence across the board, the mind-set of victors (winners) and vanquished (losers) will persist, which will lead to continued revenge cycles. Finally, failing to treat all perpetrators equally runs the risk of sending the signal that some violence is justified and permissible in transitional justice (Lemarchand, 1994).

Fambul Tok in Sierra Leone

After a brutal, terrorizing 12-year civil war, Sierra Leone instituted a Truth and Reconciliation Commission (TRC) to promote healing and restoration. As part of the negotiated peace settlement, the rebel movement, the Revolutionary United Front (RUF) was granted unconditional amnesty. In response to this amnesty, the United Nations' International Criminal Court instituted prosecutions against the Sierra Leone leaders responsible for crimes against humanity.

The TRC embarked on a truth-telling exercise seasoned with a collective historical re-write and public "'confession-apology-forgiveness'" transactions on the national level. Unfortunately, under the weight of a voluminous final report, the Sierra Leone TRC also struggled to find innovative ways to bring reconciliation to the grassroots level.

One of the most promising responses to this dearth of community-instituted healing processes is the Fambul Tok. In the local Kriol language, this is translated as "Family Talk." Fambul Tok was launched in early 2008 by a Sierra Leonean human rights organization, Forum of Conscience, with support from Catalyst of Peace, a U.S. foundation. Fambul Tok is touted as a community-driven effort that works toward "fostering sustainable peace in Sierra Leone through reviving our communities' traditions and values of confession, forgiveness, and reconciliation." The approach is based on traditional practices of conflict resolution within the family network. Organized and implemented within local villages, the encounters integrate innovative dialogue and healing measures. Called "truth-telling bonfires," the various traditional ceremonies are facilitated by local leaders/elders who provide wisdom, moral structure, and social capital. Following the ceremonies, radio-listening clubs, football games, and communal farming projects furthered healing and reconciliation. Initially, 161 Fambul Tok ceremonies were planned at the chiefdom level around the country, but the approach has spawned a demand for it at all levels of the society. There are plans for thousands of these ceremonies across the nation.

With the Sierra Leonean TRC completed, and the International Criminal Court work ending, Fambul Tok is expected to play a leading role in healing, reconciliation, and peace for the future.

Fambul Tok shows the potential of community-initiated programs over government initiatives to deliver healing, reconciliation, and justice across the nation. Fambul Tok illustrates the energy spark and creative genius of civil society and community-based innovation when allowed to dream and act out a better future.

Transitional Justice Lessons of African Experiences

Out of the African transitional justice experiences, there are a number of critical elements to consider. First, transitional justice is best served when facilitated from within its own indigenous tradition by trusted leaders. Secondly, transitional justice is necessary when there is breach of community harmony, well-being, and order. A communal response to repair the breach must include the victims, offenders, extended families, and the community. Thirdly, culturally appropriate platforms for truth telling, confession, apology, forgiveness, and reconciliation should be explored throughout the process. Fourthly, material forms of reparations, restitution, and compensation are signs of peaceful goodwill and indications of human responsibility and obligation to right the wrongs. Fifthly, symbolic gestures of ritual healing, cleansing, and resolution are an important means of offender reintegration, release for the victim-survivors, and psychosocial closure for all who have been affected by the conflict.

A Values-Based Transitional Justice Model

A restorative approach to transitional justice may be summarized in four guiding values: the need to reconstruct a unifying memory, the need to reestablish a sense of belonging and responsibility, the need to reinvest in a vibrant public participation process, and the need to reengage in a collective healing journey.

The three African cases of postwar reconstruction show that any transitional justice mechanism must be victim-sensitive, responsibility-oriented, community-driven, and compensation-based. These four characteristics are the general guiding principles of practice for transitional justice. Each of these recommended principles are connected to needs trampled on by the systems of violence that perpetrate gross human rights violations. The proposed values-based model is meant to inform the big picture vision, mission, and strategic direction of any transitional justice undertaking. The lessons from other African transitional justice efforts support each of these guiding values that are paired with the four guiding principles of practice.

These interacting values and practice principles could also be applied to the monitoring and evaluating of national and local community justice and reconciliation processes. Integrated justice, healing, and reconciliation approaches are being practiced at local and regional levels in numerous parts of the world (Cobban, 2007; Pouligny, Chesterman, & Schnabel, 2007). The following three case studies provide examples of innovative restorative transitional justice initiatives in Africa.

Case Example 1: Video Dialogue Projects in South Africa

In 1992, the Cape Town community of Crossroads was engaged in a bitter war. The regional peace committee, formed under the National Peace Accord was at a loss to bring the parties together in a forum to discuss the violence. The Media Peace Centre, a Cape Town-based NGO, used the filming of a video as a way to get parties to state their positions and reasons for fighting. This material was shared across the "enemy" lines, and a consensus was built that the film product would be useful if viewed by the adversaries together. This step introduced the notion of video dialogue—the making of a video product as a stimulus to bring parties together to talk, first to the camera and secondly to each other in a facilitated process (Wilgespruit, 1998, p. 2).

The success of the Crossroads experiment gave rise to the same idea in Kathorus, another of the most violent areas in South Africa. The resulting project was called "Simunye (we are one) Dialogues," launched in 1997 by Wilgespruit Fellowship Centre, the Media Peace Centre and Simunye, a community-based organization serving the ex-combatants of the East Rand. Video cameras were given to two former commanders of the militarized youth wings from opposing political groups. These two commanders were to tell their own and their community's story with videos. After this, a process of categorizing, editing, and putting together of one story from two was undertaken. This was a difficult and taxing process as each of these young commanders had to play down their perceived deep prejudices, myths, and stereotypes in order to produce a new joint reality that was acceptable to all.

The product of this effort was a one-and-one-half-hour video that openly and candidly outlines and analyses the past and current conflicts and offers solutions from all stakeholders. This video was successfully screened in April 1997 to a large number of community leaders. Following this, public viewings were conducted for different segments of the community, after which participants were divided into commissions and a facilitated dialogue was engaged in. This follow-on process used community resources—facilitators, video machines, church and school halls, and caterers—to interact with groups who otherwise would not have talked to each other. The overarching aim of the project was to promote a broad-based unity, restore a sense of community and assist the Kathorus community to recognize its divisions. Philip Visser, project coordinator, explained the mission:

> Through this process of visually recording the past, interlocking spheres of dialogue are constructed—slowly building understanding, restoring humanity, and initiating a process of reconciliation towards peace, respect, tolerance, and a joint future (Visser, 1998).

Case Example 2: The Brian Mitchell Story—South Africa

On Sunday, April 27, 1997, in front of about 500 community members, former police officer Brian Mitchell committed himself to rebuilding the community at Trust Feed in KwaZulu-Natal where he was involved in the massacre of 11 people in 1987. Mitchell, who was station commander at a nearby police station at the time, was sentenced to 30 years in jail for his role in the attack. He was released from prison in December 1996 after receiving amnesty from the TRC. Mitchell had a spiritual conversion in prison and expressed his sorrow to the victim's families at his amnesty hearing. He then went on to express a willingness to meet with the community to make things right. Mitchell had also expressed the wish to reunite the Trust Feed community and assist in its healing in his amnesty application. The TRC arranged this momentous meeting.

The meeting procedure was simple. It started with prayer and singing. Then community members were invited to tell their stories and ask Mitchell questions. In return, he made a statement and responded to the community's queries. Community reactions varied from anger and grief to amazement that Mitchell had the courage and bravery to face the community and how rare it was to have a former perpetrator ask for forgiveness. Although Mitchell was unemployed at the time, he committed himself to work with government, his church, and other community agencies on behalf of the community.

Bartsch and Bartsch (1997) have described the meeting's aftermath:

> The meeting ended after four hours. An old man with a cane had been listening intently from the front row. He walked forward with halting steps, took the microphone and praised the TRC for setting up this meeting. He also thanked Brian Mitchell for his bravery in coming to the community. He said he felt relieved that the process of reconciliation had begun. People then peacefully dispersed. It seemed that a start had been made. It seems that when this kind of face-to-face meeting occurs, when confession is made, when people acknowledge the humanity of one another, when the offer of restitution is made and carried out, then reconciliation can begin. Our hope and prayer is that it might happen in many more communities and in the hearts of individuals as well.

This was not the last time the Trust Feeds community ever saw Brian Mitchell. In the Pietermaritzburg Agency for Christian Social Awareness (PACSA) Easter 1999 newsletter, a short article was printed under the title "Reconciliation in Action." Above a picture of Brian Mitchell and a community woman shaking hands, the caption read, "Reconciliation Day [December 16, 1998] . . . saw a service of reconciliation in commemoration of the Trust Feed massacre. . . . The top left photo shows Mrs. Makhoba Idah telling Mr. Brian Mitchell, "'I forgive you, Brian. . . .'" Two years later, Mitchell was continuing to help rebuild the Trust Feeds community.

Case Example 3: Mashona and Matableland Reconciliation in Zimbabwe

Independent Zimbabwe suffered under severe political violence and repression from 1980 to 1987 (the Gukuruhundi period) and again from 2000 to 2008. In the early 1980s, violence was unleashed on the region of Midlands and Matabeleland in an effort to eliminate the chief opposition party, ZAPU. Approximately 20,000 people were massacred during this time (CCJP/LRF, 1997). The second period of severe violence was related to the groundswell of opposition from across the nation against the ruling ZANU-PF party because of human rights violations, financial collapse, and land redistribution. A transitional government currently governs Zimbabwe and a long-awaited "free and fair" election is scheduled for 2012. Despite the fact that Zimbabwe has not politically moved into a period of official transitional justice, many efforts to find justice and build peace are occurring at all levels of society. One hopeful initiative is described by two respondents from Matabeleland (the first from a facilitator's perspective and the second from a community leader's).

The facilitator's account:

> We are also taking pastors and leaders from Mashonaland into the deep areas of Matabeleland to meet with key leaders and to hear from community leaders what happened and for them to share what happened. And we have had a number of these. Such as one we did about five months ago, where out of about 300, over 300 people, there was not even one person who was not crying in that meeting, including these Shonas. And one elderly Shona pastor said, "I wish I could find a hole where I can hide; I can't take it anymore. Please don't continue to talk. I'm so ashamed, and I can't even stand in front of you. I'm ashamed of being a Shona." And for an Ndebele, one Ndebele elderly man stood up and he said, "Now I can die because I know and I have seen with my own eyes and heard with my own ears that there are real people in Mashonaland."

The community leader remembers

> I have been involved in this program of peace-building for the almost five years up to now. And we have been really trying to negotiate that to our own people. We even went to a point of inviting Shona pastors to come and see, even listen to these stories being told by the victims from that end. And [in the] last two months we had a service at Zbonkululu whereby we received around seventeen pastors from Mashonaland. They came to us; they gave people some chances to say out what really transpired. At the end we asked those

guys from Mashonaland, maybe to apologize on behalf their counterparts, the Shona-speaking people ... what they really did at Matabeleland. At least because of that service that took place, really people have started just forgetting some of these things.

Conclusion

The impact of these interventions is often confined to small numbers of beneficiaries who are scattered in isolated locations. It would be more beneficial if these kinds of approaches reached a wider constituency of nations, regions, and their war-affected populations. Additionally, public government and private donor partnerships would provide the necessary resources and encouragement to carry this work forward. In these troubled times, we can easily find ourselves on either end of the polemics of revenge or apathy in response to our political and legal justice needs. There is a third way—an innovative alternative process of restorative transitional justice that utilizes the social, spiritual and cultural resources of communities to transform individuals and societies who have been affected by severe violence. This is truly our only viable option for the future. Generational justice requires that we leverage a restorative approach that is able to respond to a death-dealing world with a life-giving reality. This is our hope for justice amidst the rubble.

Critical Thinking Questions

1. What can other countries learn about restorative justice proceedings from the three African nations discussed here?

2. How might transitional justice approaches be applied today for peacemaking in countries with recent rebellions and civil wars?

References

Bartsch, Karl, & Bartsch, Evelyn. (1997, October). A journey towards reconciliation. *Southern Africa Regional Newsletter*. (A publication of the Mennonite Central Committee), Number 43.

Catholic Commission for Justice and Peace (CCJP) and the Legal Resources Foundation (LRF). (1997). Breaking the silence. Building true peace: A report on the disturbances in Matabeleland and the Midlands 1980–1988. Harare, Zimbabwe: Author.

Cobban, H. (2007). *Amnesty after atrocity? Healing nations after genocide and war crimes*. Boulder, CO: Paradigm Publishers.

Ehrenreich, B. (1997). *Blood rites: Origins and history of the passions of war*. New York, NY: Metropolitan Books: Henry Holt.

Eisler, R. (1987). *The chalice and the blade: Our history, our future*. New York, NY: HarperCollins.

Girard, R. (1972). *Violence and the sacred* (Translated by Patrick Gregory). Baltimore, MD, and London, England: The John Hopkins University Press.

Hamber, B. (2009). *Transforming societies after political violence*. London/New York: Springer.

Hobbs, T. (1651). *Leviathan*.

Ignatieff, M. (1998). *The Warrior's Honour: Ethnic War and the Modern Conscience*. New York, NY: Henry Holt.

Lemarchand, R. (1994). Burundi: Ethnic conflict and genocide. Cambridge, MA: Woodrow Wilson Center Press and Cambridge University Press.

Locke, J. (1689). *Second treatise on government*.

Mamdani, M. (2001). *When victims become killers: Colonialism, nativism, and the genocide in Rwanda*. Oxford: James Curry.

Penner, D. (2000). Explaining systems: Investigating middle school students' understanding of emergent phenomena. *Journal of Research in Science Teaching, 37*(8), 784–806.

Pouligny, B., Chesterman, S., & Schnabel, A. (2007). *After mass crime: Rebuilding states and communities*. Tokyo, Japan: United Nations University Press.

Rawls, J. (1971). *A Theory of Justice*. Cambridge, MA: Harvard University Press.

Rousseau, P. (1762). *The social contract*.

Sen, A. (2009). *The idea of justice*. Cambridge, MA: The Belknap Press of Harvard University.

Tiemessen, A. (2004). After Arusha: Gacaca justice in post-genocide Rwanda. *African Studies Quarterly, 8*(1). Retrieved from http://web.africa.ufl.edu/asq/v8/v8i1a4.htm

Van der Merwe, H. (1999). The truth and reconciliation commission and community reconciliation: An analysis of competing strategies and conceptualizations (Doctoral dissertation). Fairfax, VA: George Mason University.

Visser, P. (1998, December). The media as conflict intervener: Using video dialogue in Thokoza. *Track Two Newsletter*.

Wilgespruit Fellowship Centre. (1998). Participation in Kathorus media dialogue process. Proposal to the International Committee of the Red Cross (ICRC).

Wolters, S. (2005). The gacaca process. *African Security Review, 14*(3). Retrieved from http://www.iss.co.zapubs/ASR/14No3/AWWolters.htm.

22

Truth and Reconciliation Commissions and Transitional Justice in a Restorative Justice Context

David K. Androff

David K. Androff, assistant professor of social work at Arizona State University, draws on his exhaustive research on the workings of the Truth and Reconciliation Commission in Timor Leste, a country ravaged by foreign occupation by Indonesia. Covered in this chapter are a description of guidelines provided by the UN and attempts at international peacemaking following the end of apartheid in South Africa, genocide of indigenous populations in East Timor (now Timor Leste), and mass racial violence in Greensboro, North Carolina.

Androff has shown in his previous writings how the social work value of self-determination is represented in cultural determination through the building on indigenous traditions of justice as forms of reconciliation. This value is also represented here.

The horrors of war, violence, and conflict result in millions of deaths every year. Ethnic conflict, religious strife, and political repression are the settings of massive human rights violations around the world. The tragic consequences extend beyond the loss of life, and include population displacements, the outbreak and spread of disease, economic losses, and profound social and psychological suffering. How can people and societies recover from such violence? What can a restorative justice based intervention offer to this endeavor? This chapter presents one such intervention, the truth and reconciliation commission (TRC), and uses case studies from relevant TRCs to illustrate their possibilities and potential.

Following World War II, the Nuremburg War Crimes Trials set the precedent for criminal prosecutions to be the international community's preferred method for addressing human rights violations. Since then, the field of transitional justice has emerged to address the complicated questions of justice in post-conflict settings, to address the violence and enable societies to move forward. Justice-oriented interventions are employed to right previous wrongs, contribute to reconciliation, and most importantly, to prevent future recurrences of violence and injustice. Post-conflict reconstruction is a related field that addresses efforts to rebuild communities and societies after mass violence and political repression. Post-conflict reconstruction includes efforts to maintain security, provide humanitarian relief, and attend to the needs of refugees, as well as efforts to rebuild infrastructure, public services, and encourage economic development. These interventions include war crimes trials and tribunals, the International Criminal Court, hybrid trials, truth-seeking projects, and reparations. The United Nations has published principles and guidelines for transitional justice projects (UN, 2010).

There is much debate about which interventions are most effective at rebuilding societies, and the international community has struggled to find acceptable, affordable, and sustainable ways to help communities recover from violence. While criminal prosecutions of war crimes are still an important transitional justice tool, over time several limitations with the traditional retributive justice approach have emerged. In a range of post-conflict settings, trials can be politically unfeasible, and the rule of law is often weak, underdeveloped or suffering from corruption. There are problems of jurisdiction, and the evidentiary rules governing court proceedings can limit investigation into the nature of human rights violations. Furthermore, trials are not victim-centered. In response to these problems, truth and reconciliation commissions have emerged as a restorative justice-based alternative to assist societies confront their past and are now considered a core transitional justice intervention.

Truth and Reconciliation Commissions

Truth and Reconciliation Commissions are temporary bodies that investigate past human rights abuses (Hayner, 2001). TRCs incorporate restorative justice principles by responding to victims' needs, involving multiple stakeholders, and attending to the social harm and fractured relationships caused by violence, but they can also include multiple forms of justice (Androff, 2010a). Each TRC is distinct and adaptable to local historical, political, social and cultural contexts. TRCs attempt to prevent future violence primarily through truth seeking and reconciliation. The truth-seeking function of TRCs aims to establish knowledge about the nature and extent of human rights violations through in-depth investigations including the testimony of victims, perpetrators, and community members (Chapman & Ball, 2001). Clarifying the details about violence and oppression presents opportunities for individual and collective recovery from trauma through providing acknowledgement and validation for victims and correcting the historical record. Documenting human rights abuses can also provide evidence for prosecutions as well as countering propaganda, stereotypes, and dehumanization that facilitate cycles of violence, injustice, and oppression. Unearthing the previously silenced voices of victims in a supportive environment can contribute to the narrative healing of victims from trauma by satisfying the desire to tell their stories and providing a measure of emotional relief or catharsis (Androff, in press). TRCs disseminate detailed accounts of their findings in the form of a final report that can serve to educate society about abuses and injustices that the wider public may not know about or fully accept and outline specific recommendations for institutional reform, the promotion of justice and accountability, and a platform for social recovery.

TRCs also attempt to promote reconciliation in divided communities. Reconciliation connotes dialogue and mutual tolerance between opposing groups (Minow, 1998). The social contact hypothesis of intergroup relations holds that antagonistic groups can experience cooperation and trust through interaction and dialogue (Gibson, 2004). TRCs promote reconciliation through public hearings, community restorative ceremonies, reparations, and restitution. TRCs often employ local community justice and conflict resolution strategies such as indigenous or traditional models of reconciliation and restoration. Androff (2010b) developed a model of interpersonal reconciliation based on TRCs that includes interdependent components of cognitive-affective reconciliation or changes in a person's thoughts, beliefs, attitudes, or feelings; behavioral reconciliation, or specific actions, and gestures; acknowledgements, or apologies, and social reconciliation; or the acknowledgment of another person's behavioral reconciliation.

Case Examples of Truth and Reconciliation Commissions

The following case examples are presented to illustrate the complexity, variety, and breadth of TRCs. The selected cases describe the most famous TRC, a local adaptation of a TRC in the Global South, a grassroots TRC in the U.S., and another TRC in a Western context with an innovative focus.

SOUTH AFRICA

The most famous and arguably most successful TRC is the South African Truth and Reconciliation Commission. Prior to South Africa, many TRCs in Africa and Latin America were perceived as failures and reinforced the international community's preference for war crimes trials. The South African TRC is credited with contributing to the peaceful transition from apartheid to democracy and has inspired dozens of TRCs around the world.

In 1994, the South African transition from apartheid to democracy ended decades of racial discrimination policies and violent subjugation. The negotiated peace agreement between the outgoing white apartheid government and the mainly black opposition political party established a TRC. The TRC was the result of a political compromise, necessitated by the high levels of interracial coexistence between formerly antagonistic groups, a solution short of criminal prosecutions that included amnesty for perpetrators as an incentive for their participation while providing the means to officially investigate politically motivated crimes (Gibson, 2004). The South African TRC was based on the African cultural concept of collectivity, called *ubuntu*, which loosely translates as "I am made human through my relationships with others" (Minow, 1998). Conditional amnesty was granted to perpetrators who fully disclosed the truth behind politically motivated crimes; this truth telling aided victims and their families in learning the details of how their loved ones suffered. Perpetrators who were denied amnesty were referred to the courts for prosecution. To promote this message, the South African TRC used the slogan "revealing is healing."

The South African TRC, chaired by Archbishop Desmond Tutu, included a reparations component that provided therapeutic services and material restitution for victims. The reparations wing suffered from a lack of resources and was criticized as insufficient. These criticisms underscore the limitations of truth seeking and reconciliation without concomitant social change. A common complaint about the South African TRC by the predominantly poor black African population was "you can't eat reconciliation." One TRC commissioner tells a story that illustrates the problem; after a white South African stole a bicycle from a black South African, the bicycle thief came forward to the TRC, made a statement, and apologized for his crime. The victim accepted the apology and then asked, but where is my bicycle? These limitations have encouraged subsequent TRCs to place greater emphasis on reparations and restitution for victims, as well as promoting economic development that can meet the basic needs and social welfare of communities struggling to recover.

TIMOR-LESTE

Timor-Leste, the newest nation in Asia, occupies the eastern half of a small island at the edge of the Indonesian archipelago. In 1975, Portugal withdrew after centuries of colonial rule, and after nine days of Timorese independence, Indonesia invaded and forcibly annexed Timor-Leste (Androff, 2008). The Indonesian occupation lasted until 1999 and was characterized by mass killings, rapes, displaced population, and famine (Nevins, 2005). Democratic reforms in Indonesia in the late 1990s led to a Timorese referendum on independence. Despite widespread intimidation by the Indonesian military and pro-Indonesian Timorese militias, the Timorese voted overwhelmingly for independence. As the Indonesian forces withdrew, many Timorese were massacred, thousands were forced into Indonesia, and infrastructure and cities were destroyed. United Nations peacekeepers were deployed and established a transitional government. The Democratic Republic of Timor-Leste assumed authority in 2002 and launched a TRC to examine the consequences of the occupation and to promote reconciliation.

The Timor-Leste TRC, called the Commission for Reception, Truth, and Reconciliation (CAVR) was mandated with facilitating the return of 220,000 Timorese refugees from Indonesia, establishing the truth about the human rights violations during the Portuguese decolonization and Indonesian occupation, and contributing to healing and reconciliation (CAVR, 2005). The CAVR was funded by UN and international donors, staffed by Timorese and international personnel, and led by seven Timorese commissioners. The CAVR conducted 52 public hearings across the country, collected over 7,000 statements from victims, and held national hearings on women's rights and healing where small sums were distributed to victims as symbolic reparations. The CAVR fulfilled the restorative justice principle of restoring human dignity to victims by eliciting their stories and acknowledging their suffering through their testimony at public hearings and in their statements.

The main reconciliation initiative of the CAVR was a local, culturally based restorative justice intervention to reintegrate former pro-Indonesian Timorese militia members into communities (Androff, 2008). Although most TRCs focus on reconciliation at the national level among political elites, the Community Reconciliation Process (CRP) was unique in its focus on the less serious crimes committed by militia members who were unable to face their victims and return home to their villages. The CRP built upon a traditional system of conflict resolution that was a village-based participatory process involving local leaders and elders, perpetrators, victims, community members, the courts, and CAVR representatives (Babo-Soares, 2004; Ximenes, 2004). As a restorative justice intervention, CRP ceremonies enabled perpetrators to admit responsibility for their crimes, publicly apologize, face their community, and listen to the anger, frustrations, and experiences of their victims. CRP ceremonies incorporated drumming, rituals to summon ancestors, and the use of symbolic woven mats that bound disputing parties together and solidified the final agreements. The dialogue between victims and perpetrators resulted in a determination of what act of reconciliation was required of the perpetrator to repair the social fabric, usually some form of restitution or community service. The CRP ceremonies aided thousands of former militia members to reintegrate into their villages and prevented renewed violence by settling residual anger through accountability. The CRP component of the CAVR is a powerful example of how a TRC can be adapted to the local cultural context to engage in reconciliation and social recovery from violence.

GREENSBORO, NORTH CAROLINA

The Greensboro Truth and Reconciliation Commission (GTRC) was the first TRC to be adopted in the United States and is also significant because it was completely grassroots and community based, operating without any government support or official sanction (GTRC, 2006). The GTRC was a restorative justice based response to an incident of racial violence. On November 3, 1979, a group of Ku Klux Klan (KKK) and American Nazi Party members drove to a demonstration by labor union activists in a low-income and African American neighborhood of Greensboro, North Carolina. The activists, with ties to the Communist Workers Party, had been organizing workers in local textile mills and had confronted the KKK earlier that year. The KKK and Nazis fired into the crowd, killing five demonstrators and injuring 10 others in what became known as the Greensboro Massacre. Following the attack, city authorities harassed the victims, placed them under surveillance, prevented subsequent protests, and pressured local media to distort the coverage to frame the violence as an equal shootout between two radical fringe groups rather than a one-sided attack. All-white juries acquitted the perpetrators in two criminal trials, although the attack was videotaped in broad daylight. Many suspected police complicity as an informant for the police and FBI had knowledge that the attack was planned, and the lack of meaningful justice after the violence negatively affected life in Greensboro.

The survivors continued to work to discover the truth behind the attack and for justice. In 1985, they won a federal civil suit against the perpetrators and the Greensboro Police Department for the wrongful death of one of the victims and established civil rights and social justice organizations. In 1999, influenced by the success of the South African TRC, local community organizations, consultants from the NGO International Center for Transitional Justice, and philanthropic groups began to organize a reinvestigation of the Greensboro Massacre. In 2004, the Greensboro Truth and Reconciliation Commission (GTRC) was launched with a mandate to examine the causes and consequences of the violence. The GTRC collected about 200 statements from victims, perpetrators, and community members and held three public hearings on the events leading up to the violence, the events of November 3, 1979, and the consequences of the violence (Androff, in press). In 2006, the GTRC released a final report with comprehensive findings and recommendations for institutional reform. Although the GTRC was focused on the violence of one day, the Greensboro Massacre became a lens through which to investigate patterns over decades of racism, antiunion activity, KKK activity, the legacy of slavery, and the struggle to organize for social and economic justice (Magarrell & Wesley, 2008).

The lack of official sanction of any government agency presented limitations for the GTRC. Chief among them was the inability to compel the participation of individuals and to obtain official records. Several documents released to the GTRC from federal agencies were substantially redacted, hindering the truth-seeking effort. The city government actively resisted the GTRC, claiming that racial problems in the city's past were irrelevant to contemporary life and that by dredging up the old issues, Greensboro's good image was harmed. Further, the reaction of the wider community was mixed; there was a lot of support in the form of donations and volunteers, but many in Greensboro were confused by, ignorant of, or critical of the GTRC. While the majority of GTRC participants were victims and supportive community members, a handful of perpetrators, even those critical of the GTRC, decided to participate to ensure their side of the history was told. One former Nazi expressed remorse and apologized to the widow and son of the demonstrator that he had murdered at the massacre. Some felt that the failure of more perpetrators to participate and disclose more details about law enforcement complicity in the attack hindered reconciliation (Androff, 2010b).

While the GTRC lacked formal sanction from authorities, the grassroots TRC did have a sort of moral force, a community-based sanction with its own authority. For the participants, the GTRC was a powerful example of participatory democracy, of what ordinary citizens could achieve facing their community's past in spite of government opposition. Although the GTRC was a limited success, many participants felt that the mere presence of people who used to be killing each other together in the same room without violence demonstrated the potential for reconciliation built on mutual tolerance and peaceful coexistence. The GTRC made important contributions as a community-based restorative justice intervention, and the grassroots coalitions forged in the creation and implementation of the GTRC have continued to work for political and social change in Greensboro.

CANADA

The Canadian Truth and Reconciliation Commission addresses the legacy of the Indian Residential Schools that operated from 1874 until 1996 (www.trc.ca). The Indian Residential Schools were part of a national policy of forced assimilation and the suppression of cultural identities of indigenous populations in Canada. The residential schools, first run by churches and charity organizations and later by the state child welfare systems, separated First Nations, Inuit, and other Aboriginal and indigenous children from their families and placed them into institutional boarding schools aiming to "kill the Indian in the child." Children were forbidden to speak their native languages or practice their cultural beliefs, and many cases of physical and sexual abuse occurred in the schools. Thousands of children died in the schools as a result of the abuse, inhumane living conditions, disease, and malnutrition. This experience was deeply traumatic to the indigenous populations of Canada, which continue to struggle with numerous social problems such as high rates of poverty, disease, family violence, substance abuse, and overrepresentation in the child welfare and criminal justice systems.

Years of advocacy and legal suits on behalf of indigenous communities and survivors of the Indian Residential Schools culminated in the 2006 Indian Residential Schools Settlement Agreement. This judicial agreement included reparations for survivors in the form of a lump sum "common experience payment" for anyone who spent time in a residential school and more money for those who spent multiple years in a school as well as a special fund for victims of physical and sexual abuse. To address cultural and collective harms and to ensure acknowledgment of the legacy of the Indian Residential Schools, additional funds were established for healing and commemorative programs promoting spiritual renewal, public education, memorials, and museums. The agreement also created a TRC to allow victims to testify and unearth their previously silenced stories, to encourage the validation of their experiences, and to provide a measure of emotional relief or healing.

The Canadian TRC is unique as the first TRC to be established at the national level in a Western democracy, the first to be established through a judicial decision, and the first to focus on indigenous rights and colonial harms. The Canadian TRC, whose work is ongoing, also faces significant challenges, including delays, changes in personnel, funding cuts, tension between the twin goals of accountability for perpetrators and reconciliation or healing, and ensuring that the process is viewed as legitimate by victims and satisfies their needs. Further, this TRC comes relatively late in terms of the abuses committed, and many of the survivors are passing on without the opportunity to participate. However, the Canadian TRC presents an opportunity to raise awareness of atrocities committed against indigenous peoples, and hopefully will lead to increased political power and social change for the indigenous population of Canada.

Conclusion

Truth and reconciliation commissions are important restorative justice tools in the field of transitional justice with great relevance for criminal justice and social welfare (Androff, 2010a). As evidenced by these case examples, TRCs are continuing to evolve as an intervention and continuing to inspire truth seeking, truth telling, and reconciliation programs. Communities around the world are considering implementing TRCs in Northern Ireland, the Balkans, New Orleans, and elsewhere in the southeastern United States. Descendants of a U.S. family of preeminent slave profiteers have called for a TRC to grapple with their role in the trans-Atlantic slave trade and the U.S. legacy of enslavement. The recent TRCs in North America raise the question of how the lack of a political transition affects the work of truth-seeking and reconciliation. TRCs in the context of Western democracies may be more likely to face challenges of resistance or co-option by political elites. However, they also present greater opportunities for civil society to engage in the process of facing historical injustice and building a socially just future through restorative justice.

Critical Thinking Questions

1. Senator Patrick Leahy (D-Vermont), the chairman of the Senate Judiciary Committee, made national news in 2009 when he called for a TRC to investigate torture, questionable interrogation techniques, and wrongdoings committed in the "war on terror." Do you think such a TRC would be beneficial or successful?

2. Poverty is often the context for violence; addressing material deprivation and economic development is a core aspect of post-conflict reconstruction. TRCs have struggled to attend to the material needs and social welfare of victims, but these efforts are complicated by politics and scarce resources. What international guidelines should be implemented for reparations to meet victims' needs?

References

Androff, D. (2008). Working in the mud: Community reconciliation and restorative justice in Timor-Leste. In K. van Wormer (Ed.), *Restorative Justice across the East and West* (pp. 123–44). Hong Kong: Casa Verde Publishing.

Androff, D. (in press). Narrative healing and truth and reconciliation commissions: The impact of the Greensboro Truth and Reconciliation Commission. *Families in Society*.

Androff, D. (2010a). Truth and reconciliation commissions (TRCs): An international human rights intervention and its connection to social work. *British Journal of Social Work, 40*(6), 1960–1977.

Androff, D. (2010b). "To not hate": Reconciliation among victims of violence and participants of the Greensboro Truth and Reconciliation Commission. *Contemporary Justice Review, 13*(3), 269–285.

Babo-Soares, D. (2004). Nahe Biti: The philosophy and process of grassroots reconciliation (and justice) in East Timor. *The Asia Pacific Journal of Anthropology, 5*(1), 15–33.

Chapman, A., & Ball, P. (2001). The truth of truth telling: Comparative lessons from Haiti, South Africa, and Guatemala. *Human Rights Quarterly, 23*(1), 1–43.

Commission for Reception, Truth, and Reconciliation (CAVR). (2005). Chega! The report of the Commission for Reception, Truth, and Reconciliation. Dili, Timor-Leste: CAVR. Retrieved from http://www.cavr-timorleste.org/en/chegaReport.htm

Gibson, J. (2004). *Overcoming apartheid: Can truth reconcile a divided nation?* New York, NY: Russell Sage Foundation.

Greensboro Truth and Reconciliation Commission (GTRC). (2006). Greensboro Truth and Reconciliation Commission report. Retrieved from www.greensborotrc.og.

Hayner, P. (2001). *Unspeakable truths: Confronting state terror and atrocity.* New York, NY: Routledge.

Magarrell, L., & Wesley, J. (2008). *Learning from Greensboro: Truth and reconciliation in the United States.* Philadelphia, PA: University of Pennsylvania Press.

Minow, M. (1998). *Between vengeance and forgiveness: Facing history after genocide and mass violence.* Boston, MA: Beacon.

Nevins, J. (2005). *A not-so-distant horror: Mass violence in East Timor.* Ithaca, NY: Cornell University Press.

United Nations (UN). (2010). United Nations approach to transitional justice. Guidance note of the Secretary-General. Retrieved from http://www.unrol.org/files/TJ_Guidance_Note_March_2010FINAL.pdf

Ximenes, F. B. (2004). *The unique contribution of the community-based reconciliation process in East Timor.* New York, NY: International Center for Transitional Justice, Institute for Justice and Reconciliation.

23

Social Work Values and Restorative Justice

Marta Vides Saade

Marta Vides Saade is associate professor, Law Society Program, Ramapo College of New Jersey. She has dual qualifications in theology and law. Formerly, Vides Saade was managing attorney at Legal Services for Children in San Francisco, California, where she worked in attorney/social worker teams in the representation of children. She currently serves as consultant for Eseñanza en Educación Jurídica, Programa, a USAID sponsored project (2011) in Monterrey, México. This organization trains lawyers, judges, and law professors in the implementation of a reformed criminal code, which in some Mexican states includes explicit restorative justice alternatives consistent with indigenous values. This chapter uniquely uses the concept of Shalom *to link social work values and those of restorative justice. Included in this chapter as Box 7 are guidelines that are helpful for social workers to have to help crime victims who could benefit from a restorative justice process.*

At the core of social work is a belief that individuals have the capacity to grow, develop and change.

Kropf, 2011, p. 20

When writing about restorative justice, the epistemic location of both writer and reader are important to consider in order preserve the transformational potential of restorative justice in its fullest description. In Spanish we say there are two ways to know: *saber*, to know intellectually, and *conocer*, to know in your heart. As a person of the North, a lawyer and Roman Catholic ethicist living in the United States of America, and as a person of the South, a "Nahuatl danzante" equally rooted in Cuscatlan—the country known as El Salvador after European contact—formed by stories of ancestors who migrated there from Europe and Palestine, I know that the threads of authentic justice for a person or community can weave a complicated tapestry. This modest essay is my *granito de arena* (grain of sand) added to the conversation about restorative justice and community.

Restorative justice can be conceived of as a form of social justice inasmuch as every effort is made to help repair the harm that was done to the victim-survivor and to restore a sense of well-being that might have been lost. From this perspective, restorative justice is first and foremost about healing victims from the harm that has been done and about helping restore the wrongdoer who inflicted the harm to the community.

The Concept of Shalom and Restorative Justice

The word *shalom* is Hebrew for peace. Relying on Perry B. Yoder and other Mennonite theologians, Howard Zehr describes the three dimensions of *shalom* as including (1) material or physical well-being, (2) right relationships with other people and with God, and (3) moral or ethical "straightforwardness," referring to both honesty in dealing with others and to moral integrity or a condition of being without guilt or fault (Zehr, 1990). According to this biblical alternative, the relationship between divine-human and human-human relationships is transformed by the concept of covenant, which forms the basis and model for *shalom*. *Covenant* implies mutual responsibilities as well as obligations that transcend those responsibilities. In the Jewish scriptures, adopted by both Christian and Muslim people of the Book, this happens when out of God's love, God repeatedly delivers the people, whether or not that salvation was earned or deserved. In the Christian scriptures, these relationships are transformed in Jesus in a foundation act of salvation and freedom, as well as in the doctrine of the Trinity. This covenant created the basis for a new community with its own operating principles (Zehr, 1990).

In theoretical discussions about restorative justice, the covenant and Christian origins of restorative justice are acknowledged yet not considered central to considerations of applicable justice theory or models for justice systems (Van Ness, 1993). Still, there is common ground between the concept of shalom referring to peace, honesty, and integrity and restorative justice. The secular profession of social work was founded in such values before, in fact, it was a profession or even predominantly secular. Today, the social work profession emphasizes spirituality, which refers to reverence for life rather than religion, referring to a set of beliefs and practices based on the teachings of a spiritual leader that are institutionally grounded (Umbreit & Armour, 2010).

We find a link between the concept of shalom and social work in Israel through the organization Ossim Shalom (Social Workers for Peace and Welfare), an Israeli professional nongovernmental organization (NGO) of Jewish and Arab social workers. According to its website (Ossim Shalom, n.d.), this NGO was created in Jerusalem in the summer of 1991 by a small group of Jewish and Arab social workers who believe that there is a need for pro-peace activities that will stress the interdependence of peace, welfare, and human rights. United by the values and ethics of social work, the members promote peace, human rights, and welfare to help build a democratic civil society. Ossim Shalom calls for using dialogue—a basic tool of social work—as a means to help resolve the conflict between Palestinians and Jews. The social activism and peacemaking that emerge in this Israeli platform is reminiscent of social work in its early history in the United States.

Social Work and the Correctional System: Yesterday and Today

When social work was coming into its own as a profession in the United States, social work and corrections were closely intertwined. The compatibility lasted down through the progressive 1970s, when the focus on treatment and rehabilitation was at its peak. During the 1980s, however, the national politics changed, and the two disciplines began to move in different directions. Much of the programming with its focus on changing lives was abandoned as a failed experiment, and there was a return to a much older model in which the guiding principle was how much punishment the convicted person deserved based on the crime committed. The focus was on deterrence of the self and others, often described as the educational function of punishment. Parole was abolished in some states and in the federal system. In regard to values, the vast difference between social work and criminal justice became pronounced (van Wormer, 2004).

Mandatory sentencing laws removed the emphasis on the individual and standardized the punishments; sentencing now related more directly to the crime than to the person. This move was seen as one that would be more measured, less dependent on the judge's discretion, and more reliant on the objectivity in the law. Since treatment and rehabilitation were no longer stressed, gradually social work ceded the territory to persons with a background in law enforcement.

Now, several decades later, social work students seek field placements in the juvenile and adult correctional systems, preparing to work in the field. And the realization is beginning to strike that as the social work profession was occupied elsewhere, legal experts, judges, criminologists, and religious leaders had helped to move corrections in new, more progressive directions with an emphasis on treatment (for example, substance abuse treatment in prison or through drug courts) and rehabilitation. These initiatives were primarily in response to non-violent crime, or to crimes related to substance use. The restorative justice movement that has made inroads within and alongside the criminal justice system can be viewed as a bridge between criminal justice and social work. In recent years, social work has begun to wake up, and a new awareness of this fact has begun to resonate (for the history, see van Wormer, 2004; Umbreit & Armour, 2010).

The more adversarial, winner-take-all forms of righting wrongs and even the seeming ideal of perfectly calibrated objective sentencing schedules are both out of sync with the pronounced social work values of social justice, human rights, service, and integrity. The controversial process of plea-bargaining, which serves mixed criminal justice interests, such as convicting the "big fish" criminals while letting smaller fish go, is even more incompatible with the values and ethics of social work. Conversely, the values of restorative justice and social work considerably overlap. Social workers today are using such principles of conflict resolution and reconciliation in the schools and in the child welfare system, as well as in correctional counseling (see Beck, Kropf, & Leonard, 2011; van Wormer, 2004; Umbreit & Armour, 2010).

As an academic discipline, social work still has a long way to go, however, in order to take leadership in the field of restorative justice. To take the disciplines of criminology and criminal justice as examples, restorative justice is a primary topic of research and publication. As one indication of its popularity, one can conduct a search of the Criminal Justice Abstracts database. As of April, 2012, the abstracts contained 1,535 references to restorative justice. This number reflects a tenfold increase of total references that were given according to my personal records of ten years before. The Social Work Abstracts database, in comparison, contains only 23 such references. This is also about a tenfold increase over the past decade. And that is the encouraging news. Practically all the references for social work are from the past few years, and we need to keep in mind that the social work website contains a much smaller quantity of references than does the criminal justice website. Keep in mind also that restorative justice and social work have been closely linked throughout much of the Western world and especially in the Anglo-Saxon nations of Britain, Canada, Australia, and New Zealand.

Social service agencies serve the same vulnerable and disadvantaged groups as does the criminal justice system: high-risk youth, families living with domestic violence, and the alienated poor. Practitioners in both systems balance the tension between empowerment and coercion. So a link between criminal justice and social work would be natural. Restorative justice can forge that link.

Values of Restorative Justice

How should the society (in whatever country) respond to wrongdoing? Should we seek retribution or reconciliation? How can an offender find redemption and be reintegrated into society? Can reparations be extended to a nation, to the natural environment? Above all, how can a victim's woundedness be healed? These are among the questions and issues that restorative justice seeks to address.

As defined in the *Encyclopedia of Social Work*, "*restorative justice* is a nonadversarial approach usually monitored by a trained professional who seeks to offer justice to the individual victim, the offender, and the community, all of whom have been harmed by a crime or other form of wrongdoing" (van Wormer, 2008, p. 531). This term had little or no meaning for criminologists and social workers in the United States before 1989 (Wong & Lo, 2010). Much greater strides, as mentioned previously, had been made by the social work profession in Canada, New Zealand, and Australia in helping wrongdoers repair the harm they had done through restorative strategies. Restorative strategies increasingly are being used by social workers in Asia; these strategies are consistent with the philosophy of Confucianism and therefore are easy to introduce.

In the United States today, thanks to greater international contact among social work organizations that are united through the International Federation of Social Workers (IFSW) and the International Association of Schools of Social Work (IASSW), restorative justice strategies have excited much interest among social work educators (van Wormer, 2004).

International Standards for Social Work Practice

In October 2004, the International Association of School Social Workers (IASSW) and the International Federation of Social Workers (IFSW) adopted a document entitled "Global Standards for Social Work Education and Training" (IASSW & IFSW, 2004). This document is intended to be a living document articulating a definition of social work as well as core purposes and functions of the social work profession to serve as a guideline for educating and training social work professionals. The document is useful in its articulation of standards that have been critically considered and resonate with restorative justice principles, as well as other social justice principles. The guidelines support recent scholarship that emphasizes a historical and practical purpose of empowerment as core to the social work profession, despite a lingering perception that social work is a profession that is coercive at its core with tendencies toward colonial attitudes (Burford & Adams 2004). The definition of social work contained in this international document states

> The social work profession promotes social change, problem solving in human relationships and the empowerment and liberation of people to enhance well-being. Utilising theories of human behaviour and systems, social work intervenes at the points where people interact with their environments. Principles of human rights and social justice are fundamental to social work. (IASSW & IFSW, 2004, p. 2)

Clearly the standards contain assumptions about humans and notions of freedom, responsibility, obligation, and relationship between the individual and society. Among the core purposes of social work as delineated in the document (p. 3) are to

- Address and challenge barriers, inequalities and injustices that exist in society
- Work with and mobilize individuals, families, groups, organizations, and communities to enhance their well-being and their problem-solving capacities
- Advocate for, and/or with people, the formulation and targeted implementation of policies that are consistent with the ethical principles of the profession
- Engage in social and political action to impact social policy and economic development and to effect change by critiquing and eliminating inequalities
- Enhance stable, harmonious and mutually respectful societies that do not violate people's human rights
- Promote respect for traditions, cultures, ideologies, beliefs, and religions among different ethnic groups and societies, insofar as these do not conflict with the fundamental human rights of people
- Plan, organize, administer, and manage programs and organizations dedicated to any of the purposes delineated above

Woven from the threads of contributions by colleagues throughout the world, certain values emerge in the tapestry: the importance of building the capacity of individuals to act autonomously (both in their own lives and for the advocacy of structural changes, balanced by the corresponding need to protect the otherwise excluded and all who need protection); and the social obligation as professionals to advocate for policy changes, as well create the possibility for stability and harmony in societies (respecting human rights and particular traditions, cultures, ideologies, beliefs and religions). These purposes are achievable using a restorative justice approach that includes both the informal assistance available through nonprofit family social service agencies, religious communities, neighbors, and other organizations and the formal assistance provided by state-sanctioned social services and legal services.

"Are the IFSW and IASSW referring to restorative justice?" the reader logically might ask. In fact, the IFSW and IASSW statement does mention restorative justice in one context. Schools of social work are urged to uphold, "as far as is reasonable and possible, the principles of restorative rather than retributive justice in disciplining either social work students or professional staff who violate the code of ethics" (IASSW & IFSW, 2004, p. 12). Restorative justice is defined in a footnote:

> Restorative justice reflects the following: a belief that crime violates people and relationships; making the wrong right; seeking justice between victims, offenders and communities; people are seen to be the victims; emphasis on participation, dialogue and mutual agreement; is oriented to the future and the development of responsibility. This is opposed to retributive justice which reflects: a belief that crime violates the State and its laws; a focus on punishment and guilt; justice sought between the State and the offender; the State as victim; authoritarian, technical and impersonal approaches; and orientation to the past and guilt. (p. 22)

For the first time, restorative justice has been included in the *Encyclopedia of Social Work*, and for the first time two textbooks have been published on the topic of restorative justice for social workers and social work educators (see Beck, Kropf, & Leonard, 2011; Umbreit & Armour, 2010). For years, Mark Umbreit has headed the Center for Restorative Justice and Peacemaking, a research institute housed through the University of Minnesota's School of Social Work.

However, it is only now that extensive attention has been paid to the meaning of restorative initiatives to the profession of social work, new initiatives designed to heal and bring people together rather than to further victimize and tear them apart.

This chapter ends with guidelines from the state of Iowa as a model that can be used by other states. This information is presented as Box 7 with the permission of the author, Mary Roche, the director of the Office of Victim and Restorative Justice Programs for the Iowa Department of Corrections. Roche, a licensed mental health counselor, years ago engaged in a restorative justice process. Her young husband and the father of her son had been killed in a drunk-driving accident. Following months of preparation, she met with the offender at the men's prison to describe her grief and loss and to urge him to get help for his drinking problems. Today, Roche directs the very program that was so helpful to her personally. She is a regular speaker in the first author's (van Wormer's) social work classes. As you read these guidelines in Box 7, imagine that you are a victim of crime and consider whether or not you would be willing to contact the agency based on this description of their services.

Box 7

Responding to the Needs of Those Harmed by Crime

by Mary Roche

Iowa Department of Corrections, Victim/Offender Intervention Services (VOIS)

What is VOIS?

Victim/Offender Intervention Services (VOIS) include voluntary programs that provide an opportunity for individuals directly affected by crime to actively participate in dealing with the consequences of that crime. Goals of the program are for the parties most affected by crime to have an opportunity to address

- what happened,
- how it felt when it happened,
- why it happened, and
- what is needed for restitution and/or to repair harm.
- VOIS services are "victim-centered."

What Are Program Options?

1. Victim services: Sometimes victims may have many unanswered questions after an offender has been convicted, such as restitution, the location of the offender, or the terms of supervision/custody. Most people are not familiar with the criminal justice system and may feel uncertain about their role and their rights as a crime victim. Our VOIS program is here to provide assistance. Simply contact the program director with any question or concern.

2. Indirect communication: Communication and agreements between victim(s) and offender(s) can be made indirectly through our program as well. Please refer to the information about our Apology Letter Bank further below. All indirect communication between victims and offenders is monitored and evaluated for safety and appropriateness through our program.

3. Victim/offender dialogue: Face-to-face dialogue between a victim and an offender is an option. This intervention involves careful planning and preparation and is facilitated by a trained professional. Assessing the safety and preparation needs of each participant is a vital part of this process. Follow-up procedures are also implemented to increase the likelihood that this process is beneficial to all involved.

Once a referral has been made, a trained facilitator will contact all parties involved and discuss program options. If all parties agree to an intervention, individual preparation meetings usually take place until all parties feel they are prepared, all concerns have been explored, and safety options addressed.

Common Questions About Victim/Offender Dialogue:

a. Is this program safe?

For victim/offender dialogue, preparation meetings are required. A trained facilitator conducts assessments to determine safety issues for all involved. This is a voluntary program for all participants.

(Continued)

(Continued)

    b. What does it cost?

    There is no charge for this service.

    c. Do I have to do this?

    This type of meeting is not for everyone. Only you can decide if this is something you wish to pursue, and we can explore a variety of options.

    d. Is it effective?

    Many participants report that this process is satisfying, healing, and helpful.

Potential Benefits for Victims

_ An opportunity to actively participate in the process of resolving the incident
_ An opportunity to express frustration, loss or trauma as a result of the crime
_ An increased chance of receiving restitution or reparation
_ An opportunity to be more fully informed
_ About the incident (motive, method, background of the offender)
_ About the offender (what kind of person is this?)
_ About the Criminal Justice System and its processes.
_ An opportunity to experience a sense of healing.

Potential Benefits for Offenders

_ An opportunity to be aware of the harm suffered by victims and the community
_ An opportunity to "make it right" with the victim, to acknowledge responsibility and to do whatever is reasonable and possible to make amends
_ An opportunity to fully participate in finding a fair and reasonable way to repair harm where possible

Apology Letter Bank

Sometimes, offenders wish to write apology letters to victims or victims may request letters. All letters must be screened and determined appropriate before "deposit" into the letter bank. Victims are notified that a letter exists and given the option of having the letter mailed or read over the phone. Offenders are not informed of any communication with a victim unless the victim gives permission to do so.

Restorative Justice

Restorative justice views crime as a violation of the victim and the community. It defines accountability for offenders in terms of taking responsibility for their actions, working to repair the harm caused to the victim and community, and attending to needs that both led to and were created by the offense. It provides for active participation by the victim, the offender, and the community in the process of repairing the fabric of community peace and safety.

Source: Iowa Department of Corrections. Retrieved from http://www.doc.state.ia.us/ documents/victimoffenderdialogue.pdf Reprinted with permission of Mary Roche, LMHC, director, Office of Victim and Restorative Justice Programs, Des Moines, Iowa

Conclusion

Restorative justice approaches recognize "community" as a social resource encouraging positive individual empowerment with resources to support healing. If Nils Christie is correct that the adversary legal system has "stolen away" conflicts only to have the state resolve them (Christie, 1977) in an impoverished "winner takes all" or standard "bright line" approach, then perhaps social work provides a way to "steal them back" so the parties involved in the conflict and those people most affected may use their individual autonomy in collaboration with professional facilitators to resolve their own conflicts.

The challenge for social work professionals becomes how to balance the tension between care and control or empowerment and coercion (Burford & Adams 2004).

Braithwaite's hybrid model, often illustrated as a pyramid, offers one useful framework because it allows the restorative approach to vary depending on whether the party to be regulated is a virtuous actor open to persuasion, a rational actor who will respond to efforts to be held accountable, or an incompetent or irrational actor unable to comply who must be kept safe or in a situation that keeps others safe (Braithwaite, 2002a). For Braithwaite (2002b), the threat of state intervention must remain in the background. For example, in a child welfare case involving the high level of social control that might be exerted by a social worker limiting parents' access to their children, the more prevalent regulatory formal approach would allow for an "ultimatist" social work that threatens parents with the loss of their children. Compare this to a collaborative social work that would work with the parents and others within processes such as family group conferencing to prevent escalation of the level of state intervention on the assumption that the parent is a virtuous actor open to persuasion until her actions proved otherwise (Adams & Chandler, 2004).

When working within a particular society or community, especially outside the Western European community, the difference in how culture, beliefs, religions, and customs are integrated in formal policy can be of significance in formulating models of restorative justice. Knowledge of how these belief systems might constitute resources or obstacles to growth and development or empowerment are considered core social work curricula (IASSW & IFSW, 2004).

To the extent that ethical values of social justice, self-determination, service, integrity and truth-telling, empowerment, relationship, and individual dignity and worth are values that are central to both social work and restorative justice, we can see the attraction of restorative principles and strategies to social work theorists and practitioners.

In tlaneztia in tonatiuh.

(Translation: May your sun shine brightly. Traditional Nahuatl greeting.)

Critical Thinking Questions

1. What core values do restorative justice and social work share? (Check out the NASW Code of Ethics, which is available at http://naswdc.org.)

2. What model for implementing a restorative justice option would you prefer? Why?

3. What model of restorative justice would be practical to implement as a bridge between existing legal systems and social work values?

References

Adams P., & Chandler, S. M. (2004). Responsive regulation in child welfare: Systemic challenges to mainstreaming the family group conference. *Journal of Sociology and Social Welfare, 31*(1), 93–116.

Beck, E., Kropf, N., & Leonard, P. B. (Eds.). (2011). *Social work and restorative justice: Skills for dialogue, peacemaking, and reconciliation.* New York, NY: Oxford University Press.

Braithwaite, J. (2002a). In search of restorative jurisprudence. In L. Walgrave (Ed.), *Restorative justice and the law* (pp. 150–167). Cullompton, UK: Willan Publishing.

Braithwaite, J. (2002b). *Restorative justice and responsive regulation.* New York, NY: Oxford University Press.

Burford G., & Adams P. (2004). Restorative justice, responsive regulation and social work. *Journal of Sociology and Social Welfare, 31*(1), 7–26.

Christie, N. (1977). Conflicts as property. *The British Journal of Criminology, 17*(1), 1–15.

IASSW IFSW. (2004). Global standards for social work education and training, final document adopted at the General Assemblies of IASSW and IFSW, Adelaide, Australia, in 2004. Retrieved from http://www.ifsw.org/cm_data/GlobalSocialWorkStandards2005.pdf

Kropf, N.P. (2011). Justice, restoration and social work. In E. Beck, N. P. Kropf, & P. B. Leonard (Eds.), *Social work and restorative justice: Skills for dialogue, peacemaking and reconciliation* (pp. 15–30). New York, NY: Oxford University Press.

Ossim Shalom. (n.d.). Social workers for peace and social welfare. Retrieved from http://www.ossim-shalom.org.il/home/doc.aspx?mCatID=68327

Umbreit, M., & Armour, M. (2010). *Restorative justice dialogue: An essential guide for research and practice.* New York, NY: Springer.

Van Ness, D. (1993). New wine and old wineskins: Four challenges of restorative justice, *Criminal Law Forum, 3,* (251–276).

van Wormer, K. (2004). *Confronting oppression, restoring justice: From policy analysis to direct action.* Alexandria, VA: CSWE Press.

van Wormer, K. (2008). Restorative justice. In *Encyclopedia of Social Work* (20th ed.), (pp. 531–533). Washington, DC: NASW Press.

Wong, D. S., & Lo, T. W. (2010). The recent development of restorative social work practices in Hong Kong. *International Social Work, 54*(5), 701–716.

Zehr, H. (1990). *Changing lenses: A new focus for criminal justice.* Scottdale, PA: Herald Press.

24

Restorative Justice Almost 50 Years Later: Japanese American Redress for Exclusion, Restriction, and Incarceration

Rita Takahashi

In this chapter, Rita Takahashi, professor of social work at San Francisco State University, provides an account of the belated decision by the U.S. government, after almost 50 years, to help compensate surviving Japanese Americans for the gross violation of their civil and human rights when they were restricted in movement and confined in concentration camps during World War II.

Almost 50 years after violating the human and civil rights of Japanese Americans and infringing their fundamental constitutional rights, the U.S government took actions to officially apologize, provide monetary compensation, and establish a community education fund. Although these actions do not fully compensate for the magnitude of wrongs inflicted against persons of Japanese ancestry, based solely on their ancestry, at least it addresses the wrongs by taking some form of symbolic restorative action.

On August 10, 1988, President Ronald Reagan signed the Civil Liberties Act, which authorized the government to provide a $20,000 lump-sum payment to all eligible persons who were adversely affected by the 1942 discriminatory government actions (Hata & Hata, 2011; Hatamiya, 1993; Takahashi, 1998; Takezawa, 1995). In addition, it authorized funds for community education, and an official U.S. Government apology to persons of Japanese ancestry who were wrongfully banned and removed from the U.S.'s West Coast, restricted in their movement, precluded from possessing items and property other U.S. Americans were allowed to have, and incarcerated in U.S. concentration camps during World War II (Takahashi, 1998, 2007; Yamamoto, Chon, Izumi, Kang, & Wu, F. H., 2001).

Background

On February 19, 1942, President Franklin D. Roosevelt signed Executive Order 9066, which led to the en masse exclusion of more than 120,000 persons of Japanese ancestry from the West Coast of the United States (Asahina, 2006; Daniels, 2004; Hayashi, 2004; Kashima, 2003; Muller, 2001; Robinson, 2001; Weglyn, 1976). This affected the entire state of California, the western halves of Oregon and Washington, portions of Arizona, and Alaska (Hata & Hata, 2011; Hayashi, 2004; Takahashi, 1978, 1980, 1998, 2007). In addition, many were picked up from Hawaii (Soga, 2008) and Latin American countries (Higashide, 2000; Masterson with Funada-Classen, 2004; Wegars, 2010) and forcefully detained.

All Japanese Americans faced infringed rights and most lost property. Anticipating government oppression and assuming confiscation and detention if Japanese artifacts were found, many destroyed their own made-in-Japan property (e.g., Japanese books, swords, and dolls) before government officials arrived to inspect their homes and property (Osaki, 2011). While excluded from their homes, many lost even more property when their stored goods were ransacked and stolen (Hayashi, 2011; Osaki, 2011).

This executive order was given legitimacy and strengthened by legislative actions and judicial decisions, all of which were rendered after Executive Order 9066 was signed. For example, Public Law 503, passed by Congress, made it a crime to not comply with orders emanating from Executive Order 9066. Further, the courts, including the U.S. Supreme Court, rendered several decisions that supported restrictions, exclusions, and incarcerations imposed under Executive Order 9066. The most famous among the Supreme Court cases involved Mitsue Endo, Gordon Hirabayashi, Fred Korematsu, and Minoru Yasui (Chin, 2002; Chuman, 2011; Robinson, 2001; Takahashi, 1980).

Restorative Justice

In this chapter, restorative justice relates to and applies the theory of justice whereby actions are taken to repair or rectify wrongs, injustices, or harms. While full and complete redress or restoration is usually not possible, at least some actions yielded symbolic messages that some form of restoration is at least attempted.

Collaborative and participative processes are essential to restorative justice. Persons affected and harmed by the actions of others (including governments) should be active participants in restorative measures, not passive recipients. Japanese Americans who were restricted, excluded, and incarcerated during World War II, for example, were actively involved in making the U.S. Government accountable for its discriminatory policies. Working with the legislative and executive branches of government, the victims articulated remedies and insisted on minimums: monetary compensation, U.S. government acknowledgement of wrongs; U.S. government apologies for the violations of human, civil, and constitutional rights; U.S. government publication and dissemination of information about the facts, circumstances, and implications surrounding restrictions, exclusion, and incarceration policies and programs (Takahashi, 1998).

Restorative Justice Applied to Japanese Americans

Recognizing that the restrictions, exclusion, and incarceration policies led to major hardships and losses on the part of innocent residents and citizens, the U.S. government passed the Evacuation Claims Act of 1948 (approximately three years after the U.S. Government allowed Japanese Americans to return to their West Coast homes). The purpose of this act was to at least provide some monetary relief to individuals and families who documented and verified their monetary losses resulting from the U.S. government's restrictions, exclusion, and incarceration policies. Little was actually paid; estimates were that less than 10 percent of actual monetary losses were compensated. No compensation was provided for pain, suffering, and violations to human, civil, and constitutional rights (Takahashi, 1980). Certainly, restorative justice was not the central purpose of this legislation.

The Civil Liberties Act of 1988 was very different from the Evacuation Claims Act of 1948. First, the Civil Liberties Act of 1988 reflected the recommendations of a U.S. commission that was established by Congress to study the facts and circumstances of the U.S. decision to restrict, exclude, and incarcerate all persons of Japanese ancestry. The Civil Liberties Act of 1988 acknowledged, respected, and incorporated many of the recommendations presented by the congressional commission (Hatamiya, 1993; Takahashi, 1998; Takezawa, 1995). Details about this commission's work and recommendations are presented in the next section of this study.

Secondly, the Civil Liberties Act of 1988 was different from the Evacuation Claims Act of 1948 because it did not require persons to apply for compensation. Rather, the U.S. government was responsible for locating all eligible persons and providing the $20,000 individual redress due to them. If people opted to do so, they could help the U.S. government by supplying it with needed information about their exclusion, incarceration, and other details (such as an address where a check could be sent). Thirdly, recipients did not have to document and verify losses. Recipients were made eligible to receive the lump sum of $20,000 by virtue of the fact that they were restricted, excluded, and/or incarcerated by U.S. government orders solely on the grounds of their Japanese ancestry.

Unlike the Evacuation Claims Act of 1948, there was no variation in compensation based on individual monetary losses. Fourthly, the president, on behalf of the U.S. government, acknowledged the wrongs and issued an apology to each person affected by the discriminatory U.S. policy. Fifthly, the Civil Liberties Act of 1988 authorized the establishment of community funds to educate the public and to help honor Japanese Americans collectively.

Congressional Commission Findings and Recommendations

Through an act of Congress, a bipartisan U.S. Commission on Wartime Relocation and Internment of Civilians (CWRIC) was established in 1980. The commission, which was chaired by Joan Bernstein, was directed to (1) review the facts and circumstances surrounding Executive Order Number 9066; (2) review directives of U.S. military forces requiring the relocation and, in some cases, detention in internment camps of American citizens; and (3) recommend appropriate remedies (CWRIC, 1982, Part 1, Personal Justice Denied, pp. 1–2.).

To implement its directive from Congress, the CWRIC held congressional hearings throughout the United States, gathered data from multiple federal agencies and government branches, received written and oral statements and testimonies from persons who were directly affected by government orders: public residents and citizens, government officials, agencies, and institutions across the United States. In 1983, after extensive nationwide study, the commission sent to Congress its published two-part report, *Personal Justice Denied*. The first part presented background information and included factual documentation surrounding the exclusion and incarceration of Japanese Americans from 1942 to mid-1946 (CWRIC, 1982). Part 2 of the publication stated conclusions and issued recommendations that reflected the views of the nine CWRIC commissioners.

The CWRIC concluded that "Executive Order 9066 was not justified by military necessity, and that the decisions that followed from it—exclusion, detention, the ending of detention and the ending of exclusion—were not founded upon military considerations. The Broad historical causes that shaped these decisions were race prejudice, war hysteria and a failure of political leadership. . . . A grave personal injustice was done to the American citizens and resident aliens of Japanese ancestry who, without individual review or any probative evidence against them, were excluded, removed and detained by the United States during World War II" (CWRIC, 1983, Part 2, Recommendations, p. 5).

Given the injustices, wrongs, and failures perpetrated by the U.S. government, the CWRIC recommended that U.S. governmental apologies and monetary compensation be given to each eligible person and that a community fund be established to educate the public to deter a repeat of such unjust policies in the future.

Redress for Japanese Americans

Five years after the CWRIC published its report and recommendations, the Civil Liberties Act of 1988 became law. This law provided the authorization needed for redress, but without money, redress would be incomplete. Therefore, major efforts had to be directed at getting monies appropriated so that redress would become a reality (Takahashi, 1998). It took some additional years to get monies appropriated and for the government to establish the structure and mechanisms to issue monetary redress and payments to eligible persons. The U.S. Department of Justice (DOJ), Office of Redress Administration, was established to administer the redress eligibility payment program. An established DOJ employee, Bob Bratt, became the office's first administrator/director.

By the time redress payments and apology letters began to be mailed to eligible persons, it was almost 50 years after the violations occurred (Yamamoto et al., 2001, Takahashi 1998). The road to redress was a long and arduous one for activists fighting for restorative and social justice from their government. Many forces had to come to bear to achieve redress. The effort demanded resources (people and money), networks (individuals, organizations, institutions, and communities), connections (policy-making politicians), collaborations (of all people and resources involved), and coordination (of everything and everyone involved) (Takahashi, 1998, 2007).

Lessons and Implications

The major lesson learned from the Japanese American redress experience is that one must be mindful, vigilant, determined, organized, and persistent to make wrongdoers accountable for their actions. For Japanese Americans, some form of restorative justice came 50 years after the violations, but the fight was well worth it. On principle, all must take responsibility to ensure that human rights, equity, and social justice prevail. Extensive use of time, energy, and resources are needed to achieve results.

Another lesson is that there are many forms of restorative justice. As a result, the diversity of victims will call for multiple avenues of rectifying actions. Apologies, money, and other actions cannot undo the wrongs that occurred, but they can send symbolic messages that recognize and acknowledge injustices and prevent their duplication. For some, a symbolic form of restoration may be more important than tangible and compensatory measures. For others, just saying sorry "isn't enough" (Brooks, 1999).

What is important is that the restoration should be consistent with the forms that are utilized by people and governments within the context where the wrongs occurred. In most cases, multiple types of restoration should be pursued to honor and respect the diversity of victims involved.

The implications for restorative justice are expansive. Not only does it impinge on the directly affected victims, but it also influences organizations, institutions, communities, and societies. Injustices and wrongs directed at any one component of society reverberate and affect all.

When wrongs or injustices occur or are meted out, the perpetrators should be held responsible and accountable. Whether the wrongs occur on an individual, group, organizational, institutional, or governmental level, all must be responsible for rectifying the wrong and attempting to restore rights. While one can never undo what has already occurred, one can establish solidarity (Liu, Geron, & Lai, 2008) and take action to at least symbolically acknowledge the severity of the situation and institute actions to acknowledge the wrongs or injustices, restore principles and standards of justice, and institute measures to prevent any future repeat of the same.

Governments should exist to protect the human rights of and ensure social justice for all their residents and citizens (Blau & Frezzo, 2012; Sowers and Rowe, 2007). If it fails in these duties and responsibilities and institutes injustices and wrongs, governments should (as a minimum) do the following to at least work toward restorative justice:

1. Establish government commissions to gather factual information; receive testimonies; and study and analyze the details about what happened, how, by whom, when, and for what reason(s).

2. Acknowledge the injustices and wrongs openly and publicly.

3. Publish and disseminate facts and circumstances surrounding the injustices and wrongs.

4. Apologize for all aspects and components of the injustices and wrongs.

5. Set up a mechanism whereby policy makers and citizens will be educated as to what happened, how it occurred, and what can be done to prevent repeat injustices and wrongs.

6. Provide means to study, evaluate, and disseminate what has been learned.

7. Provide remedial action(s) consistent with the country or context where the injustice or wrong occurred. The United States, for example, relies on a system of monetary compensation for wrongs, so this is what is applied for government as well as individual or group wrongs in the United States.

8. Consult with persons and groups affected by the injustices and wrongs. Craft restorative means and measures in consultation with those who have been injured or subjected to injustices and wrongs.

9. Take action (e.g., establish laws to prevent and remediate) to proactively set into place actions that enforce what is just and right.

10. Collaborate and cooperate with others (e.g., other governments) to share experiences and provide ideas for preventative and restorative justice agendas.

11. Be transparent and open. Keep agendas, actions, and decisions available to all affected by the decisions.

12. Be responsive to queries and requests. Take all input seriously.

13. Ensure that human rights are respected and protected. Be vigilant, mindful, analytical, insightful, and actionable about rights.

14. Strengthen and maintain principles and foundations of social justice. Where and when needed, invoke preventative and restorative measures.

Critical Thinking Questions

1. Identify and assess factors that contributed to the U.S. government's passage of discriminatory policies that targeted a group of color (persons of Japanese ancestry). Discuss their applications to other historically oppressed, underserved and underrepresented populations.

2. Analyze the policies and programs the U.S. government instituted to address the wrongs. Pinpoint the forces that led to the achievement of redress legislation. Evaluate the degree to which social justice was addressed and achieved.

References

Asahina, R. (2006). *Just Americans: How Japanese Americans won a war at home abroad: The story of the 100th Battalion/442nd Regimental Combat Team in World War II.* New York, NY: Gotham.

Blau, J., & Frezzo, M. (2012). *Sociology and human rights: A bill of rights for the twenty-first century.* Thousand Oaks, CA: Pine Forge.

Brooks, R. L. (1999). *When sorry isn't enough: The controversy over apologies and reparations for human injustice.* New York, NY: New York University Press.

Chin, F. (2002). *Born in the USA: A story of Japanese America, 1889–1947.* Lanham, MD: Rowman Littlefield.

Chuman, F. F. (2011). *Manzanar and beyond: Memoirs of Frank F. Chuman, Nisei attorney.* San Mateo, CA: Asian American Curriculum Project.

Daniels, R. (2004). *Prisoners without trial: Japanese Americans in World War II* (revised ed.). New York, NY: Hill and Wang.

Hata, D. T., & Hata, N. I. (2011). *Japanese Americans and World War II: Mass removal, imprisonment, and redress* (4th ed.). Wheeling, IL: Harlan Davidson.

Hatamiya, L. T. (1993). *Righting a wrong: Japanese Americans and the passage of the Civil Liberties Act of 1988.* Stanford, CA: Stanford University Press.

Hayashi, B. M. (2004). *Democratizing the enemy: The Japanese American internment.* Princeton, NJ: Princeton University Press.

Hayashi, F. M. (2011). In B.K. Dempster, (Ed.), *Making home from war: Stories of Japanese American exile and resettlement* (pp. 57–73). Berkeley, CA: Heydey Books.

Higashide, S. (2000). *Adios to tears: The memoirs of a Japanese-Peruvian internee in U.S. concentration camps.* Seattle: University of Washington Press.

Kashima, T. (2003). *Judgment without trial: Japanese American imprisonment during World War II.* Seattle: University of Washington Press.

Liu, M., Geron, K., & Lai, T. (2008). *The snake dance of Asian American activism: Community, vision, and power.* Lanham, MD: Lexington Books.

Masterson, D.M. with Funada-Classen, S. (2004). *The Japanese in Latin America.* Urbana: University of Illinois Press.

Muller, E. L. (2001). *Free to die for their country: The story of the Japanese American and draft resisters in World War II*. Chicago, IL: University of Chicago Press.

Osaki, Y. W. (2011). In B.K. Dempster, (Ed.), *Making home from war: Stories of Japanese American exile and resettlement* (pp. 99–123). Berkeley, CA: Heydey Books.

Robinson, G. (2001). *By order of the president: FDR and the internment of Japanese Americans*. Cambridge, MA: Harvard University Press.

Soga, Y. (2008). *Life behind barbed wire: The World War II internment memoirs of a Hawai'i Issei*. Honolulu: University of Hawaii Press.

Sowers, K. M., and. Rowe, W. S. (2007). *Social work practice and social justice: From local to global perspectives*. Belmont, CA: Brooks/Cole.

Takahashi, R. (1978). "Military necessity": An effective rhetorical tool for policy implementation and social change. Paper presentation. Pittsburgh, PA: University of Pittsburgh.

Takahashi, R. (1980). Comparative administration and management of five War Relocation Authority camps: America's incarceration of persons of Japanese descent during World War II (Dissertation). Pittsburgh, PA: University of Pittsburgh.

Takahashi, R. (1998). Japanese American activists speak: What the insiders know about redress [Videotape]. San Francisco, CA: San Francisco State University's Edison Uno Institute.

Takahashi, R. (2007). U.S. concentration camps and exclusion policies: Impact on Japanese American women. In G. Kirk and M. Okazawa-Rey (Eds.), *Women's lives: Multicultural perspectives*. Mountain View, CA: Mayfield.

Takezawa, Y. I. (1995). *Breaking the silence: Redress and Japanese American ethnicity*. Ithaca, NY: Cornell University Press.

U.S. Commission on Wartime Relocation and Internment of Civilians [CWRIC]. (1982). *Personal justice denied: Report of the Commission on Wartime Relocation and Internment of Civilians*. Washington, DC: U.S. Government Printing Office.

U.S. Commission on Wartime Relocation and Internment of Civilians [CWRIC]. (1983). *Personal justice denied, Part 2: Recommendations: Report of the Commission on Wartime Relocation and Internment of Civilians*. Washington, DC: U.S. Government Printing Office.

Wegars, P. (2010). *Imprisoned in paradise: Japanese internee road workers at the World War II Kooskia internment camp*. Moscow, ID: Asian American Comparative Collection, University of Idaho.

Weglyn, M. (1976). *Years of infamy: The untold story of America's concentration camps*. New York, NY: William Morrow.

Yamamoto, E. K., Chon, M., Izumi, C. L., Kang, J., & Wu, F. H. (2001). *Race, rights and reparation: Law and the Japanese American internment*. New York, NY: Aspen Law Business.

25

Speaking Earth: Environmental Restoration and Restorative Justice

Fred H. Besthorn

Fred H. Besthorn, associate professor of social work at Wichita State University, has written widely on the subject of deep ecology, which takes us into the spiritual realm with a deep appreciation for nature and for nonhuman and human life. In his contribution for this book, Besthorn constructs a model of environmental restoration as a form of environmental justice. Because we depend on nature, as the author suggests, we must work toward restoring a harmonious balance between our lifestyles and our natural resources. You don't have to be familiar with all the philosophical terms used in this contribution to appreciate the essence of its argument.

Abyproduct of the worldwide war on terror and seemingly endless escalations in horrific acts of violence is a public discourse focused on retaliation, retribution, and justice. For most, the immediate response to being harmed by another is to avenge the act to a degree that will equalize the hurt, thus balancing the ledger, but there is no meaningful way to equalize harm. A murdered family member, a lost career, or broken relationship can never be fully recompensed. However, at the level of instinct, most people do not immediately reflect on the necessity of a measured response. In the public arena, a punitive response to crime and harm that legitimizes retribution through judicial punishment is used.

While escalating cycles of violence and judicially sanctioned counterviolence are the norm, there are growing signs that many societies are attempting to find ways out of the repetitive cycles of harm and retribution. The restorative justice movement is an example. Restorative justice aims to bring a fundamental change in modern Western responses to crime and punishment. Restorative justice sprang from the civil rights, feminist, and indigenous freedom movements of the 1960s and 1970s. Its primary aim is to dismantle the *justice-industrial complex,* which executes and incarcerates ever increasing numbers of citizens in a continually more punitive and merciless atmospheres (Johnstone, 2002). Restorative justice seeks to replace the values of vengeance and retribution with humane healing, forgiveness, and restoration to "create just communities in which people who are in pain and suffering can heal with dignity" (Sullivan & Tifft, 1998, p. 21). Restorative justice pays close attention to the anguished *voice* of the victim.

Human beings are not the only constituency victimized by harm or the only ones needing to have their voices heard. The natural environment and its nonhuman members are also victimized by the violent acts of others and the sounds of nature also have been silenced (Besthorn & Canda, 2002; Canda & Furman, 2010; Coates, 2003; Zapf, 2009). Many environmental policy initiatives including the environmental restoration movement have emerged to address this situation (Katz, 1991, 1997). Restorative justice helps inform the environmental restoration movement by drawing attention to hearing the voice of the nonhuman world.

Restorative Justice: Unmuted Voices and Repaired Communities

Restorative justice has been called relational justice, restorative community justice, transformative justice and needs-based justice (Burnside & Baker, 1994; Morris, 1994; Sullivan and Tifft, 1998, 2001; Van Ness & Strong, 1997; Young, 1995). Restorative justice proponents make a distinction between restorative justice as a philosophical framework and restorative justice as a sociopolitical movement aimed at changing the current criminal justice system (Johnstone, 2002; McCold, 2000; Zehr, 1990).

Restorative justice is as much about individual values and social ideologies as it is about best methods of preventing future offenses (Daly, 2000). It is not simply a new method to control criminal behavior but rather suggests a fundamental reorientation to the manner for communities to view and respond to crime.

Katherine van Wormer (2002), social work scholar and restorative justice proponent, offers this characterization. Restorative justice

> aims to change the direction of criminal law by focusing it on the needs of victims and on repairing communities. . . . Proponents of this nonadversarial model adapt a different lens for viewing crime and rectifying the harm done by the crime (p. 16).

Restorative justice has ancient roots (Braithwaite, 2000; Findlay, 2000; Yazzie, 2000). Before establishment of the current punitive, state-sanctioned model of criminal justice, early cultures viewed crime as a breaking of community relationship. Since strong communal relationships were the lifeblood of survival, justice did not generally take the form of punishment and imprisonment. Rather, justice aimed at repairing the damage done to both parties. Crime was viewed as an offense against the community, and the offender would continue to be relationally connected.

While restitution played an important part of the early justice system, community peace, and the mending of relationships were the main responses to crime (Sullivan & Tifft, 2001). For example, indigenous populations in North America, South America, Australia and New Zealand have had various forms of *healing circles* whose aim it was to bring victim, offender, and community together to give *deep and resonant voice* to the complexity of the causes and effects of crime (Taraschi, 1998; Yazzie, 2000).

Johnstone (2002) identifies several core themes of restorative justice. The first is that modern Western patterns of criminal justice represent a relatively new orientation, which was alien to many non-Western cultural traditions (Braithwaite, 2000; Johnstone, 2002). Tribal groups did not make the same distinction between crime and conflict that modern Western societies do. Crime was a break of communal relationship, and the aim of justice was to restore peace and heal relationships.

A second core theme of restorative justice concerns not what institutionally sanctioned punishments should be but rather listening intensely to what the victim, having suffered harm, needs. Despite the increase in victim rights movements, modern criminal justice protocols only rarely hear the resonant voice of the victim because either it believes it already knows what they need or because it has not developed the skill to hear the voice of healing and reconciliation (Cowell, 1993).

A third theme concerns how communities and victims relate to the offender. Restorative justice presumes the offender and victim will be involved in ongoing connection. The offender is a member of the community rather than an alien or enemy from the outside. As such, neither the victim nor the community can be cut off from the offender.

Punitive models of justice promote segregation. This ensures the offender will be more of a threat to the community in the future. The restorative view of healing the community and offender is not a naively sympathetic view of wrongdoing nor a utopian perspective. Rather the offender must do whatever the community demands to regain full membership.

In the very process of being confronted personally with their victims and hearing first hand of the actual harm caused by their behavior—something which does not happen in the conventional criminal justice process—offenders will begin to grasp the true effect of their behavior (Johnstone, 2002, p. 13).

A final theme is the importance of community involvement in the resolution of conflicts between its members. Responsibility for crime cannot be delegated solely to the state and to professionals. It is important that the community make the offender aware of the collective consequences of bad acts. Every crime perpetrated on an individual has reverberations to the entire community. The current system of justice ostensibly acts as the agent of the community. Criminal petitions before the court are spoken in the name *of the people*, when in reality most communities have little to do with the remediation of individual criminal acts.

Restorative justice has much to offer our understanding of the relationship between victim, offender, and community before and after a harm event. It also offers environmental restoration—an environmental policy agenda to restore life and replenish what was lost.

Environmental Restoration: Unmuted Voices and Repaired Natural Communities

Environmental restoration shares similar concerns with restorative justice in that it is designed to deal with the aftermath of serious harm. It seeks to balance the *harm quotient* between victim and offender. But in the case of environmental restoration, the victim is the earth, which includes sentient physical beings and places that have sustained great harm.

Environmental restoration has been the cornerstone of western models of environmental justice for nearly a century (Baldwin, DeLuce, & Pletsch, 1994; Gunn, 1991). It is premised on an array of normative standards, but its overriding assumption is that when ecosystems are harmed, humans have the moral responsibility to restore them to a state of relative *dis-harm* (Cowell, 1993; Jackson, Lopoukhine & Hillyard, 1995).

Environmental restoration developed in the early years of the 20th century. After a half-century of rapid industrialization, population growth, and westward expansion, many American policy makers and citizens began to realize that natural resources were finite (Worster, 1994). Unless collective action was taken to manage resource extraction and, where possible, rehabilitate degraded natural systems, America would gradually outstrip the capacity of its land and resources (Hays, 1972). The answer was practical. America must manage its natural resources more effectively and where possible restore its despoiled environments (Fox, 1981; Sessions, 1995; Shi, 1985). In the 21st century, resource management and environmental restoration have dominated environmental policy conceptualization and practice. *Resourceism* (protection of natural resources for the benefit of human populations) became official policy and has legitimated governmental involvement in a full range of environmental issues (Oelschlaeger, 1991).

Several core assumptions underpin resource management and environmental restoration. The first is that natural ecosystems exist for human purposes. Human efforts at conservation management and restoration are justified because of the relative economic and survival value ecosystems have for the human species (Naess, 2008; Sessions, 1995).

Secondly, humans are fundamentally different from the rest of the natural world. At the level of culture, intelligence, consciousness, language, and rationality, humans are above the natural world (Besthorn, 2001, 2002; Capra, 1996). They rank at the pinnacle of the ontological ladder.

This anthropocentric bias of the human place in the natural order leads logically to the third assumption of resource management and environmental restoration: Solutions to environmental problems are viewed as simple technicalities fully solvable within a techno-scientific framework (Besthorn, 2000; Besthorn & Canda, 2002). Environmental solutions are technically developed and refined to better address how natural resources may be more efficiently used.

Finally, humans have a moral imperative to restore the natural environment. For example, loggers of old-growth forest have an obligation to replant trees, but the fundamental philosophy of nature's instrumental value and economic development is not questioned. Old-growth cutting is justified on the grounds that forests can be restored quite adequately or replaced by technologically designed and managed tree plantations (Brown, 2011; Drengson & Inoue, 1995). This results in the economic development of resources as quickly as technically possible. Nature's value lies only in its usefulness to humankind, and rational environmental policy involves development, management and rehabilitation of an imperfect natural world.

Environmental restoration has been criticized on several grounds. Robert Elliott argues that even if a perfect copy of a degraded environment could be restored it would still have less value than the original because it would, in fact, be a manufactured fake or forgery of much less value than the original (Elliott, 1997). Similarly, Eric Katz (1991, 1997) criticizes the anthropocentric bias of environmental restoration suggesting it leads to an *artifactual* world where things and devices without intrinsic value except for human intentions and purposes are valued. Restorative environmentalism creates the false impression that natural environments can, in fact, be restored. This human-centered focus, which creates a human culture with its omnipotence to exploit, manipulate, and manage nature, presents serious risks. The real danger with the management and restoration of nature is that it "results in the impositions of our anthropocentric purposes on areas and entities that exist outside human society" (Katz, 1997, p. 13). The only phenomena will be human phenomena, the only natural vistas will be humanly constructed, and the only voice heard will be human.

Hearing the Earth Speak

Restorative justice holds to the importance of dialogue and the essential consideration of the victim's voice. The retributive enterprise of Western justice has muted the voice of the victim while focusing on protecting the voice of the accused. The anthropocentric bias of environmental restoration has also muted the voice of the earth victims. Environmental restoration must consider ways to hear the voice of the earth's nonhuman inhabitants and entities if it is to become more than a wholly anthropocentric approach to problems of environmental degradation.

Strong cases have been made that the earth and its inhabitants speak. Contemporary phenomenologists Scott Friskics (2001), and David Abram (1996, 2010), and phenomenological theologian Henry Bugbee (1958), have suggested that the earth is not simply dead matter but a "speech actor" (Friskics, 2001, p. 393). The earth and its nonhuman inhabitants by their sheer presence and the magnitude of their influence speak to us "univocally, unisonously, formulating a tautology of infinite significance" (Bugbee, 1958, p. 141). The problem is not their speaking but rather our difficulty in hearing. How might environmental restoration look if it were to seek out and listen to the earth's voice? As we discover the vocative character of speaking earth we find ways to honor it and to do it no harm. When harm does occur, restorative efforts can seek out and consider the earth's voice rather than responding with purely anthropocentric evocations.

The essence of human existence is constituted and defined by constant involvement with a complex system of relationships or *relational events* (Friskics, 2001). To be human is to be related to concrete, material, and metaphysical reality. "There can be no thing-in-itself except as it is abstracted from the relational milieu of actual, concrete being with others" (p. 395). Relational events are physical experiences with living beings—human and nonhuman alike. Indeed, relational events preclude anything that might resemble a kind of individualized meeting of two separate ego-selves (Besthorn, 2002; Hudson, 2010). There is no way to understand the self in isolation from our relational bonds.

Relational events assume *address and response* speaking. When relationships are concrete, sense experiences are real and not abstract. Relationships are not in the mind but rather are in the senses, in the body, in the felt and speaking connections between living phenomena. This self-ness is much like the Buddhist notion of self as matter and sensation as well as perception and mental formation (Friskics, 2001). Relational events take place in the context of self-speaking fellow creatures, both sentient and nonsentient. Hearing the world and speaking to the world was the foundation ontology of ancient cultures (Friskics, 2001). Ancient Semitic tribes spoke of the mountains and hills as breaking forth into song. These were not mere figures of speech. For ancients, beingness is in essence singing, chirping, creaking, warbling, and whooshing. All these are sounds heard in the natural world.

Phenomenologists assert that to be present means to be addressed. What is around us and what occurs to us, addresses us. The beings and things we meet in the natural world, if they are not mere human artifacts, have something to say to us by their presence (Katz, 1997). When we encounter a river, a butterfly, or a tree we have encountered a relational event. We are being spoken to. "The basic mode of our participation in being with other beings is address and response. . . . *Appel et reponse*" (Bugbee, 1974, cited in Friskics, p. 395).

Observing the history and current practices of nonliterate cultures supports this view (Abram, 1996). Early nonliterate languages, still used predominantly by the ancient Koyukon people of northeastern Alaska and Aboriginal people of Australia, are "rooted in our sensorial experience of each other and of the events concurrent with our embodiment in the world and which created the context for language. To touch the coarse bark of a tree is at the same time to experience one's own tactility—to feel touched by the tree" (p. 68). We are a part of this relational event. It is no surprise that we still have vestiges of this early iconic language when describing such things as a babbling brook, the rustling wind and the pattering rain. Each of these descriptors refers back to sensuous experience with and sounds of these things. Our words are the sounds these things make. To hear a brook is to hear babbling. To hear the wind is to hear rustling.

Language is not in its essence creative but reflective (Abram, 1996). Language reflects its embodiment in the world. One could say language does not create the world; rather, the world creates language. Language can never be severed from direct experience of materiality. If we speak because of our sensing bodies then our sensing bodies are spoken to from the depths of a speaking world. Thus, language and language relationships are not just the unique property of the human species.

Yet to affirm that linguistic meaning is primarily expressive, gestural, and poetic, and that conventional and denotative meanings are inherently secondary and derivative, is to renounce the claim that "language is an exclusively human property. If language is always, in its depths, physically and sensorially resonant, then it can never be definitively separated from the evident expressiveness of birdsong or the evocative howl of a wolf late at night (Abram, 1996, p. 80).

Phenomenologists affirm that modern culture has lost much of its ability to listen to the natural world. There are many reasons for this, not the least of which is that we live in an incredibly noisy and invasive world. Televisions, radios, video games, iPhones, iPads, computers and all industrial and commercial noise usurp the quieter voices at every turn. The world of humanly created things is a cacophony of noise. It drowns out the voices of creation, which are rarely intrusive, and only occasionally deafening. When we hear other voices they are human voices and human interpretations. In the industrialized world, nature is no longer eloquent. It stands mute "a silent storehouse full of inert stuff—an inventory of lifeless stock" (Friskics, 2001, p. 401). We are involved in an interspecies monologue with ourselves.

There are ways to find a path to greater dialogical encounter with our fellow natural inhabitants. One calls for us to find our *personal vocation*—the individual actions we take with nonhuman nature that beckon our participation in a greater dialogue (Friskics, 2001). *Speaking earth* is a nature alive with calling of being to being. This calling is intensely personal, spiritual, and intuitive. It finds its deepest expression in how we seek the *native anthem* that is nature's voice calling back to us.

Another way to greater communication with earth is the process of engagement as *reinhabitation* (Abram, 1996). It is a *resonate remembering* of the particular places that humans inhabit. It is finding ways to reinhabit our places through an intimate reciprocity of the senses "as we touch the bark of a tree, we feel the tree touching us; as we lend our ears to the local sounds and ally our nose to the sensorial scents, the terrain gradually tunes us in, in turn" (p. 268).

It is through our direct interactions with the sensate land that we can ever hope to protect and restore the animate and speaking earth (Bugbee, 1958). This process starts locally and personally. Technocratic and centralized solutions will never provide for the needs of a suffering and largely unheard natural world.

Restorative Environmentalism: Listening First

Environmental restoration is challenged to consider the critical need of incorporating a core tenet of restorative justice into environmental policy initiatives. It is clear that environmental restoration, as restorative justice has long known, must consider how dedicated attention to the voice of the victim can be incorporated into comprehensive environmental policies. If humans share speaking and listening encounters with their fellow earth inhabitants, then restorative environmentalism must be careful not to succumb to the inducement to speak *for* the needs of the natural world through *purely human-centered* monologues. Humanity still knows relatively little of the multifaceted and elaborate structures of natural systems and how these interact with human systems (Brown & Garver, 2009). The assumption that human ingenuity is capable of a complete technological fix of degraded environments demonstrates the shortsightedness with which modern culture assesses the natural world.

Many environmental justice and policy advocates believe that human inventiveness can fully restore degraded ecosystems even though the destructive relationship between the technological worldview and environmental crisis has been amply demonstrated (Bender, 2003; Besthorn, in press; McKibben, 2008). The concern is not whether environmental restoration is an important practical and short-term response to environmental degradation; few believe that exploited natural environments should be left in their degraded state. Rather, the argument is that restoration based on human benefit and interests alone fails to provide an adequate ethical justification for the restoration of ecosystems. The moral dilemma is the fashioning of environmental responses on purely human grounds. The real temptation is that environmental restoration becomes an unassailable justification for degrading ecosystems in the first place because humans can restore them to their original, untrammeled perfection.

When the first requirement of environmental restoration becomes the priority of listening first and intently to the speaking earth then restoration will not only be more justly grounded, but the decision to degrade environments will be considered more cautiously. From this perspective, every part of speaking earth has the ability to communicate and establish relationship with humans. This view implies a radical equalitarianism among the beings and phenomena of nature as well as a sort of universal kinship of life in which humans do not dominate, exploit, or destroy (Besthorn, in press; Katz, 1997). Nature ceases to become simply the material of human happiness and is instead recognized as intrinsically valuable in itself. Nature becomes a manifestation of the effable *spirit presence* in all.

Truths learned from nature can serve to inform the restorative justice process. In Box 8, Laura Mirsky, the assistant director of communications and technology at the International Institute for Restorative Practices, www.iirp.edu, describes belief systems by Native American cultures that are incorporated in their process for seeking justice.

Box 8

Traditional North American Native Restorative Justice Philosophy and Practice

by Laura Mirsky

In traditional Native American (U.S.) and First Nations (Canada) justice philosophy and practice, healing, along with reintegrating individuals into their community, is more important than punishment. The traditional Native peacemaking process involves bringing together victims, offenders and their supporters to get to the bottom of a problem. The process relies on circles reflective of the circular patterns in nature. In the Native worldview, moreover, there is a deep connection between justice and spirituality, stressing the importance of maintaining or restoring harmony and balance (Mirsky, 2004a).

Consider the traditional justice processes of the Navajo Nation (of the southwestern United States). Robert Yazzie is chief justice emeritus of the Navajo Nation

Supreme Court and executive director of the Diné Policy Institute at Diné College, the public institution of higher education chartered by the Navajo Nation. Yazzie is noted for his advocacy of the use of traditional Indian law and *hozhooji naat'aanii*—Navajo for peacemaking.

"Let's say you and I got into a squabble, and you hit me over the head. In the Western world, you would be called a defendant in a criminal proceeding and would create a bad name for yourself," explains Yazzie. "The Western law way is to punish you so you don't repeat the behavior. But the Navajo way is to focus on the individual. You separate the action from the person. If you and I were to squabble and I sued you for criminal liability, civil liability, the Holy People—the *Diyin Diné'é*—would say *you* should be *respected*. What is not respected is what you *did*."

Continues Yazzie, "What matters here is, why did this act happen in the first place? If we can get to the bottom of a problem, all the other stuff will fall into place. The damage can be acknowledged by you, and I can go away happy from the process, knowing that you say that you're not going to do it again."

The peacemaking process is related to the concept of *k'e*, or respect. "K'e means to restore my dignity, to restore my worthiness," says Yazzie. "Through the peacemaking process, an offender can come to feel better, especially when the person can say, 'I'm responsible, I'm accountable.' That does a lot to the spirit, the mind and the body of those who participate in the process." What's more, not only are the victim and the offender involved in the process, like in Western law, "but the relatives and other affected parties are also involved and also get to feel relief. So there's healing at different levels."

Regarding the connection between Navajo peacemaking and restorative justice, Yazzie cites the work of psychiatrist Donald Nathanson. "He tells us that as we grow from childhood, we learn scripts—ways of responding to things that frighten or anger us. These scripts follow what Nathanson calls the 'Compass of Shame,' relying on withdrawal, avoidance, 'hurting self,' 'hurting other,' or some combination of these. If the script is an intense one, we see withdrawal into alcohol, avoidance by becoming a street person, literally hurting others, and hurting self in drug-dependence, suicide and other self-destructive behaviors. . . . Navajo peacemaking speaks precisely to the 'Compass of Shame' by subduing harmful scripts and teaching people how to avoid hurting others."

A belief system similar to that underlying Navajo peacemaking also provides a foundation to the justice processes of many First Nations of Canada, including the Wet'suwet'en of northwestern British Columbia (Mirsky, 2004b). Bonnie George, former justice coordinator of the Wet'suwet'en Unlocking Aboriginal Justice Program, says that in the Wet'suwet'en justice system both offender and victim are drawn into the process and decisions are made by consensus, aiming to restore balance and harmony in a fair, just way.

The circle is a symbol of Navajo justice because it has no beginning and end and is consistent with the forces of nature. Circles are a metaphor for how the universe operates, how the seasons come and go, and the rotation of the sun and the moon. Everything is seen as connected and unending. In the peacemaking or healing circles, equality is achieved in the circle as all participants, regardless of role or status have an equal voice. A balance is maintained in who and what are represented in the circle, including victim and offender, family members, and different points of view, and all facets of experience encompassing the spiritual, mental, and physical dimensions of being (Umbreit & Armour, 2010).

(Continued)

(Continued)

"With our system," says George, "because of our relationships and our kinship, we're all connected to each other one way or another, and those are the people that are making the decisions. They know our strengths and weaknesses, and they know the dynamics of the families and what the issues are without trying to analyze it by justice system reports—criminal records, police reports and so on."

Wet'suwet'en laws can't be codified, explains George. Decisions are made according to the nature of the offense, the relationship between the victim and the offender and the ties and kinship connections. "What I do affects my family. We have a responsibility to each other. If I get into trouble, I'm not only shaming myself, I'm shaming my family."

The Wet'suwet'en focus on restoring balance and harmony within the community reflects the harmony found in nature and contrasts with the Western system's crisis orientation (Mirsky, 2004b). "They don't act unless there's criminal activity," says George. "But we focus on support and prevention before an offense is committed. We do a lot of work within the schools with children, building self-esteem and identity." Other prevention initiatives include workshops addressing spousal abuse and traditional activities aimed at revitalizing Wet'suwet'en culture. George now teaches young children in Tachet, a village of the Lake Babine Nation, and is incorporating culture, traditions, and healthy coping skills into her lessons.

References

Mirsky, L. (2004a). Restorative justice practices of Native American, First Nation and other indigenous people of North America: Part One. *Restorative practices eForum*. Retrieved from http://www.iirp.edu/article_detail.php?article_id=NDA1

Mirsky, L. (2004b). The Wet'suwet'en unlocking Aboriginal justice program: Restorative practices in British Columbia, Canada. *Restorative Practices eForum*. Retrieved from http://www.realjustice.org/articles.html?articleId=416

Umbreit, M., & Armour, M. P. (2010). *Restorative justice dialogue: An essential guide for research and practice*. New York: Springer.

Critical Thinking Questions

1. How do terms used elsewhere in this book, such as restoration, offending, voice of the victim, relationship, reparation, and justice relate to nature and care of the earth?

2. If you can get beyond the philosophical terms, what does this chapter say to you? What might be some fundamental truths related to life suggested in this chapter?

References

Abram, D. (1996). *The spell of the sensuous: Perception and language in a more-than-human world*. New York, NY: Vintage Books.

Abram, D. (2010). *Becoming animal: An earthly cosmology*. New York, NY: Pantheon Books.

Baldwin, D., DeLuce, J., & Pletsch, C. (Eds.). (1994). *Beyond preservation: Restoring and inventing landscapes.* Minneapolis: University of Minnesota Press.

Bender, F. L. (2003). *The culture of extinction: Toward a philosophy of deep ecology.* Amherst, NY: Humanity Books.

Besthorn, F. H. (2000). Toward a deep-ecological social work: Its environmental, spiritual and political dimensions. *The Spirituality and Social Work Forum, 7*(2), 2–7.

Besthorn, F. H. (2001). Transpersonal psychology and deep ecological philosophy: Exploring linkages and applications for social work. *Social Thought: Journal of Religion in the Social Services, 22*(2), 23–44.

Besthorn, F. H. (2002). Radical environmentalism and the ecological self: Rethinking the concept of self-identity for social work practice. *Journal of Progressive Human Services, 13*(1), 53–72.

Besthorn, F. H. (in press). Deep ecology's contribution to social work: A ten-year retrospective. *International Journal of Social Welfare.*

Besthorn, F. H., & Canda, E. R. (2002). Revisioning environment: Deep ecology for education and teaching in social work. *Journal of Teaching in Social Work, 22*(2), 79–101.

Braithwaite, J. (2000). Repentance, rituals and restorative justice. *Journal of Political Philosophy, 8*(2), 115–131.

Brown, L. (2011). *World on the edge: How to prevent environmental and economic collapse.* New York, NY: W. W. Norton.

Brown, P., & Garver, G. (2009). *Right relationship: Building a whole earth economy.* San Francisco, CA: Berrett-Koehler Publishers.

Bugbee, H. (1958). *The inward morning: A philosophical exploration in journal form.* State College, PA: Bald Eagle Press.

Burnside, J., & Baker, N. (Eds.). (1994). *Relational justice: Repairing the breach.* Winchester, UK: Waterside Press.

Canda, E. R., & Furman, L. D. (2010). (2nd ed.). New York: Oxford University Press.

Capra, F. (1996). *The web of life: A new scientific understanding of living systems.* New York, NY: Anchor Books.

Coates, J. (2003). *Ecology and social work: Toward a new paradigm.* Halifax, Nova Scotia: Fernwood Publishing.

Cowell, M. (1993). Ecological restoration and environmental ethics. *Environmental Ethics, 15*(1), 19–32.

Daly, K. (2000). Revisiting the relationship between retributive and restorative justice. In H. Strang & J. Braithwaite (Eds.), *Restorative justice: Philosophy to practice* (pp. 33–53). Aldershot, UK: Ashgate / Dartmouth.

Drengson, A. R., & Inoue, Y. (Eds.). (1995). *The deep ecology movement: An introductory anthology.* Berkeley, CA: North Atlantic Press.

Elliot, R. (1997). *Faking nature: The ethics of environmental restoration.* New York, NY: Routledge.

Findlay, M. (2000). Decolonizing restoration and justice: Restoration in transitional cultures. *Howard Journal of Criminal Justice, 39*(4), 398–411.

Fox, S. (1981). *John Muir and his legacy: The American conservation movement.* Boston, MA: Little-Brown.

Friskics, S. (2001). Dialogical relations with nature. *Environmental Ethics, 23*(4), 391–410.

Gunn, A. (1991). The restoration of species and natural environments. *Environmental Ethics, 13*(3), 291–310.

Hays, S. P. (1972). *Conservation and the gospel of efficiency: The progressive conservation movement, 1890–1920.* New York, NY: Athenaeum Press.

Hudson, J. (2010). *The self in deep ecology: Insights for social work education.* Unpublished manuscript, University of Kansas, Lawrence.

Jackson, L., Lopoukhine, N., & Hillyard, D. (1995). Ecological restoration: A definition and comments. *Restoration Ecology, 3*(1), 71–75.

Johnstone, G. (2002). *Restorative justice: Ideas, values, debates.* Portland, OR: Willan Publishing.

Katz, E. (1991). The ethical significance of human intervention in nature. *Restoration and Management Notes, 9,* 90–96.

Katz, E. (1997). *Nature as subject: Human obligation and natural community.* New York, NY: Rowman & Littlefield Publishers.

McCold, P. (2000). Toward a holistic vision of restorative juvenile justice: A reply to the maximalist model. *Contemporary Justice Review, 3*(4), 357–414.

McKibben, B. (2008). *Deep economy: The wealth of communities and the durable future.* New York, NY: Holt Paperbacks.

Morris, R. (1994). *A practical path to restorative justice.* Toronto, Rittenhouse.

Naess, A. (1989). *Ecology, community and lifestyle: Outline of an ecosophy.* New York: Cambridge University Press.

Naess, A. (2008). The basics of the deep ecology movement. In A. Drengson & B. Devall (Eds.), *The ecology of wisdom* (pp. 105–119). Emeryville, CA: Counterpoint Press.

Oelschlaeger, M. (1991). *The idea of wilderness from prehistory to the age of ecology.* New Haven, CT: Yale University Press.

Sessions, G. (Ed.). (1995). *Deep ecology for the 21st century: Readings on the philosophy and practice of the new environmentalism.* Boston, MA: Shambhala.

Shi, D. E. (1985). *The simple life: Plain living and high thinking in American culture.* New York, NY: Oxford University Press.

Sullivan, D., & Tifft, L. (1998). Criminology as peacemaking: A peace-oriented perspective on crime, punishment, and justice that takes into account the needs of all. *The Justice Professional, 11*(1 & 2), 5–34.

Sullivan, D., & Tifft, L. (2001). *Restorative justice: Healing the foundations of our everyday lives.* Monsey, NY: Willow Tree Press.

Taraschi, S. (1998). Peacemaking criminology and aboriginal justice initiatives as a revitalization of justice. *Contemporary Justice Review, 1*(1), 103–121.

Van Ness, D., & Strong, K. H. (1997). *Restoring justice.* Cincinnati, OH: Anderson Publishing Co.

van Wormer, K. (2002). Restorative justice and social work. *Social Work Today, 2*(1), p. 16–21.

Worster, D. (1994). *Nature's economy: A history of ecological ideas.* New York, NY: Cambridge University Press.

Yazzie, R. (1998). Navajo peacemaking: Implications for adjudication-based systems of justice. *Contemporary Justice Review, 1*(1), 122–131.

Young, M. A. (1995). *Restorative community justice: A call to action.* Washington, DC: National Organization for Victim Assistance.

Zapf, M. (2009). *Social work and the environment: Understanding people and place.* Toronto: Canadian Scholars Press.

Zehr, H. (1990). *Changing lenses.* Scottdale, PA: Herald Press.

APPENDIX

Australian Institute of Criminology

[www.aic.gov.au/rjustice]

The Australian Institute of Criminology provides information on both Australian and international perspectives on restorative justice. It gives details of the Australian projects RISE and SAJJ, together with the full text of a report published in March 2001: "Restorative Justice Programs in Australia: a Report to the Criminology Research Council" by Heather Strang. This website also lists a number of links to international restorative justice related websites.

Restorative Justice Knowledge Base

[http://www.youth-justice-board.gov.uk/youthjusticeboard?sfgdata=4]

This website is maintained by Crime Concern in association with the Youth Justice Board. It is designed to provide Youth Offending Teams across England and Wales with information and resources, offering a discussion forum to allow practitioners to share their experiences. This website also provides links to international restorative justice websites.

Restorative Justice Online

[www.restorativejustice.org/]

A comprehensive website dedicated to all things related to restorative justice world-wide managed by Prison Fellowship International. It contains resources for those interested in researching restorative justice and for those seeking to implement a restorative justice scheme on the ground as well as case studies, conferences, and links to other restorative justice sites worldwide.

Bibliographies

Forgiveness: An Annotated Bibliography

[http://rjp.umn.edu/img/assets/13522/Forgiveness_Annotated_Bibilography.pdf]

Center for Restorative Justice & Peacemaking, School of Social Work, Saint Paul, Minnesota: University of Minnesota. Collected by Mark Umbreit. This document provides a listing of publications related to the topic of forgiveness.

Global Ministries (Methodist Church)

[http://new.gbgm-umc.org/missionstudies/restorativejustice/bibliography/]

Missouri Restorative Justice Coalition

[http://www.dps.mo.gov/Juvenile/Restorative%20Justice/Restorative_Justice_BibiliographyNina_Balsam%5B1%5D.pdf]

Victim Offender Mediation Association (VOMA)

[http://www.voma.org/bibliography.shtml]

Provides a listing of the major books in the field.

Relevant Websites

AMICUS (now RADIUS): http:www.amicususa.org

Apology & Forgiveness: www.apologyletter.org

Center for Justice and Peacebuilding, Eastern Mennonite University: www.emu.edu/ctp/ctp.html

Center for Restorative Justice and Peacemaking: http://www.cehd.umn.edu/ssw/rjphttp://www.emu.edu/cjp

Child, Youth and Family, New Zealand: http://www.justice.govt.nz/youth/fgc.html

The Compassionate Listening Project: http://www.compassionatelistening.org/

The Forgiveness Project: http://www.theforgivenessproject.com/

Hawai'i Friends of Justice & Civic Education: www.hawaiifriends.org

International Institute for Restorative Practices: http://www.iirp.edu/index.php

Lorenn Walker's website: www.lorennwalker.com

Margaret Thorsborne & Associates: http://www.thorsborne.com.au/

Minnesota Department of Corrections: www.corr.state.mn.us/rj

National Institute of Justice: Restorative Justice: http://www.ojp.usdoj.gov/nij/topics/courts/restorative-justice/welcome.htm

Restorative Justice Hosted by Tom Cavanagh: http://restorativejustice.com/
Restorative%20Justice%20-%20Dr%20Tom%20Cavanagh.html

Restorative Justice Online: www.restorativejustice.org

http://www.ojp.usdoj.gov/nij/topics/courts/restorative-justice/welcome.htm

Restorative Justice in Scotland: http://www.restorativejusticescotland.org.uk

Restorative Practices E Forum http://www.iirp.edu/pdf/lwalker04.pdf

van Wormer's website: Katherinevanwormer.com

Films on Restorative Justice

1. *Concrete Steel & Paint: A Film About Crime, Restoration and Healing.*
   New Day Films, Harriman, N.Y. [KF1328 .C652 2009] DVD, 55 min.

   When men in a prison art class agree to collaborate with victims of crime to design a mural about healing, their views on punishment, remorse, and forgiveness collide. But as the participants begin to work together, mistrust gives way to genuine moments of human contact and common purpose. Their struggle and the insights gained are reflected in the art they produce.

2. Several testimonials from victim-survivors who have engaged in RJ processes are available online from the Restorative Justice Council, UK, for example, *The Meeting, Jo's Story: Surviving Rape,* which can be viewed online at http://www .restorativejustice.org.uk/resource/rjc_video_wall/

3. *A Healing River* is a collection of passionate voices and heartfelt stories that take you on a journey through the paradigm shift that some call restorative justice. The film, which focuses on First Nations People, takes a thought provoking look at the issues of trauma, recovery and the psychological foundations of restorative process. Available at http://www.heartspeakproductions.ca/a -healingriver/

4. *Introducing Restorative Justice: A Positive Approach in the Schools.* This British film is available for purchase at http://www.incentiveplus.co.uk/introducing-restorative -justice-dvd-13861

5. Repairing the Harm: Restorative Justice. NEWIST/CESA 7 Productions, WI [KF1328 .R452 2007] DVD, 30 min. with 35-page guide. Documents restorative justice process as it is used in prisons, communities, and schools.

6. *Restorative Practices in Hull: The First Restorative City.* Produced by Nova Studios in partnership with Neighbourhood Training & Resource Centre, Department for Communities and Local Government, Goodwin Development Trust and Hull Centre for Restorative Practices. Order at http://www.iirp.edu/oscommerce2.3.1/ catalog/product_info.php?cPath=61&products_id=154

7. *Victim Offender Mediation and Conferencing: A Multi-Method Approach.* University of Minnesota Center for Restorative Justice & Peacemaking. [KF1328 .R472 2005] DVD, 22 min.

8. *Victim Sensitive Offender Dialogue in Crimes of Severe Violence.* Center for Restorative Justice & Peacemaking, University of Minnesota. [KF1328 .R472 2005] DVD, 70 min.

9. The Forgiveness Project in London, England, collects and tells stories of people who have forgiven many of the cruel and horrific injustices they have suffered. It has also produced films on people in prison who explore how restorative justice has helped them: http://theforgivenessproject.com/projects/films/

10. International Institute of Restorative Practices (IIRP) produces and distributes good films on restorative justice, including *Facing the Demons,* an award-winning Australian film about a young Pizza Hut employee and the men who shot him in a robbery. An IIRP list of many films: http://www.iirp.edu/oscommerce-2.3.1/catalog/index.php?cPath=61&osCsid=745v8c8rtiqst671cdpnsnlfn7

Index

About the Contributors

David K. Androff, MSW, Ph.D., assistant professor of social work at Arizona State University.

Fred H. Besthorn, MSW, Ph.D. is associate professor of social work at Wichita State University. Besthorn is the coauthor of *Human Behavior and the Social Environment, Macro Level.*

Gale Burford, MSW, Ph.D., is professor of social work at the University of Vermont. He is the coauthor with Joe Hudson of *Family Group Conferencing: New Directions in Community-Centered Child and Family Practice.*

Micky Duxbury, journalist and author of *Making Room in Our Hearts: Keeping Family Ties Through Open Adoption.*

Burt Galaway, MA, Ph.D., is retired professor of social work at the University of Manitoba and the University of Minnesota. Galaway has authored and coauthored a number of books including *Family Group Conferences: Perspectives on Policy and Practice.*

Theo Gavrielides, LL.M, Ph.D., is the founder and director of Independent Academic Research Studies (IARS). He is also a visiting professorial research fellow at Panteion University of Social & Political Science (Greece), a visiting senior research fellow at the International Centre for Comparative Criminological Research (ICCCR) at Open University (UK) and a visiting scholar at the Centre for Criminology and Justice Research, Department of Justice, Mount Royal University (Canada).

Rebecca Greening, JD, is a juvenile court public defender in Boston, Massachusetts, working for the Committee for Public Counsel Services. She clerked for Lorenn Walker and Hawai'i Friends of Justice & Civic Education Law, assisting in the provision of solution-focused reentry circles in the Hawai'i prisons, and is coauthor of *Reentry & Transition Planning Circles for Incarcerated People.* She received a JD from Northeastern University School of Law, a BS in social work from New York University, and she is a graduate of Boston Latin school.

Anne Hayden, Ph.D., is cofounder of the Homicide Survivors Support Group (NZ) Inc., and author of the Restorative Conferencing Manual of Aotearoa New Zealand (2000), which was commissioned by the District Courts of New Zealand.

Amy Holloway, MSW, is director of victim services at the Vermont Department of Corrections.

Ida Hydle, MD, Ph.D., who is an anthropologist as well as a physician, is a senior researcher at the Norwegian Institute for Research on Child Development, Welfare, and Aging (NOVA) and professor at the Center for Peace Studies, University of Tromsø, Norway.

Andrew Johnson, M.A., is a doctoral candidate in the Sociology Department at the University of Minnesota. As part of his dissertation research, he spent two weeks living inside the cells, as a recuperando, in two APAC institutions.

Rudi Kauffman, MEd, Ph.D., is assistant professor of restorative justice at Bluffton University in Ohio.

Heather Koontz, MSW, is assistant professor of social work at Bluffton University in Ohio.

Gabrielle Maxwell, Ph.D., senior associate at the Institute of Policy Studies, University of Victoria, New Zealand. Maxwell is the coauthor of several books including *Respectful Schools: Restorative Practices in Education.*

Stacey Miller, MA, EdD, director of residential life and special assistant to the president for Multicultural Initiatives at the University of Vermont.

Laura Mirsky, MFA, is assistant director of communications and technology, International Institute for Restorative Practices, www.iirp.edu. Mirsky has written numerous articles on restorative justice, including articles on North American Native rituals and concepts.

Kay Pranis, is a Peace Circles trainer and the former restorative justice planner, Minnesota Department of Corrections, and is a consultant for the National Institute of Corrections and the National Institute of Justice. Pranis is the author of *The Little Book of Circle Processes: A New/Old Approach to Peacemaking.*

Mary Roche, MA, is director of the Office of Victim and Restorative Justice Programs for the Iowa Department of Corrections.

Marta Vides Saade, MDiv., JD, Ph.D., associate professor, Law Society Program, Ramapo College of New Jersey, is a consultant for Eseñanza en Educación Jurídica, Programa, a USAID-sponsored project in Monterrey, México.

Ted Sakai, MBA, is the retired warden of WCF, and former director of the Hawai'i Department of Public Safety, which oversees all Hawai'i prisons.

Mona Schatz, MSW, DSW, is director of the Division of Social Work at the University of Wyoming. Schatz is a c-author of *147 Practical Tips for Teaching Diversity.*

Carl Stauffer, Ph.D., assistant professor of Development and Justice Studies, Eastern Mennonite University.

Rita Takahashi, MSW, Ph.D., professor of social work at San Francisco State University, has been a civil rights lobbyist in Washington, DC.

Margaret Thorsborne, Dip.Ed., Graduate Diploma in Counseling, is a founding director and current vice chair of Restorative Practices International, a worldwide association of restorative practitioners. She is a fellow of the Australian Institute of Management and is the managing director of Transformative Justice Australia. Thorsborne is the author of several books, including *Restorative Practices Bullying*.

Ted Wachtel, a former high school teacher and founder and president of the International Institute for Restorative Practices, Wachtel is the author of *Real Justice*.

David Wexler, Ph.D., is professor of law and director, International Network on Therapeutic Jurisprudence, University of Puerto Rico, and distinguished research professor of law, emeritus, University of Arizona. Wexler is credited with first discussing the therapeutic jurisprudence perspective. He is a consultant on therapeutic jurisprudence to the National Judicial Institute of Canada. Wexler is the author of a number of books, including *Rehabilitating Lawyers: Principles of Therapeutic Jurisprudence for Criminal Law Practice.*

Mary E. White, JD, Yuma County assistant district attorney, promotes restorative justice strategies in the courts.

Dennis, S. W. Wong, Dip(Swk), Ph.D., associate professor, Department of Applied Social Studies at the City University of Hong Kong. Wong is a restorative justice pioneer in Hong Kong and author of numerous books, including *School Bullying and Tackling Strategies.*

Howard Zehr, MA, Ph.D., is professor of restorative justice, Eastern Minnesota University. Zehr has been called "the godfather of restorative justice" and is the author of the groundbreaking *Changing Lenses: A New Focus for Crime and Justice,* a book that helped shape the restorative justice movement.

SSAGE researchmethods

The essential online tool for researchers from the world's leading methods publisher

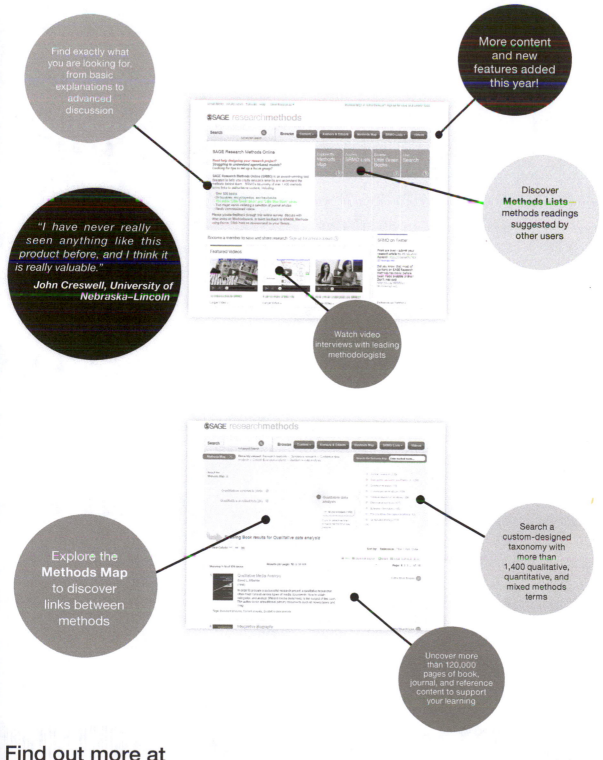

Find exactly what you are looking for, from basic explanations to advanced discussion

More content and new features added this year!

Discover **Methods Lists** — methods readings suggested by other users

"I have never really seen anything like this product before, and I think it is really valuable."

John Creswell, University of Nebraska–Lincoln

Watch video interviews with leading methodologists

Explore the **Methods Map** to discover links between methods

Search a custom-designed taxonomy with more than 1,400 qualitative, quantitative, and mixed methods terms

Uncover more than 120,000 pages of book, journal, and reference content to support your learning

Find out more at
www.sageresearchmethods.com

CPSIA information can be obtained
at www.ICGtesting.com
Printed in the USA
FFHW010326241218
49947709-54612FF